Microsoft® Word 2002

Illustrated Introductory

Microsoft® Word 2002

Illustrated Introductory

Jennifer A. Duffy

APPROVED COURSEWARE

COURSE
TECHNOLOGY
THOMSON LEARNING

Australia • Canada • Mexico • Singapore • Spain • United Kingdom • United States

COURSE TECHNOLOGY
THOMSON LEARNING

Microsoft Word 2002 - Illustrated Introductory

Jennifer A. Duffy

Managing Editor: Nicole Jones Pinard	**Product Manager:** Emily Heberlein	**Associate Product Manager:** Emeline Elliott
Production Editor: Aimee Poirier	**Developmental Editor:** Pamela Conrad	**Editorial Assistant:** Christina Kling Garrett
QA Manuscript Reviewers: John Freitas, Ashlee Welz, Alex White, Harris Bierhoff, Serge Palladino, Holly Schabowski, Jeff Schwartz	**Text Designer:** Joseph Lee, Black Fish Design	**Composition House:** GEX Publishing Services

The Illustrated Series Vision

Teaching and writing about computer applications can be extremely rewarding and challenging. How do we engage students and keep their interest? How do we teach them skills that they can easily apply on the job? As we set out to write this book, our goals were to develop a textbook that:

- ▶ works for a beginning student

- ▶ provides varied, flexible and meaningful exercises and projects to reinforce the skills

- ▶ serves as a reference tool

- ▶ makes your job as an educator easier, by providing resources above and beyond the textbook to help you teach your course

Our popular, streamlined format is based on advice from instructional designers and customers. This flexible design presents each lesson on a two-page spread, with step-by-step instructions on the left, and screen illustrations on the right. This signature style, coupled with high-caliber content, provides a comprehensive yet manageable introduction to Microsoft Word 2002 — it is a teaching package for the instructor and a learning experience for the student.

ACKNOWLEDGMENTS

I wish to express particular thanks to Pam Conrad for her tireless help and keen editorial sensibilities. I am also deeply grateful for the support of my husband, Fred Eliot, and our daughter, Isabella, who patiently waited to be born until this book was nearly finished.

Thanks to the reviewers who provided invaluable feedback and ideas to us, especially Janis Cox and Joe LaMontagne.

Jennifer A. Duffy
and the Illustrated Team

Preface

Welcome to *Microsoft Word 2002–Illustrated Introductory*. Each lesson in the book contains elements pictured to the right in the sample two-page spread.

▶ How is the book organized?
The book is organized into eight units on Word, covering creating, editing, and formatting text and documents. Students also learn how to create and format tables and Web sites, add graphics, and merge Word documents.

▶ What kinds of assignments are included in the book? At what level of difficulty?
The lesson assignments use MediaLoft, a fictional chain of bookstore cafés, as the case study. The assignments on the blue pages at the end of each unit increase in difficulty. Project files and case studies, with many international examples, provide a great variety of interesting and relevant business applications for skills. Assignments include:

- **Concepts Reviews** include multiple choice, matching, and screen identification questions.

- **Skills Reviews** provide additional hands-on, step-by-step reinforcement.

- **Independent Challenges** are case projects requiring critical thinking and application of the skills learned in the unit. The Independent Challenges increase in difficulty, with the first Independent Challenge in each unit being the easiest (most step-by-step with detailed instructions). Independent Challenges 2 and 3 become increasingly open-ended, requiring more independent thinking and problem solving.

- **E-Quest Independent Challenges** are case projects with a Web focus. E-Quests require the use of the World Wide Web to conduct research to complete the project.

- **Visual Workshops** show a completed file and require that the file be created without any step-by-step guidance, involving problem solving and an independent application of the unit skills.

Each 2-page spread focuses on a single skill.

Concise text that introduces the basic principles in the lesson and integrates the brief case study (indicated by the paintbrush icon).

Unit D · Word 2002 · Editing Headers and Footers

To change header and footer text or to alter the formatting of headers and footers you must first open the Header and Footer areas. You can open headers and footers using the Header and Footer command on the View menu, or by double-clicking a header or footer in Print Layout view. Alice modifies the header by adding a small circle symbol between "Buzz" and the date. She also adds a border under the header text to set it off from the rest of the page. Finally, she removes the header and footer text from the first page of the document.

Steps

Trouble?
If the Header and Footer toolbar is in the way, click its title bar and drag it to a new location.

1. Place the insertion point at the top of page 2, position the pointer over the header text at the top of page 2, then double-click
The Header and Footer areas open.

2. Place the insertion point between the two spaces after Buzz, click Insert on the menu bar, then click Symbol
The Symbol dialog box opens and is similar to Figure D-13. Symbols are special characters, such as graphics, shapes, and foreign language characters, that you can insert into a document. The symbols shown in Figure D-13 are the symbols included with the (normal text) font. You can use the Font list arrow on the Symbols tab to view the symbols included with each font on your computer.

3. Scroll the list of symbols if necessary to locate the black circle symbol shown in Figure D-13, select the black circle symbol, click Insert, then click Close
A circle symbol is added at the location of the insertion point.

QuickTip
You can enter different text in the First Page Header and First Page Footer areas.

4. With the insertion point in the header text, click Format on the menu bar, then click Borders and Shading
The Borders and Shading dialog box opens.

TABLE D-3: Buttons on the Header and Footer toolbar

button	function
Insert AutoText	Inserts an AutoText entry, such as a field for the filename, or the author's name
Insert Page Number	Inserts a field for the page number so that the pages are numbered automatically
Insert Number of Pages	Inserts a field for the total number of pages in the document
Format Page Number	Opens the Page Number Format dialog box; use to change the numbering format or to begin automatic page numbering with a specific number
Insert Date	Inserts a field for the current date
Insert Time	Inserts a field for the current time
Page Setup	Opens the Page Setup dialog box
Switch Between Header and Footer	Moves the insertion point between the Header and Footer areas

▶ WORD D-12 FORMATTING DOCUMENTS

Hints as well as troubleshooting advice, right where you need it – next to the step itself.

Quickly accessible summaries of key terms, toolbar buttons, or keyboard alternatives connected with the lesson material. Students can refer easily to this information when working on their own projects at a later time.

Every lesson features large, full-color representations of what the screen should look like as students complete the numbered steps.

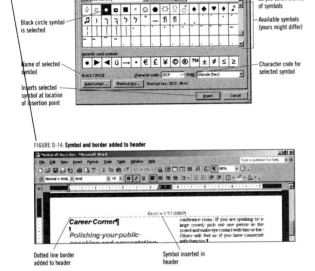

FIGURE D-13: Symbol dialog box

Black circle symbol is selected

Name of selected symbol

Inserts selected symbol at location of insertion point

The subset changes as you scroll the list of symbols

Available symbols (yours might differ)

Character code for selected symbol

FIGURE D-14: Symbol and border added to header

Dotted line border added to header

Symbol inserted in header

Inserting and creating AutoText entries

In addition to inserting AutoText entries into headers and footers, you can use the AutoText command on the Insert menu to insert AutoText entries into any part of a document. Word includes a number of built-in AutoText entries, including salutations and closings for letters, as well as information for headers and footers. To insert a built-in AutoText entry at the location of the insertion point, point to AutoText on the Insert menu, point to a category on the AutoText menu, then click the AutoText entry you want to insert. You can also use the Insert AutoText button on the Header and Footer toolbar to insert an AutoText entry from the Header/Footer category into a header or footer.

Word's AutoText feature also allows you to store text and graphics that you use frequently so that you can easily insert them in a document. To create a custom AutoText entry, enter the text or graphic you want to store—such as a company name or logo—in a document, select it, point to AutoText on the Insert menu, and then click New. In the Create AutoText dialog box, type a name for your AutoText entry, then click OK. The text or graphic is saved as a custom AutoText entry. To insert a custom AutoText entry in a document, point to AutoText on the Insert menu, click AutoText, select the entry name on the AutoText tab in the AutoCorrect dialog box, click Insert, then click OK.

Clues to Use boxes provide concise information that either expands on the major lesson skill or describes an independent task that in some way relates to the major lesson skill.

The pages are numbered according to unit. D indicates the unit, 13 indicates the page.

► Is this book MOUS Certified?

Microsoft Word 2002 – Illustrated Introductory covers the Core objectives for Word and has received certification approval as courseware for the MOUS program. When used in conjunction with *Microsoft Word 2002 – Illustrated Second Course*, this book is approved courseware for the Expert Exam for Word. See the inside front cover for more information on other Illustrated titles meeting MOUS certification.

The first page of each unit includes ⎣MOUS⎤ symbols to indicate which unit skills are MOUS skills. A grid in the back of the book lists all the exam objectives and cross-references them with the lessons and exercises.

► What online content solutions are available to accompany this book?

Visit www.course.com for more information on our online content for Illustrated titles. Options include:

MyCourse.com

Need a quick, simple tool to help you manage your course? Try MyCourse.com, the easiest to use, most flexible syllabus and content management tool available. MyCourse.com offers you brand new content, including Topic Reviews, Extra Case Projects, and Quizzes, to accompany this book.

WebCT

Course Technology and WebCT have partnered to provide you with the highest quality online resources and Web-based tools for your class. Course Technology offers content for this book to help you create your WebCT class, such as a suggested Syllabus, Lecture Notes, Practice Test questions, and more.

Blackboard

Course Technology and Blackboard have also partnered to provide you with the highest quality online resources and Web-based tools for your class. Course Technology offers content for this book to help you create your Blackboard class, such as a suggested Syllabus, Lecture Notes, Practice Test questions, and more.

Instructor Resources

The Instructor's Resource Kit (IRK) CD is Course Technology's way of putting the resources and information needed to teach and learn effectively into your hands. All the components are available on the IRK, (pictured below), and many of the resources can be downloaded from www.course.com.

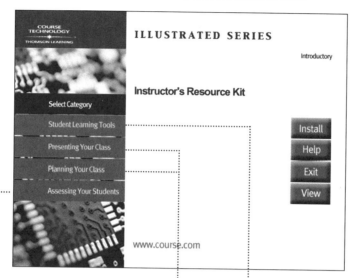

ASSESSING YOUR STUDENTS

Solution Files
Solution Files are Project Files completed with comprehensive sample answers. Use these files to evaluate your students' work. Or distribute them electronically or in hard copy so students can verify their own work.

ExamView
ExamView is a powerful testing software package that allows you to create and administer printed, computer (LAN-based), and Internet exams. ExamView includes hundreds of questions that correspond to the topics covered in this text, enabling students to generate detailed study guides that include page references for further review. The computer-based and Internet testing components allow students to take exams at their computers, and also save you time by grading each exam automatically.

PRESENTING YOUR CLASS

Figure Files
Figure Files contain all the figures from the book in .jpg format. Use the figure files to create transparency masters or in a PowerPoint presentation.

STUDENT TOOLS

Project Files and Project Files List
To complete most of the units in this book, your students will need **Project Files**. Put them on a file server for students to copy. The Project Files are available on the Instructor's Resource Kit CD-ROM, the Review Pack, and can also be downloaded from www.course.com.

Instruct students to use the **Project Files List** at the end of the book. This list gives instructions on copying and organizing files.

PLANNING YOUR CLASS

Instructor's Manual
Available as an electronic file, the Instructor's Manual is quality-assurance tested and includes unit overviews, detailed lecture topics for each unit with teaching tips, comprehensive sample solutions to all lessons and end-of-unit material, and extra Independent Challenges. The Instructor's Manual is available on the Instructor's Resource Kit CD-ROM, or you can download it from www.course.com.

Sample Syllabus
Prepare and customize your course easily using this sample course outline (available on the Instructor's Resource Kit CD-ROM).

SAM, Skills Assessment Manager for Microsoft Office XP
SAM is the most powerful Office XP assessment and reporting tool that will help you gain a true understanding of your students' proficiency in Microsoft Word, Excel, Access, and PowerPoint 2002. (Available separately from the IRK CD.)

TOM, Training Online Manager for Microsoft Office XP
TOM is Course Technology's MOUS-approved training tool for Microsoft Office XP. Available via the World Wide Web and CD-ROM, TOM allows students to actively learn Office XP concepts and skills by delivering realistic practice through both guided and self-directed simulated instruction.

Brief Contents

Contents

Word 2002

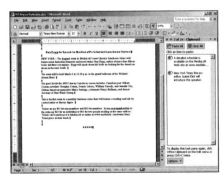

Contents

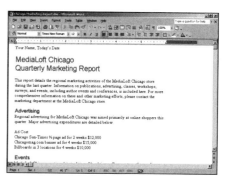

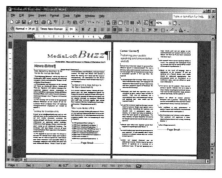

Illustrating Documents with Graphics   WORD F-1

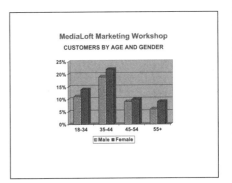

Creating a Web Site   WORD G-1

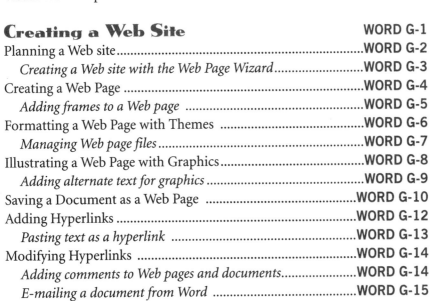

Contents

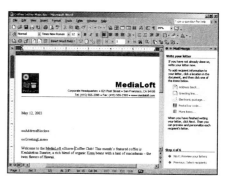

Read This Before You Begin

Software Information and Required Installation

This book was written and tested using Microsoft Office XP - Professional Edition, with a typical installation on Microsoft Windows 2000, with Internet Explorer 5.0 or higher.

What are Project Files?

To complete many of the units in this book, you need to use Project Files. You use a Project File, which contains a partially completed document used in an exercise, so you don't have to type in all the information you need in the document. Your instructor will either provide you with a copy of the Project Files or ask you to make your own copy. Detailed instructions on how to organize your files, as well as a complete listing of all the files you'll need and will create, can be found in the back of the book (look for the yellow pages) in the Project Files List.

Why is my screen different from the book?

1. Your Desktop components and some dialog box options might be different if you are using an operating system other than Windows 2000

2. Depending on your computer hardware capabilities and the Windows Display settings on your computer, you may notice the following differences:
   - Your screen may look larger or smaller because of your screen resolution (the height and width of your screen)
   - The colors of the title bar in your screen may be a solid blue

3. Depending on your Office settings, your toolbars may display on a single row and your menus may display with a shortened list of frequently used commands. Office menus and toolbars can modify themselves to your working style by displaying only the most frequently used buttons and menu commands.

To view buttons not currently displayed, click a Toolbar Options button ⬛ at the end of either the Standard or Formatting toolbar. To view the full list of menu commands, click the double arrow at the bottom of the menu.

Toolbars on one row

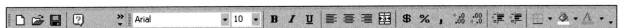

In order to have your toolbars display on two rows, showing all buttons, and to have the full menus display, you must turn off the personalized menus and toolbars feature. Click Tools on the menu bar, Click Customize, select the show Standard and Formatting toolbars on two rows and Always show full menus check boxes on the Options tab, then click Close. This book assumes you are displaying toolbars on two rows and full menus.

Toolbars on two rows

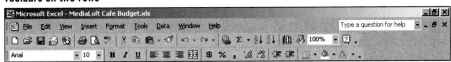

Getting
Started with Word 2002

Objectives

► Understand word processing software
► Start Word 2002
► Explore the Word program window
► Start a document
⌐MOUS⌐ ► Save a document
⌐MOUS⌐ ► Print a document
► Use the Help system
► Close a document and exit Word

Microsoft Word 2002 is a word processing program that makes it easy to create a variety of professional-looking documents, from simple letters and memos to newsletters, research papers, Web pages, business cards, resumes, financial reports, and other documents that include multiple pages of text and sophisticated formatting. In this unit, you will explore Word's editing and formatting features and learn how to start Word and create a document. ✎ Alice Wegman is the marketing manager at MediaLoft, a chain of bookstore cafés that sells books, music, and videos. Alice familiarizes herself with Word and uses it to create a memo to the marketing staff. You will work with Alice as she creates her memo.

Understanding Word Processing Software

A **word processing program** is a software program that includes tools for entering, editing, and formatting text and graphics. Microsoft Word is a powerful word processing program that allows you to create and enhance a wide range of documents quickly and easily. Figure A-1 shows the first page of a report created using Word and illustrates some of the Word features you can use to enhance your documents. The electronic files you create using Word are called **documents**. One of the benefits of using Word is that document files are stored on a disk, making them easy to transport and revise. ◣ Alice needs to write a memo to the marketing staff to inform them of an upcoming meeting. Before beginning her memo, she explores Word's editing and formatting capabilities.

You can use Word to accomplish the following tasks:

► **Type and edit text**

Word's editing tools make it simple to insert and delete text in a document. You can add text to the middle of an existing paragraph, replace text with other text, undo an editing change, and correct typing, spelling, and grammatical errors with ease.

► **Copy and move text from one location to another**

Using Word's more advanced editing features you can copy or move text from one location and insert it in a different location in a document. You also can copy and move text between documents. Being able to copy and move text means you don't have to retype text that is already entered in a document.

► **Format text and paragraphs with fonts, colors, and other elements**

Word's sophisticated formatting tools allow you to make the text in your documents come alive. You can change the size, style, and color of text, add lines and shading to paragraphs, and enhance lists with bullets and numbers. Using text-formatting features creatively helps you highlight important ideas in your documents.

► **Format and design pages**

Word's page-formatting features give you power to design attractive newsletters, create powerful resumes, and produce documents such as business cards, CD labels, and books. You can change the paper size and orientation of your documents, add headers and footers to pages, organize text in columns, and control the layout of text and graphics on each page of a document.

► **Enhance documents with tables, charts, diagrams, and graphics**

Using Word's powerful graphic tools you can spice up your documents with pictures, photographs, lines, shapes, and diagrams. You also can illustrate your documents with tables and charts to help convey your message in a visually interesting way.

► **Create Web pages**

Word's Web page design tools allow you to create documents that others can read over the Internet or an intranet. You can enhance Web pages with themes and graphics, add hyperlinks, create online forms, and preview Web pages in your Web browser.

► **Use Mail Merge to create form letters and mailing labels**

The Word Mail Merge feature allows you to easily send personalized form letters to many different people. You can also use Mail Merge to create mailing labels, directories, e-mail messages, and many other types of documents.

Format the size and appearance of text

Insert graphics

Create columns of text

Add bullets to lists

Create tables

Add headers to every page

Align text in paragraphs evenly

Add lines

Create charts

Add page numbers

MediaLoft Book Buyer Survey

In an effort to develop an economic profile of the MediaLoft book buyers, the marketing department hired the market research firm Takeshita Consultants, Inc. to create and administer a survey of the MediaLoft customer base. A secondary goal of the survey was to identify the areas in which MediaLoft can improve its service and products in the book department. Over 20,000 people completed the survey, which was distributed at MediaLoft stores, the Chicago Book Fair, the Modern Language Association annual meeting, the San Diego Literary Festival, and other events.

Book-buyer Profile

A typical MediaLoft book-buyer is a 42-year-old professional with an annual household income between $40,000 and $60,000. He or she has graduated from college and has one child. The typical book-buyer works in the city and owns a home in an urban or suburban area.

- 42% graduated from college.
- 32% have a graduate level degree.
- 26% have completed high school.
- 60% earn more than $40,000 per year.
- 8% earn more than $70,000 per year.
- 60% are employed as professionals.
- 20% work in clerical/service industries.
- 20% work in trades.

Survey Methods

The survey was distributed to purchasing and non-purchasing customers at MediaLoft stores during January and February 2003. Surveys were distributed at other events as they were held. The table below shows the distribution of surveys by location and by sex. Roughly equal numbers of surveys were completed at the eight MediaLoft stores.

Survey Location	Male	Female
MediaLoft stores	6,657	7,801
Chicago Book Fair	1,567	1,238
MLA annual meeting	563	442
SD Literary Festival	398	487
Other	865	622
Total	**10,050**	**10,590**
	Grand Total	20,640

Purchasing Habits

Respondents report they purchase one or two books a month. 80% purchase books online, but 68% prefer to shop for reading material in bookstores.

Preferred Genres

14% 25% 18% 16% 19% 8%

- Fiction
- Biography/Memoir
- Professional
- Non-Fiction
- Technical
- Children's

Customer Satisfaction

On the whole, MediaLoft book customers gave the book department a favorable review. Customers rated the quality of book offerings as excellent, the quantity of titles as very good, and the subject coverage as excellent. Equally favorable ratings were given to the sales staff and the physical appearance of MediaLoft stores. Book-buyers did express interest in seeing a wider selection of non-fiction titles and deeper discounts for computer and professional titles. The organization and variety of titles in the children's and juvenile departments could also be improved.

1▶

CLUES TO USE

Planning a document

Before you create a new document, it's a good idea to spend time planning it. Identify the message you want to convey, the audience for your document, and the elements, such as tables or charts, you want to include. You should also think about how you want your document to sound and look—is it a business letter, which should be written in a pleasant, but serious tone and have a formal appearance, or are you creating a flyer that must be colorful, eye-catching, and fun to read?

The purpose and audience for your document will determine the appropriate design. Planning the layout and design of a document involves deciding how to organize the text, selecting the fonts to use, identifying the graphics to include, and selecting the formatting elements that will enhance its message and appeal. For longer documents, such as newsletters, it can be useful to sketch the layout and design of each page before you begin.

Word 2002

Word 2002

Starting Word 2002

Before starting Word, you must start Windows by turning on your computer. Once Windows is running, you can start Word or any other application by using the Start button on the Windows taskbar. You can also start Word by clicking the Word icon on the Windows desktop or the Word icon on the Microsoft Office Shortcut bar, if those items are available on your computer. Alice uses the Start button to start Word so she can familiarize herself with its features.

1. Click the **Start button** ⊞Start on the Windows taskbar
The Start menu opens on the desktop.

2. Point to **Programs** on the Start menu
The Programs menu opens, as shown in Figure A-2. The Programs menu displays the list of programs installed on your computer. If you are using personalized menus in Windows, your Programs menu might display only the most frequently used programs; click the double arrow at the bottom of the Programs menu to expand the menu and display the complete list of programs.

Trouble?

If Microsoft Word is not on your Programs menu, ask your technical support person for assistance.

3. Click **Microsoft Word** on the Programs menu
The **Word program window** opens and displays a blank document and the New Document task pane, as shown in Figure A-3. The blank document opens in the most recently used view. **Views** are different ways of displaying a document in the document window. Figure A-3 shows a blank document in Print Layout view. The lessons in this unit will use Print Layout view.

4. Click the **Print Layout View button** ▣ as shown in Figure A-3
If your blank document opened in a different view, the view changes to Print Layout view.

Trouble?

If your toolbars are on one row, click the Toolbar Options button » at the end of the Formatting toolbar, then click Show Buttons on Two Rows.

5. Click the **Zoom list arrow** on the Standard toolbar as shown in Figure A-3, then click **Page Width**
The blank document fills the document window. Your screen should now match Figure A-3. The blinking vertical line in the upper-left corner of the document window is the **insertion point**. It indicates where text will appear when you type.

6. Move the mouse pointer around in the Word program window
The mouse pointer changes shape depending on where it is in the Word program window. In the document window in Print Layout view, the mouse pointer changes to an **I-beam pointer** I or a **click and type pointer** I☰. You use these pointers to move the insertion point in the document or to select text to edit. Table A-1 describes common mouse pointers.

7. Place the mouse pointer over a toolbar button
When you place the pointer over a button or some other element of the Word program window, a ScreenTip appears. A **ScreenTip** is a label that identifies the name of the button or feature.

TABLE A-1: **Common Word pointers**

pointer	use to
I	Move the insertion point in a document or to select text
I☰ or I̱	Move the insertion point in a blank area of a document in Print Layout or Web Layout view; automatically applies the paragraph formatting required to position text at that location in the document
▷	Click a button, menu command, or other element of the Word program window; appears when you point to elements of the Word program window
◁	Select a line or lines of text; appears when you point to the left edge of a line of text in the document window
⊕	Open a hyperlink; appears when you point to a hyperlink in the task pane or a document

FIGURE A-2: Starting Word from the Programs menu

Displays menu of programs installed on your computer

Start button

Click to start Word

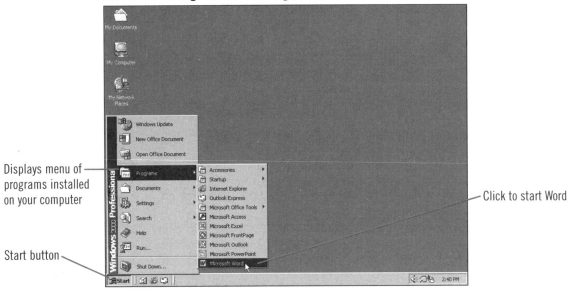

FIGURE A-3: Word program window in Print Layout view

Insertion point

I-beam pointer

Blank document in document window in Print Layout view

Print Layout view button

Zoom list arrow

New Document task pane; the items listed in your task pane might differ

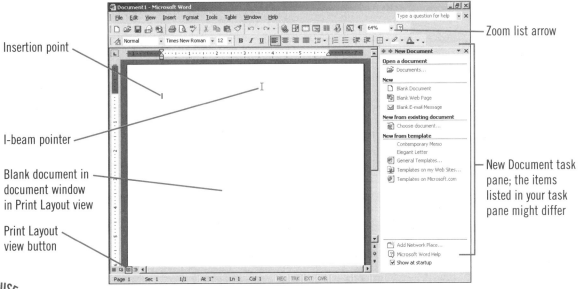

CLUES TO USE

Using Word document views

Each Word view provides features that are useful for working on different types of documents. The default view, Print Layout view, displays a document as it will look on a printed page. Print Layout view is helpful for formatting text and pages, including adjusting document margins, creating columns of text, inserting graphics, and formatting headers and footers. Also useful is Normal view, which shows a simplified layout of a document, without margins, headers and footers, or graphics. When you want to quickly type, edit, and format text, it's often easiest to work in Normal view. Web Layout view allows you to accurately format Web pages or documents that will be viewed on a computer screen. In Web Layout view, a document appears just as it will when viewed with a Web browser. Finally, Outline view is useful for editing and formatting longer documents that include multiple headings. Outline view allows you to reorganize text by moving the headings.

You switch between views by clicking the view buttons on the horizontal scroll bar or by using the commands on the View menu. Changing views does not affect how the printed document will appear. It simply changes the way you view the document in the document window.

Word 2002

Exploring the Word Program Window

When you start Word, a blank document appears in the document window and the New Document task pane appears. Alice examines the elements of the Word program window.

Using Figure A-4 as a guide, find the elements described below in your program window.

► The **title bar** displays the name of the document and the name of the program. Until you give a new document a different name, its temporary name is Document1. The title bar also contains resizing buttons and the program Close button, common to all Windows programs.

► The **menu bar** contains the names of the Word menus. Clicking a menu name opens a list of commands from which you can choose. The menu bar also contains the Ask a Question box and the Close Window button. You use the **Ask a Question box** to access the Word Help system.

► The **toolbars** contain buttons for the most commonly used commands. The **Standard toolbar** contains buttons for frequently used operating and editing commands, such as saving a document, printing a document, and cutting, copying, and pasting text. The **Formatting toolbar** contains buttons for commonly used formatting commands, such as changing font type and size, applying bold to text, and changing paragraph alignment. The Clues to Use in this lesson provides more information about working with Word's toolbars.

► The **New Document task pane** contains shortcuts for opening a document and for creating new documents. The blue words in the New Document task pane are **hyperlinks** that provide quick access to existing documents, document templates, and dialog boxes used for creating and opening documents. As you learn more about Word, you will work with other task panes that provide shortcuts to Word formatting and editing features. Clicking a hyperlink in a task pane can be quicker than using menu commands and toolbar buttons to accomplish a task.

► The **document window** displays the current document. You enter text and format your document in the document window.

► The horizontal and vertical rulers appear in the document window in Print Layout view. The **horizontal ruler** displays left and right document margins as well as the tab settings and paragraph indents, if any, for the paragraph in which the insertion point is located. The **vertical ruler** displays the top and bottom document margins.

► The **vertical and horizontal scroll bars** are used to display different parts of the document in the document window. The scroll bars include **scroll boxes** and **scroll arrows**, which you can use to easily move through a document.

► The **view buttons** at the left end of the horizontal scroll bar allow you to display the document in Normal, Web Layout, Print Layout, or Outline view.

► The **status bar** displays the page number and section number of the current page, the total number of pages in the document, and the position of the insertion point in inches, lines, and characters. The status bar also indicates the on/off status of several Word features, including tracking changes, overtype mode, and spelling and grammar checking.

FIGURE A-4: Elements of the Word program window

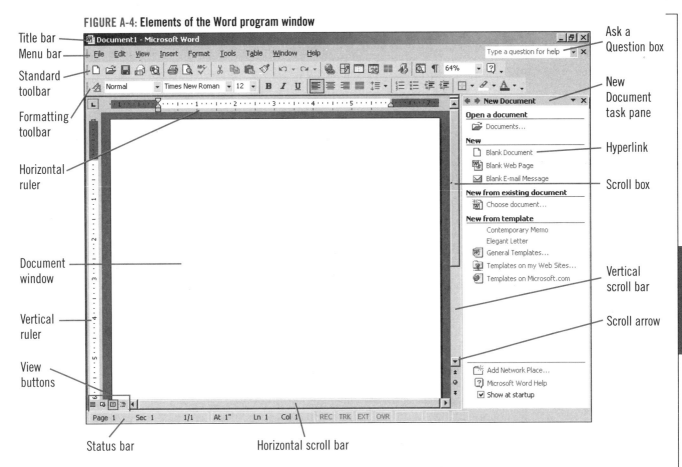

Title bar
Menu bar
Standard toolbar
Formatting toolbar
Horizontal ruler
Document window
Vertical ruler
View buttons
Status bar
Horizontal scroll bar

Ask a Question box
New Document task pane
Hyperlink
Scroll box
Vertical scroll bar
Scroll arrow

CLUES TO USE

Working with toolbars and menus in Word 2002

The lessons in this book assume you are working with full menus and toolbars visible, which means the Standard and Formatting toolbars appear on two rows and display all the buttons, and the menus display the complete list of menu commands.

You can also set Word to use personalized toolbars and menus that modify themselves to your working style. When you use personalized toolbars, the Standard and Formatting toolbars appear on the same row and display only the most frequently used buttons. To use a button that is not visible on a toolbar, click the Toolbar Options button ⚟ at the end of the toolbar, and then click the button you want on the Toolbar Options list. As you work, Word adds the

buttons you use to the visible toolbars, and moves the buttons you haven't used recently to the Toolbar Options list. Similarly, Word menus adjust to your work habits, so that the commands you use most often appear on shortened menus. You click the double arrow at the bottom of a menu to view additional menu commands.

To work with full toolbars and menus visible, you must turn off the personalized toolbars and menus features. To turn off personalized toolbars and menus, click Tools on the menu bar, click Customize, select the Show Standard and Formatting toolbars on two rows and Always show full menus check boxes on the Options tab, and then click Close.

Word 2002

Steps 1234

Starting a Document

You begin a new document by simply typing text in a blank document in the document window. Typing with a word processor is easy because word processors include a **word-wrap** feature, which means as you reach the edge of the page when you type, Word automatically moves the insertion point to the next line of the document. You need only press [Enter] when you want to start a new paragraph or insert a blank line. Also, you can easily edit text in a document by inserting new text or by deleting existing text. ✒ Alice types a quick memo to the marketing staff to inform them of the agenda and schedule for the next marketing meeting.

1. Click the **Close button** in the New Document task pane
The task pane closes and the blank document fills the screen.

QuickTip

If you press the wrong key, press [Backspace] to erase the mistake, then try again.

2. Type **Memorandum**, then press **[Enter]** four times
Each time you press [Enter] the insertion point moves to the start of the next line.

3. Type **DATE:**, then press **[Tab]** twice
Pressing [Tab] moves the insertion point several spaces to the right. You can use the [Tab] key to align the text in a memo header or to indent the first line of a paragraph.

QuickTip

Smart tags and other automatic feature markers appear on screen, but do not print.

4. Type **April 21, 2003**, then press **[Enter]**
When you press [Enter], a purple dotted line appears under the date. This dotted underline is a **smart tag**. It indicates that Word recognizes the text as a date. If you move the mouse pointer over the smart tag, a **Smart Tag Actions button** ⑤ appears above the date. Smart tags are just one of many automatic features you will encounter as you type. Table A-2 describes other automatic features available in Word. You can ignore the smart tags in your memo.

5. Type: **TO: [Tab] [Tab] Marketing Staff [Enter]**
          FROM: [Tab] Your Name [Enter]
          RE: [Tab] [Tab] Marketing Meeting [Enter] [Enter]
Red or green wavy lines may appear under the words you typed. A red, wavy line means the word is not in Word's dictionary and might be misspelled. A green, wavy line indicates a possible grammar error. You can correct any typing errors you make later.

QuickTip

To reverse an AutoCorrect adjustment, immediately click the Undo button ↺ on the Standard toolbar.

6. Type **The next marketing meeting will be held May 6th at 10 a.m. in the Bloomsbury room on the ground floor.**
As you type, notice that the insertion point moves automatically to the next line of the document. You also might notice that Word corrects typing errors or makes typographical adjustments as you type. This feature is called **AutoCorrect**. AutoCorrect automatically detects and adjusts typos, certain misspelled words (such as "taht" for "that"), and incorrect capitalization as you type. For example, in the memo, Word automatically changed "6th" to "6th."

QuickTip

Type just one space after a period at the end of a sentence when typing with a word processor.

7. Type **Heading the agenda will be a discussion of our new cafe music series, scheduled for August. Please bring ideas for promoting this exciting new series to the meeting**.
When you type the first few characters of "August," Word's AutoComplete feature displays the complete word in a ScreenTip. **AutoComplete** suggests text to insert quickly into your documents. You can ignore AutoComplete for now. Your memo should resemble Figure A-5.

8. Position the pointer ⌶ after **for** (but before the space) in the second sentence, then click
Clicking moves the insertion point after "for."

9. Press **[Backspace]** three times, then type **to debut in**
Pressing [Backspace] removes the character before the insertion point.

10. Move the insertion point before **marketing** in the first sentence, then press **[Delete]** ten times to remove the word marketing and the space after it
Pressing [Delete] removes the character after the insertion point. Figure A-6 shows the revised memo.

FIGURE A-5: Memo text in the document window

Blank lines between paragraphs

Purple dotted underline indicates a smart tag

Red, wavy underline indicates a possible misspelled word (your memo will show your name)

Text wraps to the next line (yours might differ)

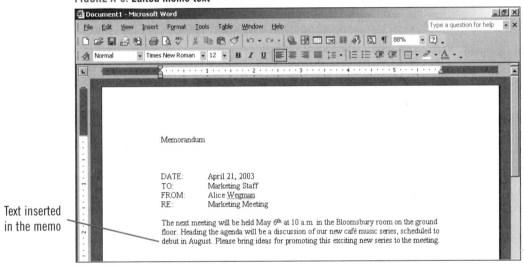

FIGURE A-6: Edited memo text

Text inserted in the memo

TABLE A-2: Word's automatic features

feature	what appears	to use
AutoComplete	A ScreenTip suggesting text to insert appears as you type	Press [Enter] to insert the text suggested by the ScreenTip; continue typing to reject the suggestion
Spelling and grammar	A red, wavy line under a word indicates a possible misspelling; a green wavy line under text indicates a possible grammatical error	Right-click red- or green-underlined text to display a shortcut menu of correction options; click a correction to accept it and remove the wavy underline
AutoCorrect	A small blue box appears when you place the pointer under text corrected by AutoCorrect; an AutoCorrect Options button appears when you point to the corrected text	Word automatically corrects typos, minor spelling errors, and capitalization, and adds typographical symbols (such as © and ™) as you type; to reverse an AutoCorrect adjustment, click the AutoCorrect Options button, then click Undo
Smart tag	A purple dotted line appears under text Word recognizes as a date, name, address, or place; a Smart Tag Actions button appears when you point to a smart tag	Click the Smart Tag Actions button to display a shortcut menu of options (such as adding a name to your address book in Outlook or opening your Outlook calendar to a date); to remove a smart tag, click Remove this Smart Tag on the shortcut menu

Word 2002

Saving a Document

To store a document permanently so you can open and edit it in the future, you must save a document as a **file** on your computer. When you **save** a document you give it a name, called a **filename**, and indicate the location where you want to store the file. Files can be saved to your computer's internal hard disk, to a floppy disk, or to a variety of other locations. You can save a document using the Save button on the Standard toolbar or the Save command on the File menu. Once you have saved a document for the first time, you should save it again every few minutes and always before printing so that the saved file is updated to reflect your latest changes. ✐ Alice saves her memo with the filename Marketing Memo.

Trouble?
If you don't see the extension .doc on the filenames in the Save As dialog box, don't worry. Windows can be set to display or not to display the file extensions.

1. **Click the Save button 🖫 on the Standard toolbar**
   The first time you save a document, the Save As dialog box opens, as shown in Figure A-7. The default filename, Memorandum, appears in the File name text box. The default filename is based on the first few words of the document. The ".doc" extension is assigned automatically to all Word documents to distinguish them from files created in other software programs. To save the document with a different filename, type a new filename in the File name text box, and use the Save in list arrow to select where you want to store the document file. You do not need to type .doc when you type a new filename. Table A-3 describes the functions of the buttons in the Save As dialog box.

2. **Type Marketing Memo in the File name text box**
   The new filename replaces the default filename. It's a good idea to give your documents brief filenames that describe the contents.

Trouble?
This book assumes your Project Files are stored in drive A. Substitute the correct drive or folder if this is not the case.

3. **Click the Save in list arrow, then navigate to the drive or folder where your Project Files are located**
   The drive or folder where your Project Files are located appears in the Save in list box. Your Save As dialog box should resemble Figure A-8.

4. **Click Save**
   The document is saved to the location you specified in the Save As dialog box, and the title bar displays the new filename, "Marketing Memo."

5. **Place the insertion point before August in the second sentence, type early, then press [Spacebar]**
   You can continue to work on a document after you have saved it with a new filename.

6. **Click 🖫**
   Your change to the memo is saved. Saving a document after you give it a filename saves the changes you make to a document. You also can click File on the menu bar, and then click Save to save a document.

Recovering lost document files

Sometimes while you are working on a document, Word might freeze, making it impossible to continue working, or you might experience a power failure that shuts down your computer. Should this occur, Word has a built-in recovery feature that allows you to open and save the files that were open during the interruption. When you restart Word after an interruption, the Document Recovery task pane opens on the left side of your screen and lists both the original and the recovered versions of the Word files. If you're not sure which file to open (original or recovered), it's usually better to open the recovered file because it includes your latest changes to the document. You can, however, open and review all the versions of the file that were recovered and select the best one to save. Each file listed in the Document Recovery task pane has a list arrow with options that allow you to open the file, save the file, delete the file, or show repairs made to the file.

FIGURE A-7: **Save As dialog box**

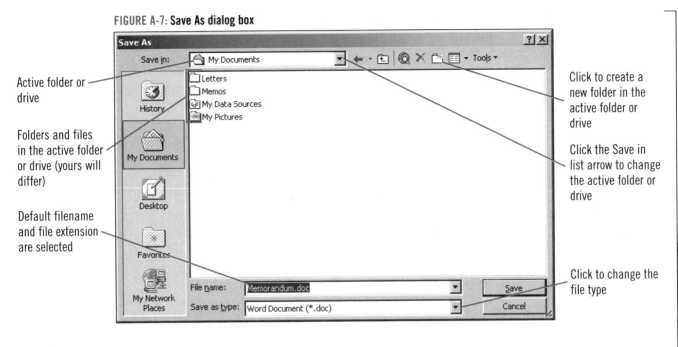

Active folder or drive

Folders and files in the active folder or drive (yours will differ)

Default filename and file extension are selected

Click to create a new folder in the active folder or drive

Click the Save in list arrow to change the active folder or drive

Click to change the file type

FIGURE A-8: **File to be saved to drive A**

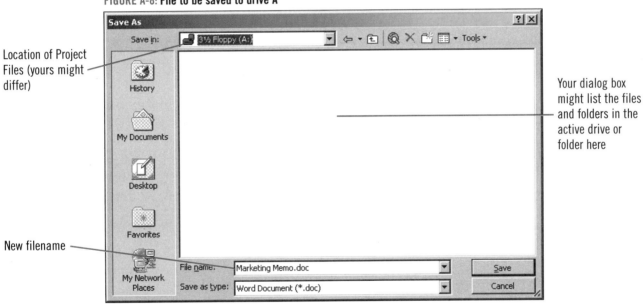

Location of Project Files (yours might differ)

New filename

Your dialog box might list the files and folders in the active drive or folder here

TABLE A-3: **Save As dialog box buttons**

button	use to
⬅ Back	Navigate to the drive or folder previously shown in the Save in list box; click the Back list arrow to navigate to a recently displayed drive or folder
🔼 Up One Level	Navigate to the next highest level in the folder hierarchy (to the drive or folder that contains the current folder)
🔍 Search the Web	Connect to the World Wide Web to locate a folder or file
✕ Delete	Delete the selected folder or file
📁 Create New Folder	Create a new folder in the current folder or drive
▦ ▾ Views	Change the way folder and file information is shown in the Save As dialog box
Tools ▾ Tools	Open a menu of commands related to the selected drive, folder, or file

Word 2002

Printing a Document

Before you print a document, it's a good habit to examine it in Print Preview to see what it will look like when printed. When you are ready, you can print a document using the Print button on the Standard toolbar or the Print command on the File menu. When you use the Print button, the document prints using the default print settings. If you want to print more than one copy of a document or select other printing options, you must use the Print command. Alice displays her memo in Print Preview and then prints a copy.

Steps

1. Click the **Print Preview button** on the Standard toolbar

The document appears in Print Preview. It is useful to examine a document carefully in Print Preview so that you can correct any problems before printing it.

QuickTip

You can also use the Zoom list arrow on the Print Preview toolbar to change the magnification in the Print Preview window.

2. Move the pointer over the memo text until it changes to 🔍, then click the memo

Clicking with the ⊕ pointer magnifies the document in the Print Preview window and changes the pointer to ⊖. The memo appears in the Print Preview window exactly as it will look when printed, as shown in Figure A-9. Clicking with 🔍 reduces the size of the document in the Print Preview window.

3. Click the **Magnifier button** on the Print Preview toolbar

Clicking the Magnifier button turns off the magnification feature and allows you to edit the document in Print Preview. In edit mode, the pointer changes to Ⅰ. The Magnifier button is a **toggle button**, which means you can use it to switch back and forth between magnification mode and edit mode.

4. Compare the text on your screen with the text in Figure A-9, examine your memo carefully for typing or spelling errors, correct any mistakes, then click the **Close Preview button** Close on the Print Preview toolbar

Print Preview closes and the memo appears in the document window.

5. Click the **Save button** on the Standard toolbar

If you made any changes to the document since you last saved it, the changes are saved.

6. Click **File** on the menu bar, then click **Print**

The Print dialog box opens, as shown in Figure A-10. Depending on the printer installed on your computer, your print settings might differ slightly from those in the figure. You can use the Print dialog box to change the current printer, change the number of copies to print, select what pages of a document to print, and modify other printing options.

7. Click **OK**

The dialog box closes and a copy of the memo prints using the default print settings. You can also click the Print button on the Standard toolbar or the Print Preview toolbar to print a document using the default print settings.

FIGURE A-9: Memo in the Print Preview window

Magnifier
button

Close
Preview
button

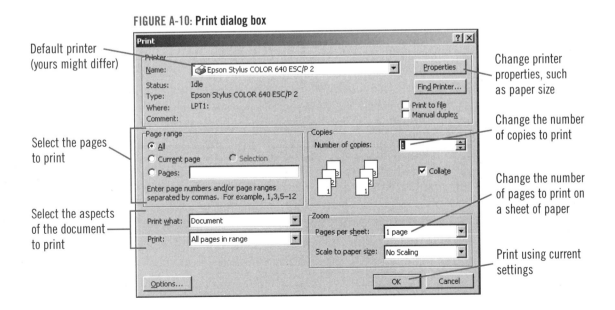

Marketing Memo.doc (Preview) - Microsoft Word

File   Edit   View   Insert   Format   Tools   Table   Window   Help

Type a question for help

100%   Close

Memorandum

DATE: April 21, 2003
TO: Marketing Staff
FROM: Alice Wegman
RE: Marketing Meeting

The next meeting will be held May 6th at 10 a.m. in the Bloomsbury room on the ground
floor. Heading the agenda will be a discussion of our new café music series, scheduled to
debut in early August. Please bring ideas for promoting this exciting new series to the
meeting.

Page 1   Sec 1   1/1   At 3.1"   Ln 12   Col 16   REC   TRK   EXT   OVR

FIGURE A-10: Print dialog box

Default printer
(yours might differ)

Print

Printer
Name: Epson Stylus COLOR 640 ESC/P 2   Properties

Status: Idle   Find Printer...
Type: Epson Stylus COLOR 640 ESC/P 2
Where: LPT1:   □ Print to file
Comment: □ Manual duplex

Change printer
properties, such
as paper size

Select the pages
to print

Page range
⊙ All
○ Current page   ○ Selection
○ Pages:

Enter page numbers and/or page ranges
separated by commas. For example, 1,3,5–12

Copies
Number of copies: 1

☑ Collate

Change the number
of copies to print

Select the aspects
of the document
to print

Print what: Document
Print: All pages in range

Zoom
Pages per sheet: 1 page

Scale to paper size: No Scaling

Change the number
of pages to print on
a sheet of paper

Print using current
settings

Options...   OK   Cancel

Using the Help System

Word includes an extensive Help system that provides immediate access to definitions, instructions, and useful tips for working with Word. You can quickly access the Help system by typing a question in the Ask a Question box on the menu bar, or by clicking the Microsoft Word Help button on the Standard toolbar. Table A-4 describes the many ways to get help while using Word. Alice is curious to learn more about typing with AutoCorrect and viewing a document in Print Preview. She searches the Word Help system to discover more about these features.

Steps

1. Type AutoCorrect in the Ask a Question box on the menu bar, then press [Enter]
A drop-down menu of help topics related to AutoCorrect opens. You can select a topic from this menu or click See more… to view additional help topics related to your query.

2. Click About automatic corrections on the drop-down menu
The Microsoft Word Help window opens, as shown in Figure A-11. The left pane of the Help window contains the Contents, Answer Wizard, and Index tabs, which you can use to search for and display information on help topics. The right pane of the Help window displays the "About automatic corrections" help topic you selected. The blue text in the Help window indicates a link to a definition or to more information about the topic. Notice that the pointer changes to ⟨ᵐ⟩ when you move it over the blue text.

3. Read the information in the Help window, then click the blue text hyperlinks
Clicking the link expands the help topic to display more detailed information. A definition of "hyperlink" appears in green text in the Help window.

4. Read the definition, then click hyperlinks again to close the definition

5. Click Using AutoCorrect to correct errors as you type, then read the expanded information, clicking the down scroll arrow as necessary to read the entire help topic
Clicking the up or down scroll arrow allows you to navigate through the help topic when all the text does not fit in the Help window. You can also scroll by clicking the scroll bar above and below the scroll box, or by dragging the scroll box up or down in the scroll bar.

6. Click the Answer Wizard tab in the left pane if necessary, type print a document in the What would you like to do? text box, then click Search
When you click Search, a list of help topics related to your query appears in the Select topic to display box on the Answer Wizard tab, as shown in Figure A-12. The active help topic—the topic selected in the Select topic to display box—appears in the right pane.

7. Click the Index tab, type print preview in the Type keywords text box, then click Search
As you type, notice that Word automatically supplies possible keywords in the Type keywords box. When you click Search, a list of help topics related to Print Preview appears in the Choose a topic box. You can use the Index tab to narrow the scope of the help topics related to your query by searching for topics related to specific words or phrases.

8. Click Edit text in print preview in the Choose a topic box
The help topic appears in the right pane of the Help window.

9. Click the Close button on the Help window title bar to close Help

FIGURE A-11: Microsoft Word Help window

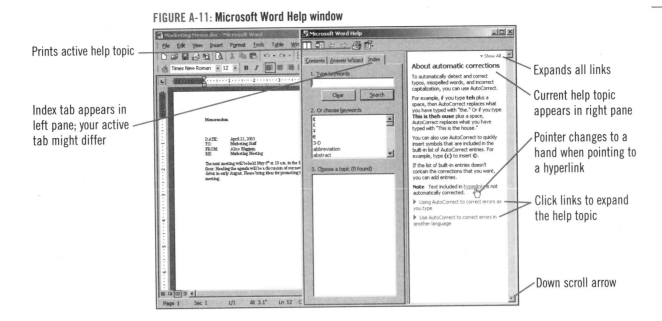

Prints active help topic

Index tab appears in left pane; your active tab might differ

Expands all links

Current help topic appears in right pane

Pointer changes to a hand when pointing to a hyperlink

Click links to expand the help topic

Down scroll arrow

FIGURE A-12: Answer Wizard tab in the Microsoft Word Help window

Query used to search for topic

List of help topics related to query

Close button

Active help topic

TABLE A-4: Word resources for getting Help

resource	function	to use
Ask a Question box	Provides quick access to the Help system	Type a word or question in the Ask a Question box, then press [Enter]
Office Assistant	Displays tips and Help topics related to your current task and provides access to the Help system	Press [F1] or click the Microsoft Word Help button ❓ on the Standard toolbar, select a Help topic or type a word or question in the Office Assistant dialog box, then click Search
Microsoft Word Help window	Catalogs and displays the detailed Help topics included in the Help system	Browse the table of contents on the Contents tab, type a question in the text box on the Answer Wizard tab, or search for topics related to a keyword on the Index tab
What's This?	Displays information about elements of the Word program window in ScreenTips	Press [Shift][F1] or click the What's This? command on the Help menu, then use the ⬚? pointer to click the element for which you want help
Help on the World Wide Web	Connects to the Microsoft Office Web site, where you can search for information on a topic	Click the Office on the Web command on the Help menu

Word 2002

Closing a Document and Exiting Word

When you finish working on a document and have saved your changes, you can close the document using the Close Window button on the menu bar or the Close command on the File menu. Closing a document closes the document only, it does not close the Word program window. To close the Word program window and exit Word, you can use the Close button on the title bar or the Exit command on the File menu. Using the Exit command closes all open documents. It's good practice to save and close your documents before exiting Word. Figure A-14 shows the Close buttons on the title bar and menu bar. ✎ Alice closes the memo and exits Word.

Steps

1. Click **File** on the menu bar, then click **Close**

If you saved your changes to the document before closing it, the document closes. If you did not save your changes, an alert box opens asking if you want to save the changes.

QuickTip

Click the New Blank Document button ☐ on the Standard toolbar to create a new blank document.

2. Click **Yes** if necessary

The document closes, but the Word program window remains open, as shown in Figure A-15. You can create or open another document, access Help, or close the Word program window.

3. Click **File** on the menu bar, then click **Exit**

The Word program window closes. If any Word documents were still open when you exited Word, Word would close all open documents, prompting you to save changes to those documents if necessary.

CLUES TO USE

Using the Office Assistant to get Help

The **Office Assistant**, shown in Figure A-13, is an animated character that appears on your screen to provide tips while you work. For example, when you begin typing a letter, the Office Assistant anticipates what you are doing and opens to offer help writing a letter. You can accept this help or continue working on your own. The Office Assistant also appears when you use the Microsoft Word Help button ⯑ to access the Word Help system. In this case, the Office Assistant displays a list of help topics related to tasks you have recently completed and provides space for you to search for information on other topics. Selecting a help topic in the Office Assistant displays that topic in the Microsoft Help window. When you finish working with the Office Assistant, right-click it and then click Hide to close it. You also can turn off the Office Assistant: right-click it, click Options, deselect the Use the Office Assistant check box on the Options tab in the Office Assistant dialog box, and then click OK. To turn it on again, click Show Office Assistant on the Help menu.

FIGURE A-13: Office Assistant

FIGURE A-14: Close and Close Window buttons

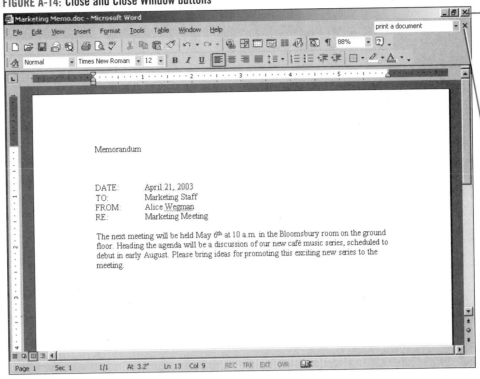

Close button on title bar closes all open documents and exits Word

Close Window button closes the current document

FIGURE A-15: Word program window with no documents open

New Blank Document button

Practice

► Concepts Review

Label the elements of the Word program window shown in Figure A-16.

FIGURE A-16

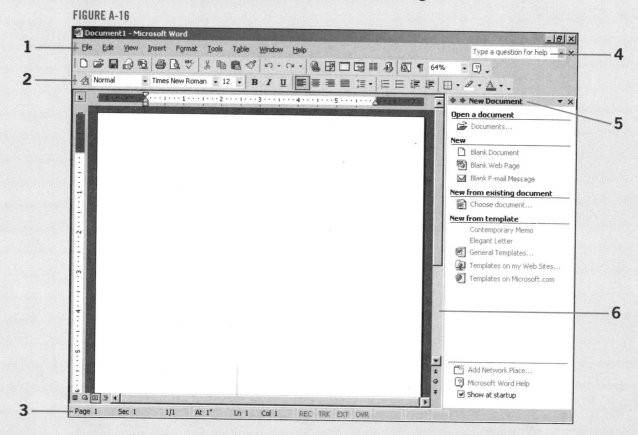

Match each term with the statement that best describes it.

7. Print Preview
8. Office Assistant
9. Status bar
10. Menu bar
11. AutoComplete
12. Horizontal ruler
13. AutoCorrect
14. Normal view

a. Suggests text to insert into a document
b. Provides access to Word commands
c. Displays the document exactly as it will look when printed
d. Provides tips on using Word and displays Help topics
e. Fixes certain errors as you type
f. Displays the number of pages in the current document
g. Displays a simple layout view of a document
h. Displays tab settings and document margins

Select the best answer from the list of choices.

15. **Which element of the Word program window contains hyperlinks to help you quickly accomplish a task?**
    a. Formatting toolbar
    b. Menu bar
    c. New Document task pane
    d. Status bar

16. **Which button is found on the Formatting toolbar?**
    a. Underline button
    b. Drawing button
    c. Format Painter button
    d. Tables and Borders button

17. **What is the function of the Exit command on the File menu?**
    a. To save changes to and close the current document
    b. To close the current document without saving changes
    c. To close all open documents and the Word program window
    d. To close all open programs

18. **Which view would you use if you want to adjust the margins in a document?**
    a. Outline view
    b. Print Layout view
    c. Normal view
    d. Web Layout view

19. **Which of the following does *not* appear on the status bar?**
    a. The current page number
    b. The current line number
    c. The Overtype mode status
    d. The current tab settings

20. **Which of the following is *not* used to access Word Help topics?**
    a. The Ask a Question box
    b. The Search task pane
    c. The Office Assistant
    d. The Answer Wizard

▶ ## Skills Review

1. **Start Word 2002.**
   a. Start Word using the Programs menu.
   b. Switch to Print Layout view if necessary.
   c. Change the zoom level to Page Width if necessary.

2. **Explore the Word program window.**
   a. Identify as many elements of the Word program window as you can without referring to the unit material.
   b. Click each menu name on the menu bar and drag the pointer through the menu commands.
   c. Point to each button on the Standard and Formatting toolbars and read the ScreenTips.
   d. Point to each hyperlink in the New Document task pane.
   e. Click the view buttons to view the blank document in Normal, Web Layout, Print Layout, and Outline view.
   f. Return to Print Layout view.

3. **Start a document.**
   a. Close the New Document task pane.
   b. In a new blank document, begin typing a fax to one of your customers at Plateau Tours and Travel in Montreal.
   c. Type FAX at the top of the page, then press [Enter] four times.

  d. Type the following, pressing [Tab] as indicated and pressing [Enter] at the end of each line:
  To: [Tab] **Dr. Monique Lacasse**
  From: [Tab] **Your Name**
  Date: [Tab] **Today's Date**
  Re: [Tab] **Travel arrangements**
  Pages: [Tab] **1**
  Fax: [Tab] **(514) 555-3948**

  e. Press [Enter], then type **I have reserved a space for you on the February 4-18 Costa Rica Explorer tour. You are scheduled to depart Montreal's Dorval Airport on Plateau Tours and Travel charter flight 234 at 7:45 a.m. on February 4th, arriving in San Jose at 4:30 p.m. local time.**

  f. Press [Enter] twice, then type **Please call me at (514) 555-4983 or stop by our offices on rue St-Denis.**

  g. Insert this sentence at the beginning of the second paragraph: **I must receive full payment within 48 hours to hold your reservation.**

  h. Using the [Backspace] key, delete **Travel** in the Re: line, then type **Costa Rica tour.**

  i. Using the [Delete] key, delete **48** in the last sentence, then type **72.**

4. Save a document.

  a. Click File on the menu bar, then click Save.

  b. Save the document as **Lacasse Fax** to the drive and folder where your Project Files are located.

  c. After your name, type a comma, a space, and then type **Plateau Tours and Travel.**

  d. Click the Save button to save your changes to the document.

5. Print a document.

  a. Click the Print Preview button to view the document in Print Preview.

  b. Click the word FAX to zoom in on the document, then proofread the fax.

  c. Click the Magnifier button to switch to edit mode, then correct any typing errors in your document.

  d. Close Print Preview, then save your changes to the document.

  e. Print the fax using the default print settings.

6. Use the Help system.

  a. Click the Microsoft Word Help button to open the Office Assistant. (*Hint*: If the Help window opens instead of the Office Assistant, close the Help window, click Help on the menu bar, click Show the Office Assistant, then click the Microsoft Word Help button again.)

  b. Type **save a document** in the Office Assistant text box, then click Search.

  c. Click the topic Save a document.

  d. Read about saving documents in Word by clicking the links to expand the help topic.

  e. Click the Contents tab, then double-click the topic Viewing and Navigating Documents.

  f. Click the topic Zoom in on or out of a document, then read the help topic.

  g. Close the Microsoft Word Help window.

7. Close a document and exit Word.

  a. Close the Lacasse Fax document, saving your changes if necessary.

  b. Exit Word.

▶ Independent Challenge 1

You are a performance artist, well known for your innovative work with computers. The Missoula Arts Council president, Jeb Zobel, has asked you to be the keynote speaker at an upcoming conference in Missoula, Montana, on the role of technology in the arts. You are pleased at the invitation, and write a letter to Mr. Zobel accepting the invitation and confirming the details. Your letter to Mr. Zobel should reference the following information:

- The conference will be held October 10–12, 2003 at the civic center in Missoula.
- You have been asked to speak for one hour on Saturday, October 11, followed by a half hour for questions.
- Mr. Zobel suggested the lecture topic "Technology's Effect on Art and Culture."
- Your talk will include a 20-minute slide presentation.
- The Missoula Arts Council will make your travel arrangements.
- Your preference is to arrive in Missoula on Friday, October 10, and depart on Sunday, October 12.
- You want to fly in and out of the airport closest to your home.

a. Start Word.

b. Save a new blank document as **Zobel Letter** to the drive and folder where your Project Files are located.

c. Model your letter to Mr. Zobel after the sample business letter shown in Figure A-17: there are 3 blank lines after the date, 1 blank line after the inside address, 1 blank line after the salutation, 1 blank line after each body paragraph, and 3 blank lines between the closing and your typed name.

d. Begin the letter by typing today's date.

e. Type the inside address. Be sure to include Mr. Zobel's title and the name of the organization. Make up a street address.

f. Type a salutation.

g. Using the information listed above, type the body of the letter:

- In the first paragraph, accept the invitation to speak and confirm the important conference details.
- In the second paragraph, confirm your lecture topic and provide any relevant details.
- In the third paragraph, state your travel preferences.
- Type a short final paragraph.

h. Type a closing, then include your name in the signature block.

i. Save your changes.

j. Preview and print the letter, then close the document and exit Word.

FIGURE A-17

July 8, 2003

Dr. Amanda Russell
Department of Literature and Creative Writing
Nashua State College
Nashua, NH 03285

Dear Dr. Russell:

Thank you for the invitation to speak at your upcoming seminar on "The Literature of Place." I will be happy to do so. I understand that the seminar will be held from 2:30 p.m. to 4:30 p.m. on September 17 in the Sanders Auditorium. As you suggested, I will address the topic "Writers of the Monadonock Region."

I appreciate your invitation and I look forward to working with you on September 17.

Sincerely,

Jessica Grange

▶ Independent Challenge 2

Your company has recently installed Word 2002 on its company network. As the training manager it's your responsibility to teach employees how to use the new software productively. Since installing Word 2002, several employees have asked you about smart tags. In response to their queries, you decide to write a memo to all employees and explain how to use the smart tag feature. You know that smart tags are designed to help users perform tasks in Word that normally would require opening a different program, such as Microsoft Outlook (a desktop information-management program that includes e-mail, calendar, and address book features). Before writing your memo, you'll learn more about smart tags by searching the Word Help system.

FIGURE A-18

WORD TRAINING MEMORANDUM

To: All employees
From: Your Name, Training Manager
Date: Today's date
Re: Smart tags in Word 2002

a. Start Word and save a new blank document as **Smart Tags Memo** to the drive and folder where your Project Files are located.

b. Type **WORD TRAINING MEMORANDUM** at the top of the document, press [Enter] four times, then type the memo heading information shown in Figure A-18. Make sure to include your name in the From line and the current date in the Date line.

c. Press [Enter] twice to place the insertion point where you will begin typing the body of your memo.

d. Search the Word Help system for information on working with smart tags.

e. Type your memo after completing your research. In your memo, define smart tags, then explain what they look like, how to use smart tags, and how to remove smart tags from a document.

f. Save your changes, preview and print the memo, then close the document and exit Word.

▶ Independent Challenge 3

Yesterday you interviewed for a job as marketing director at Komata Web Designs. You spoke with several people at Komata, including Hiro Kobayashi, Director of Operations, whose business card is shown in Figure A-19. You need to write a follow-up letter to Mr. Kobayashi, thanking him for the interview and expressing your interest in the company and the position. He also asked you to send him some samples of your marketing work, which you will enclose with the letter.

FIGURE A-19

Hiro Kobayashi
Director of Operations

Komata Web Designs

5-8, Edobori 4-chome
Minato-ku
Tokyo 108-0034 Japan

Phone: (03) 5555-3299
Fax: (03) 5555-7028
Email: hkoba@komata.co.jp

a. Start Word and save a new blank document as **Komata Letter** to the drive and folder where your Project Files are located.

b. Begin the letter by typing today's date.

c. Four lines below the date, type the inside address, referring to Figure A-19 for the address information. Be sure to include the recipient's title, company name, and full mailing address in the inside address. (*Hint*: When typing a foreign address, type the name of the country in capital letters by itself on the last line.)

d. Two lines below the inside address, type the salutation.

e. Two lines below the salutation, type the body of the letter according to the following guidelines:

• In the first paragraph, thank him for the interview. Then restate your interest in the position and express your desire to work for the company. Add any specific details you think will enhance the power of your letter.

- In the second paragraph, note that you are enclosing three samples of your work and explain something about the samples you are enclosing.
- Type a short final paragraph.

f. Two lines below the last body paragraph, type a closing, then four lines below the closing, type the signature block. Be sure to include your name in the signature block.

g. Two lines below the signature block, type an enclosure notation. (*Hint*: An enclosure notation usually includes the word "Enclosures" or the abbreviation "Enc." followed by the number of enclosures in parentheses.)

h. Save your changes.

i. Preview and print the letter, then close the document and exit Word.

Independent Challenge 4

Unlike personal letters or many e-mail messages, business letters are formal in tone and format. The World Wide Web is one source for information on writing styles, proper document formatting, and other business etiquette issues. In this independent challenge, you will research guidelines and tips for writing effective and professional business letters. Your online research should seek answers to the following questions: What is important to keep in mind when writing a business letter? What are the parts of a business letter? What are some examples of types of business letters? What are some useful tips for writing business letters?

a. Use your favorite search engine to search the Web for information on writing and formatting business letters. Use the keywords **business letters** to conduct your search. If your search does not result in links to information on business letters, try looking at the following Web sites: www.eHow.com, www.business-letters.com, or www.about.com.

b. Review the Web sites you find. Print at least two Web pages that offer useful guidelines for writing business letters.

c. Start Word and save a new blank document as **Business Letters** to the drive and folder where your Project Files are located.

d. Type your name at the top of the document, then press [Enter] twice.

e. Type a brief report on the results of your research. Your report should answer the following questions:
- What are the URLs of the Web sites you visited to research guidelines for writing a business letter? (*Hint*: A URL is a Web page's address. An example of a URL is www.eHow.com.)
- What is important to keep in mind when writing a business letter?
- What are the parts of a business letter?
- In what situations do people write business letters? Provide as many examples as you can think of.

f. Save your changes to the document, preview and print it, then close the document and exit Word.

▶ **Visual Workshop**

Create the cover letter shown in Figure A-20. Since you plan to print the letter on your letterhead, you do not need to include your return address. Save the document with the name **Publishing Cover Letter** to the drive and folder where your Project Files are stored, print a copy of the letter, then close the document and exit Word.

FIGURE A-20

June 16, 2003

Ms. Olivia Johansen
Managing Editor
Conway Press
483 Grove Street
Wellesley, MA 02181

Dear Ms. Johansen:

I read of the opening for an editorial assistant on the June 15 edition of Boston.com, and I would like to be considered for the position. A recent graduate of Whitfield College, I am interested in pursuing a career in publishing.

My desire for a publishing career springs from my interest in writing and editing. At Whitfield College, I was a frequent contributor to the student newspaper and was involved in creating a Web site for student poetry and short fiction.

I have a wealth of experience using Microsoft Word in professional settings. For the past several summers I worked as an office assistant for Packer Investment Consultants, where I used Word to create newsletters and financial reports for clients. During the school year, I also worked part-time in the Whitfield College admissions office. Here I used Word's mail merge feature to create form letters and mailing labels.

My enclosed resume details my talents and experience. I would welcome the opportunity to discuss the position and my qualifications with you. I can be reached at 617-555-3849.

Sincerely,

Your Name

Enc.

Editing
Documents

Word's sophisticated editing features make it easy to revise and polish your documents. In this unit, you learn how to open an existing file, revise it by replacing, copying, and moving text, and then save the document as a new file. You also learn to perfect your documents using Word's proofing tools, and to quickly create attractive, professionally designed documents using wizards and templates. Alice Wegman needs to create a press release about a new MediaLoft lecture series in New York. The press release should provide information about the series so that newspapers, radio stations, and other media outlets can announce it to the public. Alice also needs to create a fax coversheet to use when she faxes the press release to her list of press contacts. You will work with Alice as she creates these documents.

Opening a Document

Word 2002

Sometimes the easiest way to create a document is to edit an existing document and save it with a new filename. To modify a document, you must first **open** it so that it displays in the document window. Word offers several methods for opening documents, described in Table B-1. Once you have opened a file, you can use the Save As command to create a new file that is a copy of the original. You can then edit the new file without making changes to the original. ![pencil] Rather than write her press release from scratch, Alice decides to modify a press release written for a similar event. She begins by opening the press release document and saving it with a new filename.

Steps

Trouble?

If the New Document task pane is not open, click File on the menu bar, then click New.

QuickTip

You also can use the Open button ![icon] on the Standard toolbar or the Open command on the File menu to open the Open dialog box.

QuickTip

You also can double-click a filename in the Open dialog box to open the file.

1. Start Word

Word opens and a blank document and the New Document task pane appear in the program window, as shown in Figure B-1. The New Document task pane contains links for opening existing documents and for creating new documents.

2. Click the Documents or More Documents hyperlink under Open a document in the New Document task pane

The Open dialog box opens. You use the Open dialog box to locate and select the file you want to open. The Look in list box displays the current drive or folder.

3. Click the Look in list arrow, then click the drive containing your Project Files

A list of Project Files appears in the Open dialog box, as shown in Figure B-2. If your Project Files are located in a folder, double-click the folder to display its contents.

4. Click the filename WD B-1 in the Open dialog box, then click Open

The document opens. Notice that the filename WD B-1 appears in the title bar. Once you have opened a file, you can edit it and use the Save or the Save As command to save your changes. You use the **Save** command when you want to save the changes you make to a file, overwriting the file that is stored on a disk. You use the **Save As** command when you want to create a new file with a different filename, leaving the original file intact.

5. Click File on the menu bar, then click Save As

The Save As dialog box opens. By saving a file with a new filename, you create a document that is identical to the original document. The original filename is selected (highlighted) in the File name text box. Any text you type will replace the selected text.

6. Type NY Press Release in the File name text box, then click Save

The original file closes and the NY Press Release file is displayed in the document window. Notice the new filename in the title bar. You can now make changes to the press release file without affecting the original file.

TABLE B-1: Methods for opening documents

use	to	if you want to
The Open button ![icon] on the Standard toolbar, Open command on the File menu, or [Ctrl][O]	Open the Open dialog box	Open an existing file; a fast way to open a document when the New Document task pane is not displayed
The Documents or More Documents hyperlink in the New Document task pane	Open the Open dialog box	Open an existing file; a fast way to open a document when the New Document task pane is displayed
A filename hyperlink in the New Document task pane	Open the file in the document window	Open the file; a fast way to open a file that was recently opened on your computer
The Choose a document hyperlink in the New Document task pane	Open the New From Existing Document dialog box	Create a copy of an existing file; a fast way to open a document you intend to save with a new filename

FIGURE B-1: **New Document task pane**

Open button

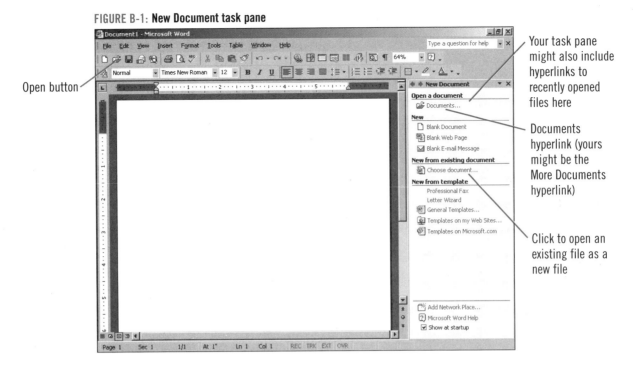

Your task pane might also include hyperlinks to recently opened files here

Documents hyperlink (yours might be the More Documents hyperlink)

Click to open an existing file as a new file

FIGURE B-2: **Open dialog box**

Current drive or folder

Click to quickly open the My Documents folder

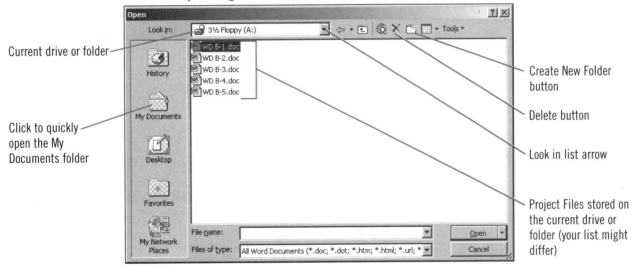

Create New Folder button

Delete button

Look in list arrow

Project Files stored on the current drive or folder (your list might differ)

Managing files and folders

The Open and Save As dialog boxes include powerful tools for navigating, creating, and deleting files and folders on your computer, a network, or the Web. By selecting a file or folder and clicking the Delete button ☒, you can delete the item and send it to the Recycle Bin. You can also create a new folder for storing files by clicking the Create New Folder button 🗀 and typing a name for the folder. The new folder is created in the current folder.

Using the Save As dialog box, you can also create new files that are based on existing files. You can create a new file by saving an existing file with a different filename or by saving it in a different location on your system. You also can save a file in a different file format so that it can be opened in a different software program. To save a file in a different format, click the Files of type list arrow, then click the type of file you want to create. For example, you can save a Word document (which has a .doc file extension) as a plain text file (.txt), as a Web page file (.htm), or in a variety of other file formats.

Selecting Text

Before deleting, editing, or formatting text, you must **select** the text. Selecting text involves clicking and dragging the I-beam pointer across text to highlight it. You also can click with the ⬧ pointer in the blank area to the left of text to select lines or paragraphs. Table B-2 describes the many ways to select text. Alice revises the press release by selecting text and replacing it with new text.

Steps

Trouble?

If you make a mistake, you can deselect the text by clicking anywhere in the document window.

1. Click before **December 9, 2002** and drag the I pointer over the text to select it
The date is selected, as shown in Figure B-3.

2. Type **January 13, 2003**
The text you type replaces the selected text.

3. Double-click **James**, type your first name, double-click **Callaghan**, then type your last name
Double-clicking a word selects the entire word.

4. Place the pointer in the margin to the left of the phone number so that the pointer changes to ⬧, click to select the phone number, then type **(415) 555-8293**
Clicking to the left of a line of text with the ⬧ pointer selects the entire line.

5. Click the **down scroll arrow** at the bottom of the vertical scroll bar until the headline Guy Fogg to Speak ... is at the top of your document window
The scroll arrows or scroll bars allow you to **scroll** through a document. You scroll through a document when you want to display different parts of the document in the document window.

6. Select **SAN FRANCISCO**, then type **NEW YORK**

QuickTip

If you delete text by mistake, immediately click the Undo button 🔄 on the Standard toolbar to restore the deleted text to the document.

7. In the fourth body paragraph, select the sentence **All events will be held at the St. James Hotel.**, then press **[Delete]**
Selecting text and pressing [Delete] removes the text from the document.

8. Select and replace text in the second and last paragraphs using the following table:

select	type
February 12	March 6
St. James Hotel in downtown San Francisco	Waldorf-Astoria Hotel
National Public Radio's Helen DeSaint	New York Times literary editor Isabel Eliot

The edited press release is shown in Figure B-4.

9. Click the **Save button** 💾 on the Standard toolbar
Your changes to the press release are saved. Always save before and after editing text.

CLUES TO USE

Replacing text in Overtype mode

Normally you must select text before typing to replace the existing characters, but by turning on Overtype mode you can type over existing characters without selecting them first. To turn Overtype mode on and off on your computer, double-click OVR in the status bar.

On some computers you also can turn Overtype mode on and off by pressing [Insert]. When Overtype mode is on, OVR appears in black in the status bar. When Overtype mode is off, OVR is dimmed.

FIGURE B-3: **Date selected in the press release**

Selected text

Left document margin

Down scroll arrow

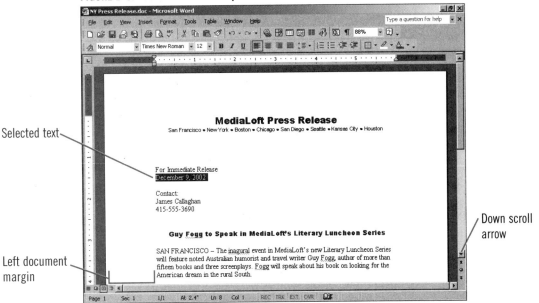

FIGURE B-4: **Edited press release**

Replacement text

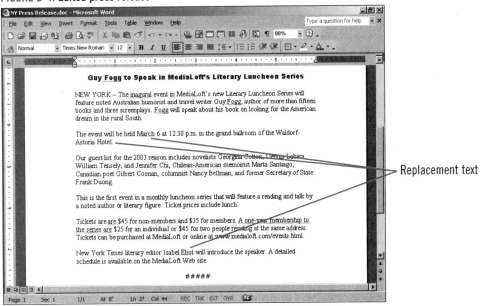

TABLE B-2: **Methods for selecting text**

to select	use the mouse pointer to
Any amount of text	Drag over the text
A word	Double-click the word
A line of text	Click with the ⟍ pointer to the left of the line
A sentence	Press and hold [Ctrl], then click the sentence
A paragraph	Triple-click the paragraph or double-click with the ⟍ pointer to the left of the paragraph
A large block of text	Click at the beginning of the selection, press and hold [Shift], then click at the end of the selection
Multiple nonconsecutive selections	Select the first selection, then press and hold [Ctrl] as you select each additional selection
An entire document	Triple-click with the ⟍ pointer to the left of any text, click Select All on the Edit menu, or press [Ctrl][A]

Cutting and Pasting Text

Word's editing features allow you to move text from one location to another in a document. The operation of moving text is often called **cut and paste**. When you cut text from a document, you remove it from the document and add it to the **Clipboard**, a temporary storage area for text and graphics that you cut or copy from a document. You cut text by selecting it and using the Cut button or the Cut command on the Edit menu. To insert the text from the Clipboard into the document, you place the insertion point where you want to insert the text, and then use the Paste button or the Paste command on the Edit menu to paste the text at that location. You also can move text by dragging it to a new location using the mouse. Alice reorganizes the information in the press release by moving text using the cut and paste and dragging methods.

1. Click the **Show/Hide ¶ button ¶** on the Standard toolbar

Formatting marks appear in the document window. **Formatting marks** are special characters that appear on your screen and do not print. Common formatting marks include the paragraph symbol (¶), which shows the end of a paragraph—wherever you press [Enter]; the dot symbol (•), which represents a space—wherever you press [Spacebar]; and the arrow symbol (→), which shows the location of a tab stop—wherever you press [Tab]. Working with formatting marks turned on can help you to select, edit, and format text with precision.

Trouble?

If the Clipboard task pane opens, close it.

2. In the third paragraph, select **Canadian poet Gilbert Coonan,** (including the comma and the space after it), then click the **Cut button** on the Standard toolbar

The text is removed from the document and placed on the Clipboard. Word uses two different clipboards: the **system Clipboard** (the Clipboard), which holds just one item, and the **Office Clipboard**, which holds up to 24 items. The last item you cut or copy is always added to both clipboards. You'll learn more about the Office Clipboard in a later lesson.

3. Place the insertion point before **novelists** (but after the space) in the first line of the third paragraph, then click the **Paste button** on the Standard toolbar

The text is pasted at the location of the insertion point, as shown in Figure B-5. The Paste Options button appears below text when you first paste it in a document. You'll learn more about the Paste Options button in the next lesson. For now, you can ignore it.

4. Press **[Ctrl]**, then click the sentence **Ticket prices include lunch.** in the fourth paragraph

The entire sentence is selected.

Trouble?

If you make a mistake, click the Undo button on the Standard toolbar, then try again.

5. Press and hold the mouse button over the selected text until the pointer changes to , then drag the pointer's vertical line to the end of the fifth paragraph (between the period and the paragraph mark) as shown in Figure B-6

The pointer's vertical line indicates the location the text will be inserted when you release the mouse button.

6. Release the mouse button

The selected text is moved to the location of the insertion point. It's convenient to move text using the dragging method when the locations of origin and destination are both visible on the screen. Text is not removed to the Clipboard when you move it using the dragging method.

7. Deselect the text, then click the **Save button** on the Standard toolbar

Your changes to the press release are saved.

FIGURE B-5: Moved text with Paste Options button

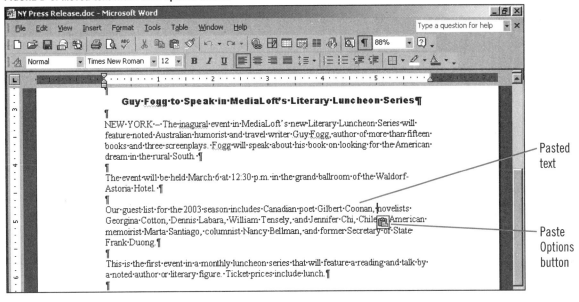

Pasted text

Paste Options button

FIGURE B-6: Text being dragged to a new location

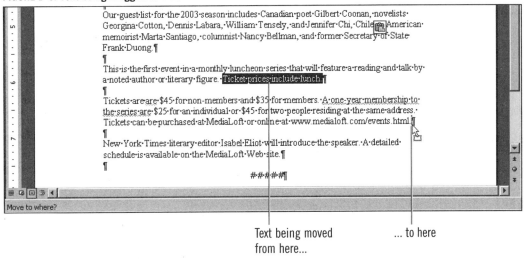

Text being moved from here...

... to here

Using keyboard shortcuts

Instead of using the Cut, Copy, and Paste commands to edit text in Word, you can use the keyboard shortcuts [Ctrl][X] to cut text, [Ctrl][C] to copy text, and [Ctrl][V] to paste text. A **shortcut key** is a function key, such as [F1], or a combination of keys, such as [Ctrl][S], that you press to perform a command. For example, pressing [Ctrl][S] saves changes to a document just as clicking the Save button or using the Save command on the File menu saves a document. Becoming skilled at using keyboard shortcuts can help you to quickly accomplish many of the tasks you perform frequently in Word. If a keyboard shortcut is available for a menu command, then it is listed next to the command on the menu. To find a more extensive list of shortcut keys, search the Help system using the keyword "shortcuts."

Word 2002

Copying and Pasting Text

Copying and pasting text is similar to cutting and pasting text, except that the text you copy is not removed from the document. Rather, a copy of the text is placed on the Clipboard, leaving the original text in place. You can copy text to the Clipboard by using the Copy command on the Edit menu or the Copy button, or you can copy text by pressing [Ctrl] as you drag the selected text from one location to another. ✍ Alice continues to edit the press release by copying text from one location to another.

Steps

Trouble?

If the Clipboard task pane opens, close it.

1. In the headline, select **Literary Luncheon**, then click the **Copy button** 📋 on the Standard toolbar
A copy of the text is placed on the Clipboard, leaving the text you copied in place.

2. Place the insertion point before **season** in the third body paragraph, then click the **Paste button** 📋 on the Standard toolbar
"Literary Luncheon" is inserted before "season," as shown in Figure B-7. Notice that the pasted text is formatted differently than the paragraph in which it was inserted.

QuickTip

If you don't like the result of a paste option, try another option or click the Undo button and then paste the text again.

3. Click the **Paste Options button** 📋▾, then click **Match Destination Formatting**
The Paste Options button allows you to change the formatting of pasted text. The formatting of "Literary Luncheon" is changed to match the rest of the paragraph. The options available on the Paste Options menu depend on the format of the text you are pasting and the format of the surrounding text. Table B-3 summarizes the commands used for pasting text.

4. Scroll down if necessary so that the last two paragraphs are visible on your screen

5. In the fifth paragraph, select **www.medialoft.com**, press and hold [**Ctrl**], then press the mouse button until the pointer changes to 📋

6. Drag the pointer's vertical line to the end of the last paragraph, placing it between **site** and the period, release the mouse button, then release [Ctrl]
The text is copied to the last paragraph. Since the formatting of the text you copied is the same as the formatting of the paragraph in which you inserted it, you can ignore the Paste Options button. Text is not copied to the Clipboard when you copy it using the dragging method.

7. Place the insertion point between **site** and **www.medialoft.com** in the last paragraph, type **at** followed by a space, then click the **Save button** 📋 on the Standard toolbar
Compare your document with Figure B-8.

CLUES TO USE

Using the Undo, Redo, and Repeat commands

Word remembers the editing and formatting changes you make so that you can easily reverse or repeat them. You can reverse the last action you took by clicking the Undo button 📋 on the Standard toolbar, or you can undo a series of actions by clicking the Undo list arrow 📋▾ and selecting the action you want to reverse. When you undo an action using the Undo list arrow, you also undo all the actions above it in the list; that is, all actions that were performed after the action you selected. Similarly, you can keep the changes you just reversed by using the Redo button 📋 and the Redo list arrow 📋▾.

If you want to repeat a change you just made, use the Repeat command on the Edit menu. The name of the Repeat command changes depending on the last action you took. For example, if you just typed "thank you," the name of the command will be Repeat Typing. Clicking the Repeat Typing command will insert "thank you" at the location of the insertion point. You also can repeat the last action you took by pressing [F4].

FIGURE B-7: Text pasted in document

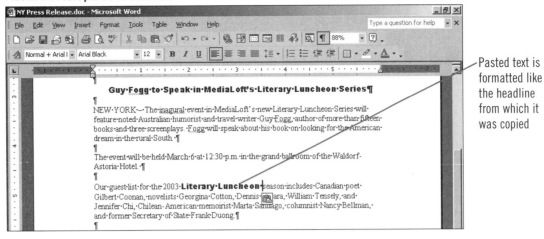

Pasted text is formatted like the headline from which it was copied

FIGURE B-8: Copied text in press release

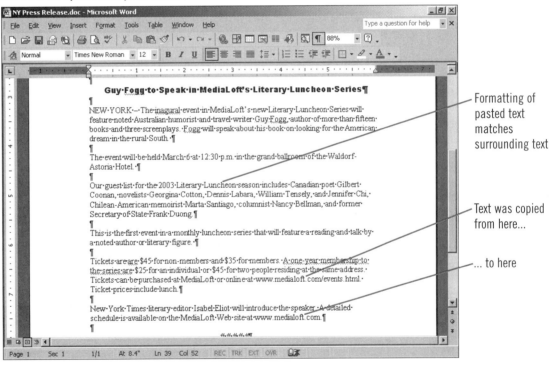

Formatting of pasted text matches surrounding text

Text was copied from here...

... to here

TABLE B-3: Commands used for pasting text

command	use to
Paste command on the Edit menu, Paste button on the Standard toolbar, or [Ctrl][V]	Insert the last item you cut or copied at the location of the insertion point; use the Paste Options button to change the format of the pasted text
Paste Special command on the Edit menu	Insert an item copied or cut from another Office program into a Word document; allows you to embed the object so that you can edit it in its original program; also allows you to create a link to the source file so that changes to the source file are reflected in the Word document
Paste as Hyperlink command on the Edit menu	Paste text so that it is formatted as a hyperlink that jumps to the location from where text was copied; can be used only in conjunction with the Copy command

Using the Office Clipboard

The Office Clipboard allows you to collect text and graphics from files created in any Office Program and insert them into your Word documents. It holds up to 24 items and, unlike the system Clipboard, the items on the Office Clipboard can be viewed. By default, the Office Clipboard opens automatically when you cut or copy two items consecutively. You can also use the Office Clipboard command on the Edit menu to manually display the Office Clipboard if you prefer to work with it open. You add items to the Office Clipboard using the Cut and Copy commands. The last item you collect is always added to both the system Clipboard and the Office Clipboard. Alice uses the Office Clipboard to move several sentences in her press release.

1. In the last paragraph, select the sentence **New York Times literary editor…** (including the space after the period), then click the **Cut button** 🔏 on the Standard toolbar
The sentence is cut to the Clipboard.

2. Select the sentence **A detailed schedule is…** (including the ¶ mark), then click 🔏
The Office Clipboard opens in the Clipboard task pane, as shown in Figure B-9. It displays the items you cut from the press release. The 🗐 icon next to each item indicates the items are from a Word document.

3. Place the insertion point at the end of the second paragraph (before the ¶ mark after Hotel.), then click the **New York Times literary editor…** item on the Office Clipboard
Clicking an item on the Office Clipboard pastes the item in the document at the location of the insertion point. Notice that the item remains on the Office Clipboard even after you pasted it. Items remain on the Office Clipboard until you delete them or close all open Office programs. Also, if you add a 25th item to the Office Clipboard, the first item is deleted.

4. Place the insertion point at the end of the third paragraph (after Duong.), then click the **A detailed schedule is…** item on the Office Clipboard
The sentence is pasted in the document.

5. Select the fourth paragraph, which contains the sentence **This is the first event…** (including the ¶ mark), then click 🔏
The sentence is cut to the Office Clipboard. Notice that the last item collected displays at the top of the Clipboard task pane. The last item collected is also stored on the system Clipboard.

6. Place the insertion point at the beginning of the third paragraph (before Our…), click the **Paste button** 📋 on the Standard toolbar, then press **[Backspace]**
The "This is the first …" sentence is pasted at the beginning of the "Our guest list …" paragraph. You can paste the last item collected using either the Paste command or the Office Clipboard.

7. Place the insertion point at the end of the third paragraph (before the ¶ mark), then press **[Delete]** twice
The ¶ symbols and the blank line between the third and fourth paragraphs are deleted.

8. Click the **Show/Hide ¶ button** ¶ on the Standard toolbar
Compare your press release with Figure B-10.

9. Click the **Clear All button** on the Office Clipboard to remove the items from it, close the Clipboard task pane, press **[Ctrl][Home]**, then click the **Save button** 💾
Pressing [Ctrl][Home] moves the insertion point to the top of the document.

FIGURE B-9: Office Clipboard in Clipboard task pane

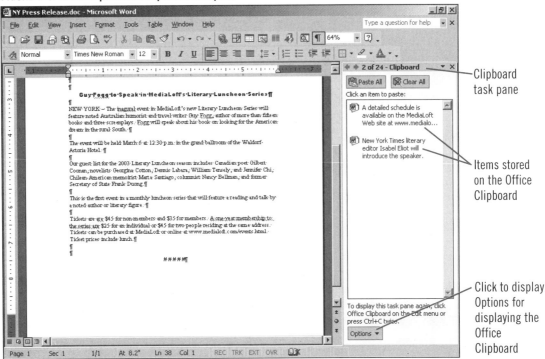

Clipboard task pane

Items stored on the Office Clipboard

Click to display Options for displaying the Office Clipboard

FIGURE B-10: Revised press release

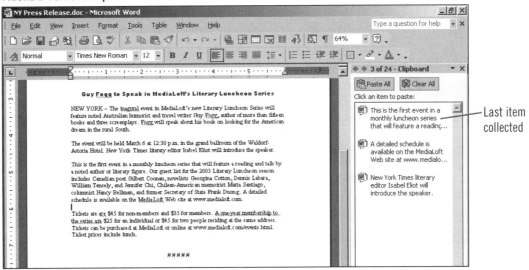

Last item collected

Copying and moving items between documents

The system and Office Clipboards also can be used to copy and move items between Word documents. To copy or cut text from one Word document and paste it into another, first open both documents in the program window. When a document is open in the program window, a Word program button labeled with its filename appears on the taskbar. With multiple documents open, you can copy and move text between documents by copying or cutting the item(s) from one document and then switching to another document and pasting the item(s). To switch between open documents, click the button on the taskbar for the document you want to appear in the document window. The Office Clipboard stores all the items collected from all files, regardless of which document is displayed in the document window. The system Clipboard stores the last item collected from any file.

Word 2002

Using the Spelling and Grammar Checker and the Thesaurus

When you finish typing and revising a document, you can use the Spelling and Grammar command to search the document for misspelled words and grammatical errors. The Spelling and Grammar checker flags possible mistakes, suggests correct spellings, and offers remedies for grammatical errors such as subject-verb agreement, repeated words, and punctuation. Word also includes a Thesaurus, which you can use to look up synonyms for awkward or repetitive words. Alice uses the Spelling and Grammar checker to search her press release for errors. Before beginning the search, she sets the Spelling and Grammar checker to ignore words, such as Fogg, she knows are spelled correctly. She also uses the Thesaurus to find a synonym for "noted."

Trouble?

If Word flags your name or "MediaLoft" as misspelled, right-click those words, then click Ignore All.

1. Right-click **Fogg** in the headline

A shortcut menu that includes suggestions for correcting the spelling of "Fogg" opens. You can correct individual spelling and grammar errors by right-clicking text that is underlined with a red or green wavy line and selecting a correction. Although "Fogg" is not in Word's dictionary, it is spelled correctly in the document.

2. Click **Ignore All**

Clicking Ignore All tells Word not to flag "Fogg" as misspelled.

QuickTip

To change the language used by Word's proofing tools, click Tools on the menu bar, point to Language, then click Set Language.

3. Press **[Ctrl][Home]**, then click the **Spelling and Grammar button** on the Standard toolbar

The Spelling and Grammar: English (U.S.) dialog box opens, as shown in Figure B-11. The dialog box identifies "inagural" as misspelled and suggests possible corrections for the error. The word selected in the Suggestions box is the correct spelling.

4. Click **Change**

Word replaces the misspelled word with the correctly spelled word. Next, the dialog box indicates "are" is repeated in a sentence.

Trouble?

You might need to correct other spelling and grammatical errors.

5. Click **Delete**

Word deletes the second occurrence of the repeated word. Next, the dialog box flags a subject-verb agreement error and suggests using "is" instead of "are," as shown in Figure B-12. The phrase selected in the Suggestions box is correct.

QuickTip

If Word does not offer a valid correction, correct the error yourself.

6. Click **Change**

The word "is" replaces the word "are" in the sentence and the Spelling and Grammar dialog box closes. Keep in mind that the spelling and grammar feature identifies many common errors, but you cannot rely on it to find and correct all spelling and grammatical errors in your documents. Always proofread your documents carefully.

7. Click **OK** to complete the spelling and grammar check, then scroll up until the headline is displayed at the top of your screen

QuickTip

You also can right-click a word and point to Synonyms on the shortcut menu to see a list of synonyms for a word.

8. In the first sentence of the third paragraph, select **noted**, click **Tools** on the menu bar, point to **Language**, then click **Thesaurus**

The Thesaurus: English (U.S.) dialog box opens, as shown in Figure B-13. Possible synonyms for "noted" appear in the dialog box.

9. Click **distinguished** in the Replace with Synonym list box, then click **Replace**

The dialog box closes and "distinguished" replaces "noted" in the press release.

10. Press **[Ctrl][Home]**, then click the **Save button** on the Standard toolbar

FIGURE B-11: **Spelling and Grammar: English (U.S.) dialog box**

Spelling and Grammar: English (U.S.)
Not in Dictionary:
NEW YORK – The inagural event in MediaLoft's new Literary Luncheon Series will feature noted Australian humorist and travel writer Guy Fogg, author of more than
Suggestions:
inaugural
inaugurals
Check grammar
Ignore Once
Ignore All
Add to Dictionary
Change
Change All
AutoCorrect
Options...
Undo
Cancel
Word identified as misspelled
Suggested corrections
Adds the misspelled word and the correction to the AutoCorrect list
Ignores this occurrence of the word
Leaves all occurrences of the word unchanged
Adds the word to Word's dictionary
Changes the word to the selected correction
Changes all occurrences of the word to the selected correction

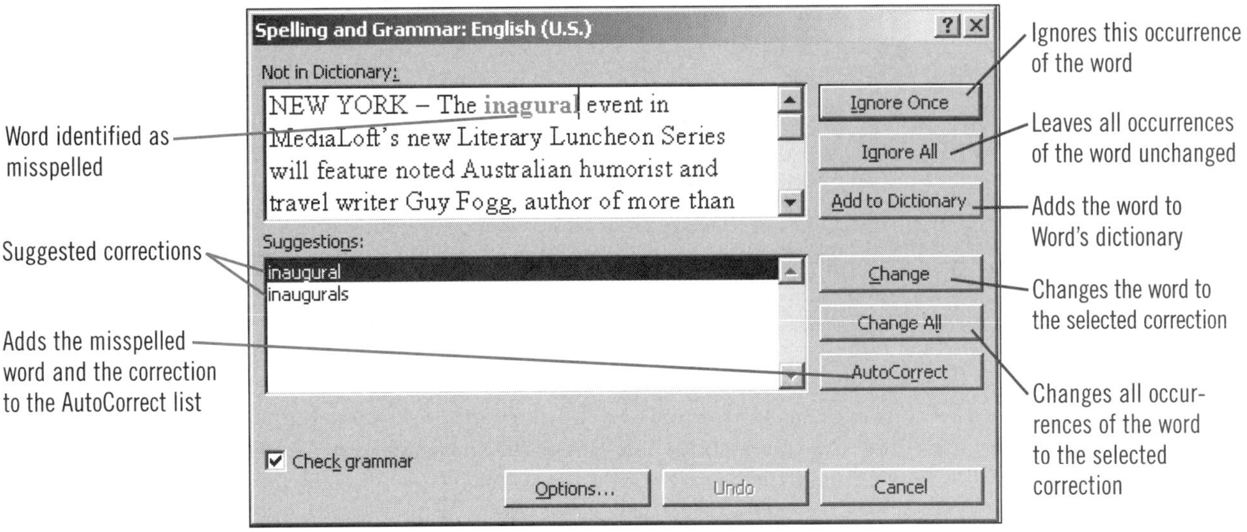

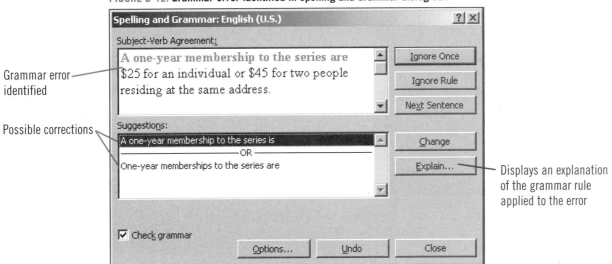

FIGURE B-12: **Grammar error identified in Spelling and Grammar dialog box**

Spelling and Grammar: English (U.S.)
Subject-Verb Agreement:
A one-year membership to the series are $25 for an individual or $45 for two people residing at the same address.
Suggestions:
A one-year membership to the series is
OR
One-year memberships to the series are
Check grammar
Ignore Once
Ignore Rule
Next Sentence
Change
Explain...
Options...
Undo
Close
Grammar error identified
Possible corrections
Displays an explanation of the grammar rule applied to the error

FIGURE B-13: **Thesaurus: English (U.S.) dialog box**

Thesaurus: English (U.S.)
Looked Up:
noted
Meanings:
renowned (adj.)
Related Words
Replace with Synonym:
renowned
renowned
well-known
famous
distinguished
celebrated
illustrious
eminent
prominent
Replace
Look Up
Previous
Cancel
Word in the document
Possible meanings for the word
Replaces the word with the selected synonym
Synonyms for the selected meaning of the word

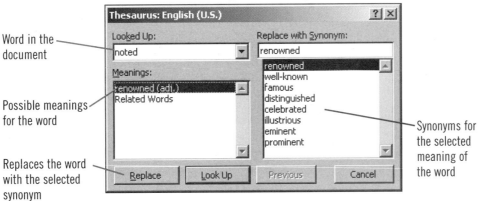

Finding and Replacing Text

Word's Find and Replace feature allows you to automatically search for and replace all instances of a word or phrase in a document. For example, you might need to substitute "bookstore" for "store," and it would be very time-consuming to manually locate and replace each instance of "store" in a long document. Using the Replace command you can automatically find and replace all occurrences of specific text at once, or you can choose to find and review each occurrence individually. You also can use the Find command to locate and highlight every occurrence of a specific word or phrase in a document. MediaLoft has decided to change the name of the New York series from "Literary Luncheon Series" to "Literary Limelight Series." Alice uses the Replace command to search the document for all instances of "Luncheon" and replace them with "Limelight."

1. **Click Edit on the menu bar, click Replace, then click More in the Find and Replace dialog box**
   The Find and Replace dialog box opens, as shown in Figure B-14.

2. **Click the Find what text box, then type Luncheon**
   "Luncheon" is the text that will be replaced.

3. **Press [Tab], then type Limelight in the Replace with text box**
   "Limelight" is the text that will replace "Luncheon."

4. **Click the Match case check box in the Search Options section to select it**
   Selecting the Match case check box tells Word to find only exact matches for the uppercase and lowercase characters you entered in the Find what text box. You want to replace all instances of "Luncheon" in the proper name "Literary Luncheon Series." You do not want to replace "luncheon" when it refers to a lunchtime event.

> **QuickTip**
> Click Find Next to find, review, and replace each occurrence individually.

5. **Click Replace All**
   Clicking Replace All changes all occurrences of "Luncheon" to "Limelight" in the press release. A message box reports three replacements were made.

6. **Click OK to close the message box, then click Close to close the Find and Replace dialog box**
   Word replaced "Luncheon" with "Limelight" in three locations, but did not replace "luncheon."

7. **Click Edit on the menu bar, then click Find**
   The Find and Replace dialog box opens with the Find tab displayed. The Find command allows you to quickly locate all instances of text in a document. You can use it to verify that Word did not replace "luncheon."

8. **Type luncheon in the Find what text box, click the Highlight all items found in check box to select it, click Find All, then click Close**
   The Find and Replace dialog box closes and "luncheon" is selected in the document.

9. **Deselect the text, click the Save button 🖫 on the Standard toolbar, then click the Print button 🖨 on the Standard toolbar**
   A copy of the finished press release prints. Compare your document to Figure B-15.

10. **Click File on the menu bar, then click Close**

FIGURE B-14: **Replace tab in the Find and Replace dialog box**

Replace only exact matches of uppercase and lowercase characters

Find only complete words

Use wildcards (*) in a search string

Find words that sound like the Find what text

Find and replace all forms of a word

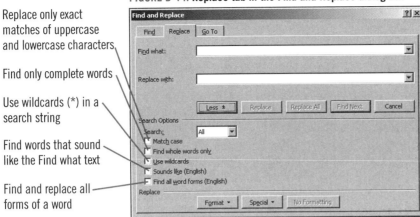

FIGURE B-15: **Completed press release**

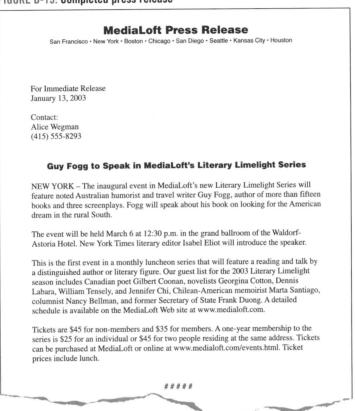

Inserting text with AutoCorrect

As you type, AutoCorrect automatically corrects many commonly misspelled words. By creating your own AutoCorrect entries, you also can set Word to quickly insert text that you type often, such as your name or contact information, or to correct words you frequently misspell. For example, you could create an AutoCorrect entry so that "Alice Wegman" is automatically inserted whenever you type "aw" followed by a space. To create an AutoCorrect entry, click AutoCorrect Options on the Tools menu. On the AutoCorrect tab in the AutoCorrect dialog box, type the text you want to be automatically corrected in the Replace text box (such as "aw"), type the text you want to be automatically inserted in its place in the With text box (such as "Alice Wegman"), then click Add. The AutoCorrect entry is added to the list. Note that Word inserts an AutoCorrect entry in a document only when you press [Spacebar] after typing the text you want Word to correct. For example, Word will insert "Alice Wegman" when you type "aw" followed by a space, but not when you type "awful."

Word 2002

Using Wizards and Templates

Word includes many templates that you can use to quickly create memos, faxes, letters, reports, brochures, and other professionally designed documents. A **template** is a formatted document that contains placeholder text. To create a document that is based on a template, you replace the placeholder text with your own text and then save the document with a new filename. A **wizard** is an interactive set of dialog boxes that guides you through the process of creating a document. A wizard prompts you to provide information and select formatting options, and then it creates the document for you based on your specifications. You can create a document with a wizard or template using the New command on the File menu. Alice will fax the press release to her list of press contacts, beginning with the *New York Times*. She uses a template to create a fax coversheet for the press release.

Steps

1. **Click File on the menu bar, then click New**
   The New Document task pane opens.

2. **Click the General Templates hyperlink in the New Document task pane**
   The Templates dialog box opens. The tabs in the dialog box contain icons for the Word templates and wizards.

3. **Click the Letters & Faxes tab, then click the Professional Fax icon**
   A preview of the Professional Fax template appears in the Templates dialog box, as shown in Figure B-16.

   QuickTip

   Double-clicking an icon in the Templates dialog box also opens a new document based on the template.

4. **Click OK**
   The Professional Fax template opens as a new document in the document window. It contains placeholder text, which you can replace with your own information.

5. **Drag to select Company Name Here, then type MediaLoft**

6. **Click the Click here and type return address and phone and fax numbers placeholder**
   Clicking the placeholder selects it. When a placeholder says Click here... you do not need to drag to select it.

7. **Type MediaLoft San Francisco, press [Enter], then type Tel: (415) 555-8293**
   The text you type replaces the placeholder text.

   QuickTip

   Delete any placeholder text you do not want to replace.

8. **Replace the remaining placeholder text with the text shown in Figure B-17**
   Word automatically inserted the current date in the document. You do not need to replace the current date with the date shown in the figure.

9. **Click File on the menu bar, click Save As, use the Save in list arrow to navigate to the drive or folder where your Project Files are located, type NYT Fax in the File name text box, then click Save**
   The document is saved with the filename NYT Fax.

10. **Click the Print button 🖨 on the Standard toolbar, click File on the menu bar, then click Exit**
    A copy of the fax coversheet prints and the document and Word close.

FIGURE B-16: Letters & Faxes tab in Templates dialog box

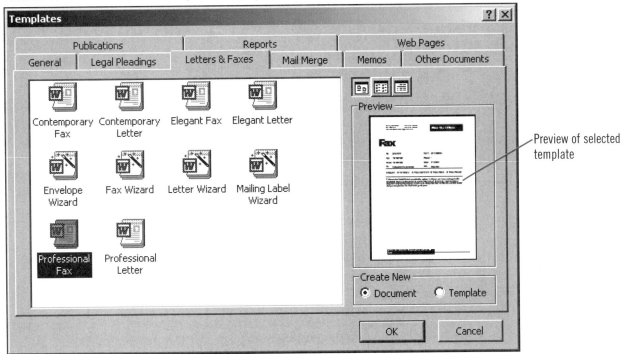

Preview of selected template

FIGURE B-17: Completed fax coversheet document

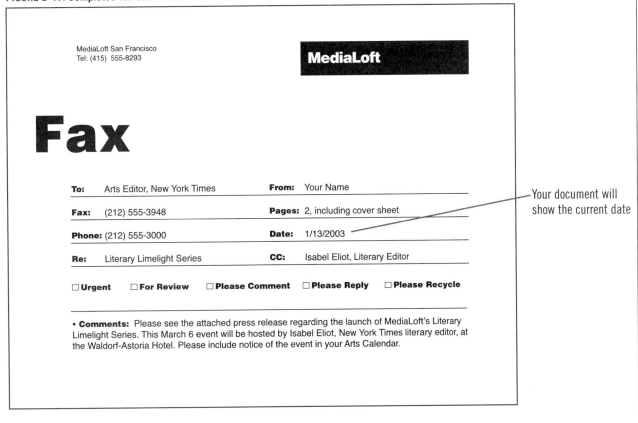

Your document will show the current date

Word 2002

Practice

► Concepts Review

Label the elements of the Open dialog box shown in Figure B-18.

FIGURE B-18

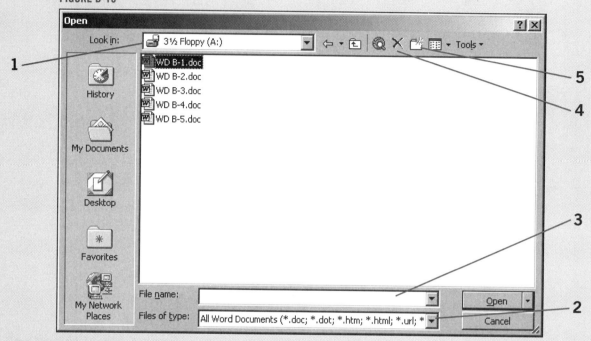

Match each term with the statement that best describes it.

6. **System Clipboard**
7. **Show/Hide**
8. **Select**
9. **Thesaurus**
10. **Undo**
11. **Template**
12. **Office Clipboard**
13. **Paste**
14. **Replace**

a. Feature used to suggest synonyms for words
b. Command used to insert text stored on the Clipboard into a document
c. Command used to reverse the last action you took in a document
d. Temporary storage area for only the last item cut or copied from a document
e. Document that contains placeholder text
f. Temporary storage area for up to 24 items collected from any Office file
g. Command used to locate and replace occurrences of specific text in a document
h. Action that must be taken before text can be cut, copied, or deleted
i. Command used to display formatting marks in a document

Select the best answer from the list of choices.

15. Which of the following is *not* used to open an existing document?
   a. Documents or More documents hyperlink in the New Document task pane
   b. Open command on the Edit menu
   c. Blank document hyperlink in the New Document task pane
   d. Open button on the Standard toolbar

16. **To locate and change all instances of a word in a document, which command do you use?**
    a. Replace
    b. Find
    c. Search
    d. Paste

17. **Which of the following statements is *not* true?**
    a. The last item cut or copied from a document is stored on the system Clipboard.
    b. The Office Clipboard can hold more than one item.
    c. You can view the contents of the Office Clipboard.
    d. When you move text by dragging it, a copy of the text you move is stored on the system Clipboard.

18. **Which Word feature corrects errors as you type?**
    a. AutoCorrect
    b. Thesaurus
    c. Spelling and Grammar
    d. Undo and Redo

19. **Which command do you use to paste an item created in a different Office program into a Word document so that changes to the source file are reflected in the Word document?**
    a. Paste
    b. Paste Special
    c. Paste as Hyperlink
    d. Office Clipboard

20. **What does the symbol ¶ represent when it is displayed in the document window?**
    a. Text that is pasted
    b. A space
    c. The end of a paragraph
    d. A tab stop

▶ Skills Review

1. **Open a document.**
   a. Start Word, click the Open button, then open the file WD B-2 from the drive and folder where your Project Files are located.
   b. Save the document with the filename **CAOS Press Release**.

2. **Select text.**
   a. Select **Today's Date** and replace it with the current date.
   b. Select **Your Name** and **Your Phone Number** and replace them with the relevant information.
   c. Scroll down, then select and replace text in the body of the press release using the following table as a guide:

in paragraph	select	replace with
1	16 and 17	13 and 14
1	fifth	eighth
4	open his renovated Pearl St studio for the first time this year	offer a sneak-preview of his Peace sculpture commissioned by the city of Prague

   d. In the fourth paragraph, delete the sentence **Exhibiting with him will be sculptor Francis Pilo**.
   e. Save your changes to the press release.

3. Cut and paste text.

a. Display paragraph and other formatting marks in your document if they are not already displayed.

b. Use the Cut and Paste buttons to switch the order of the two sentences in the fourth paragraph (which begins New group shows...).

c. Use the drag method to switch the order of the second and third paragraphs.

d. Adjust the spacing if necessary so that there is one blank line between paragraphs, then save your changes.

4. Copy and paste text.

a. Use the Copy and Paste buttons to copy CAOS 2000 from the headline and paste it before the word map in the third paragraph.

b. Change the formatting of the pasted text to match the formatting of the third paragraph, then insert a space between 2000 and map if necessary.

c. Use the drag method to copy CAOS from the third paragraph and paste it before the word group in the second sentence of the fourth paragraph, then save your changes.

5. Use the Office Clipboard.

a. Use the Office Clipboard command on the Edit menu to open the Office Clipboard in the task pane.

b. Scroll so that the first body paragraph is displayed at the top of the document window.

c. Select the fifth paragraph (which begins Studio location maps...) and cut it to the Office Clipboard.

d. Select the third paragraph (which begins Cambridgeport is easily accessible...) and cut it to the Office Clipboard.

e. Use the Office Clipboard to paste the Studio location maps... item as the new fourth paragraph.

f. Use the Office Clipboard to paste the Cambridgeport is easily accessible... item as the new fifth paragraph.

g. Use any method to switch the order of the two sentences in the fourth paragraph (which begins Studio location maps...).

h. Adjust the spacing if necessary so that there is one blank line between each of the six body paragraphs.

i. Turn off the display of formatting marks, clear and close the Office Clipboard, then save your changes.

6. Use the Spelling and Grammar checker and the Thesaurus.

a. Set Word to ignore the spelling of Cambridgeport, if necessary. (*Hint*: Right-click Cambridgeport.)

b. Move the insertion point to the top of the document, then use the Spelling and Grammar command to search for and correct any spelling and grammatical errors in the press release.

c. Use the Thesaurus to replace thriving in the second paragraph with a different suitable word.

d. Save your changes to the press release.

7. Find and replace text.

a. Using the Replace command, replace all instances of 2000 with 2003.

b. Replace all instances of the abbreviation St with Street, taking care to replace whole words only when you perform the replace. (*Hint*: Click More to expand the Find and Replace dialog box.)

c. Use the Find command to find all instances of st in the document, and make sure no errors occurred when you replaced St with Street.

d. Proofread your press release, correct any errors, save your changes, print a copy, then close the document.

8. Use wizards and templates.

a. Use the New command to open the New Documents task pane.

b. Use the General Templates hyperlink to open the Templates dialog box.

c. Create a new document using the Elegant Fax template.

d. Replace the placeholder text in the document using Figure B-19 as a guide. Delete any placeholders that do not apply to your fax. The date in your fax will be the current date.

e. Scroll to the bottom of the document and replace the placeholder text with your return address.

f. Save the document as **CAOS Fax**, print a copy, close the document, then exit Word.

FIGURE B-19

C A O S 2 0 0 3

FACSIMILE TRANSMITTAL SHEET

TO:	FROM:
Pat Zabko, Listings Editor	Your Name
COMPANY:	DATE:
Boston Phoenix	9/12/2003
FAX NUMBER:	TOTAL NO. OF PAGES INCLUDING COVER:
(617) 555-2980	2
PHONE NUMBER:	SENDER'S REFERENCE NUMBER:
RE:	YOUR REFERENCE NUMBER:
Cambridgeport Artists Open Studios	

☐ URGENT   ☐ FOR REVIEW   ☐ PLEASE COMMENT   ☐ PLEASE REPLY   ☐ PLEASE RECYCLE

NOTES/COMMENTS:

A press release regarding the 2003 Cambridgeport Artists Open Studios is included with this fax. Please include this information in the Phoenix Listings.

► Independent Challenge 1

FIGURE B-20

Because of your success in revitalizing a historic theatre in Hobart, Tasmania, you were hired as the director of The Wellington Lyric Theatre in Wellington, New Zealand, to breathe life into its theatre revitalization efforts. After a year on the job, you are launching your first major fund-raising drive. You'll create a fund-raising letter for the Lyric Theatre by modifying a letter you wrote for the theatre in Hobart.

a. Start Word, open the file WD B-3 from the drive and folder where your Project Files are located, then save it as **Lyric Theatre Letter**.

b. Replace the theatre name and address, the date, the inside address, and the salutation with the text shown in Figure B-20.

c. Use the Replace command to replace all instances of **Hobart** with **Wellington**.

d. Use the Replace command to replace all instances of **Tasmanians** with **New Zealanders**.

e. Use the Find command to locate the word **considerable**, then use the Thesaurus to replace the word with a synonym.

f. Create an AutoCorrect entry that inserts **Wellington Lyric Theatre** whenever you type **wlt**.

g. Select each XXXXX and the space that follows it, then type **wlt** followed by a space.

h. Move the fourth body paragraph so that it becomes the second body paragraph.

The Wellington Lyric Theatre
72-74 Hobson Street, Thorndon, Wellington, New Zealand

September 12, 2003

Mr. Colin Fuller
168 Cuba Street
Wellington

Dear Mr. Fuller,

i. Replace Your Name with your name in the signature block.

j. Use the Spelling and Grammar command to check for and correct spelling and grammar errors.

k. Proofread the letter, correct any errors, save your changes, print a copy, close the document, then exit Word.

▶ Independent Challenge 2

An advertisement for job openings in Scotland caught your eye and you have decided to apply. The ad, shown in Figure B-21, was printed in last weekend's edition of your local newspaper. You'll use the Letter Wizard to create a cover letter to send with your resume.

a. Read the ad shown in Figure B-21 and decide which position to apply for. Choose the position that most closely matches your qualifications.

b. Start Word and open the Templates dialog box.

c. Double-click Letter Wizard on the Letters & Faxes tab, then select Send one letter in the Office Assistant balloon or Letter Wizard dialog box.

d. In the Letter Wizard—Step 1 of 4 dialog box, choose to include a date on your letter, select Elegant Letter for the page design, select Modified block for the letter style, include a header and footer with the page design, then click Next.

e. In the Letter Wizard—Step 2 of 4 dialog box, enter the recipient's name (Ms. Hillary Price) and the delivery address, referring to the ad for the address information. Also enter the salutation **Dear Ms. Price** using the business style, then click Next.

f. In the Letter Wizard—Step 3 of 4 dialog box, include a reference line in the letter, enter the appropriate position code (see Figure B-21) in the Reference line text box, then click Next.

g. In the Letter Wizard—Step 4 of 4 dialog box, enter your name as the sender, enter your return address (including your country), and select an appropriate complimentary closing. Then, because you will be including your resume with the letter, include one enclosure. Click Finish when you are done.

h. Click Cancel to close the Office Assistant, if necessary. Then save the letter with the filename **Global Dynamics Letter** to the drive and folder where your Project Files are located.

i. Replace the placeholder text in the body of the letter with three paragraphs that address your qualifications for the job:

- In the first paragraph, specify the job you are applying for, indicate where you saw the position advertised, and briefly state your qualifications and interest in the position.

FIGURE B-21

*Global*Dynamics

Career Opportunities in Scotland

Global Dynamics, an established software development firm with offices in North America, Asia, and Europe, is seeking candidates for the following positions in its new Edinburgh facility:

Instructor

Responsible for delivering software training to our expanding European customer base. Duties include delivering hands-on training, keeping up-to-date with product development, and working with the Director of Training to ensure the high quality of course materials. Successful candidate will have excellent presentation skills and be proficient in Microsoft PowerPoint and Microsoft Word. **Position B12C6**

Administrative Assistant

Proficiency with Microsoft Word a must! Administrative office duties include making travel arrangements, scheduling meetings, taking notes and publishing meeting minutes, handling correspondence, and ordering office supplies. Must have superb multi-tasking abilities, excellent communication, organizational, and interpersonal skills, and be comfortable working with e-mail and the Internet. **Position B16F5**

Copywriter

The ideal candidate will have marketing or advertising writing experience in a high tech environment, including collateral, newsletters, and direct mail. Experience writing for the Web, broadcast, and multimedia is a plus. Fluency with Microsoft Word required. **Position C13D4**

Positions offer salary, excellent benefits, moving expenses, and career growth opportunities.

Send resume and cover letter referencing position code to:

**Hillary Price
Director of Recruiting
Global Dynamics
24 Castle Terrace
Edinburgh EH3 9SH
United Kingdom**

- In the second paragraph, describe your work experience and skills. Be sure to relate your experience and qualifications to the position requirements listed in the ad.
- In the third paragraph, politely request an interview for the position and provide your phone number and e-mail address.

j. When you are finished typing the letter, check it for spelling and grammar errors and correct any mistakes.

k. Save your changes to the letter, print a copy, close the document, then exit Word.

▶ Independent Challenge 3

As administrative director of continuing education, you drafted a memo to instructors asking them to help you finalize the course schedule for next semester. Today you'll examine the draft and make revisions before printing it.

a. Start Word and open the file WD B-4 from the drive and folder where your Project Files are located.

b. Open the Save As dialog box, navigate to the drive and folder where your Project Files are located, use the Create New Folder button to create a new folder called **Memos**, then save the document as **Computer Memo** in the Memos folder.

c. Replace Your Name with your name in the From line.

d. Use the Cut and Paste buttons to move the sentence **If you are planning to teach ...** from the first body paragraph to become the first sentence in the last paragraph of the memo.

e. Use the [Delete] key to merge the first two paragraphs into one paragraph.

f. Use the Office Clipboard to reorganize the list of twelve-week courses so that the courses are listed in alphabetical order. (*Hint*: Use the Zoom list arrow to enlarge the document as needed.)

g. Use the dragging method to reorganize the list of one-day seminars so that the seminars are listed in alphabetical order.

h. Use the Spelling and Grammar command to check for and correct spelling and grammar errors.

i. Clear and close the Office Clipboard, save your changes, print a copy, close the document, then exit Word.

℮ Independent Challenge 4

Reference sources—dictionaries, thesauri, style and grammar guides, and guides to business etiquette and procedure—are essential for day-to-day use in the workplace. Much of this reference information is available on the World Wide Web. In this independent challenge, you will locate reference sources on the Web and use some of them to look up definitions, synonyms, and antonyms for words. Your goal is to familiarize yourself with online reference sources so you can use them later in your work.

a. Start Word, open the file WD B-5 from the drive and folder where your Project Files are located, and save it as **Web References**. This document contains the questions you will answer about the Web reference sources you find. You will type your answers to the questions in the document.

b. Replace the placeholder text at the top of the Web References document with your name and the date.

c. Use your favorite search engine to search the Web for grammar and style guides, dictionaries, and thesauri. Use the keywords **grammar**, **usage**, **dictionary**, **glossary**, and **thesaurus** to conduct your search. If your search does not result in links to appropriate reference sources, try the following Web sites: www.bartleby.com, www.dictionary.com, or www.thesaurus.com.

d. Complete the Web References document, then proofread it and correct any mistakes.

e. Save the document, print a copy, close the document, then exit Word.

▶ **Visual Workshop**

Using the Contemporary Letter template, create the letter shown in Figure B-22. Save the document as **Visa Letter**. Check the letter for spelling and grammar errors, then print a copy.

FIGURE B-22

35 Hardy Street
Vancouver, BC V6C 3K4
Tel: (604) 555-8989
Fax: (604) 555-8981

Your Name

March 10, 2003

Embassy of Australia
Suite 710
50 O'Connor Street
Ottawa, Ontario K1P 6L2

Dear Sir or Madam:

I am applying for a long-stay (six-month) tourist visa to Australia, valid for four years. I am scheduled to depart for Sydney on June 1, 2003, returning to Vancouver on November 23, 2003.

While in Australia, I plan to conduct research for a book I am writing on coral reefs. I am interested in a multiple entry visa valid for four years so that I can return to Australia after this trip to follow-up on my initial research. I will be based in Cairns, but will be traveling frequently to other parts of Australia to meet with scientists, policy-makers, and environmentalists.

Enclosed please find my completed visa application form, my passport, a passport photo, a copy of my return air ticket, and the visa fee. Please let me know if I can provide further information.

Sincerely,

Your Name

Enclosures (5)

Formatting
Text and Paragraphs

Objectives

- MOUS ▶ **Format with fonts**
- MOUS ▶ **Change font styles and effects**
- MOUS ▶ **Change line and paragraph spacing**
- MOUS ▶ **Align paragraphs**
- MOUS ▶ **Work with tabs**
- MOUS ▶ **Work with indents**
- MOUS ▶ **Add bullets and numbering**
- MOUS ▶ **Add borders and shading**

Formatting can enhance the appearance of a document, create visual impact, and help illustrate a document's structure. The formatting of a document can also add personality and lend a degree of professionalism to your document. In this unit you learn how to format text using different fonts and font-formatting options. You also learn how to change the alignment, indentation, and spacing of paragraphs, and how to spruce up documents with borders, shading, bullets, and other paragraph-formatting effects. ✎━ Isaac Robinson is the marketing director at the MediaLoft Chicago store. Isaac has drafted a quarterly marketing report to send to MediaLoft's headquarters. He now needs to format the report so it is attractive and highlights the significant information. You will work with Isaac as he formats the report.

Formatting with Fonts

Formatting text with different fonts is a quick and powerful way to enhance the appearance of a document. A **font** is a complete set of characters with the same typeface or design. Arial, Times New Roman, Comic Sans, Courier, and Tahoma are some of the more common fonts, but there are hundreds of others, each with a specific design and feel. Another way to alter the impact of text is to increase or decrease its **font size**, which is measured in points. A **point** is ½ of an inch. When formatting a document with fonts, it's important to pick fonts that augment the document's purpose. You can apply fonts and font sizes to text by selecting the text and using the Formatting toolbar. Isaac changes the font and font size of the title and headings in his report, selecting a font that enhances the business tone of the document. By formatting the title and headings in a font different from the body text, he helps to visually structure the report for readers.

Steps

1. Start **Word**, open the file **WD C-1** from the drive and folder where your Project Files are located, then save it as **Chicago Marketing Report**
   The file opens in Print Layout view.

2. Click the **Normal View button** on the horizontal scroll bar, click the **Zoom list arrow** on the Standard toolbar, then click **100%** if necessary
   The document switches to Normal view, a view useful for simple text formatting. The name of the font used in the document, Times New Roman, is displayed in the Font list box on the Formatting toolbar. The font size, 12, appears next to it in the Font Size list box.

3. Select the title **MediaLoft Chicago Quarterly Marketing Report**, then click the **Font list arrow** on the Formatting toolbar
   The Font list showing the fonts available on your computer opens, as shown in Figure C-1. Fonts you have used recently appear above the double line. All the fonts on your computer are listed in alphabetical order below the double line.

4. Click **Arial**
   The font of the report title changes to Arial.

5. Click the **Font Size list arrow** on the Formatting toolbar, then click **20**
   The font size of the title increases to 20 points.

6. Click the **Font Color list arrow** on the Formatting toolbar
   A palette of colors opens.

7. Click **Dark Blue** on the Font Color palette as shown in Figure C-2, then deselect the text
   The color of the report title text changes to dark blue. The active color on the Font Color button also changes to dark blue.

8. Select the heading **Advertising**, click the **Font list arrow**, click **Arial**, click the **Font Size list arrow**, click **14**, click the **Font Color button**, then deselect the text
   The heading is formatted in 14-point Arial with a dark blue color.

9. Scroll down the document and format each of the following headings in 14-point Arial with a dark blue color: **Events**, **Classes & Workshops**, **Publications**, and **Surveys**

10. Press **[Ctrl][Home]**, then click the **Save button** on the Standard toolbar
    Pressing [Ctrl][Home] moves the insertion point to the beginning of the document. Compare your document to Figure C-3.

QuickTip

There are two types of fonts: serif fonts have a small stroke, called a serif, at the ends of characters; sans serif fonts do not have a serif. Times New Roman is a serif font. Arial is a sans serif font.

QuickTip

For a clean look, limit the number of fonts you use in a document to two or three.

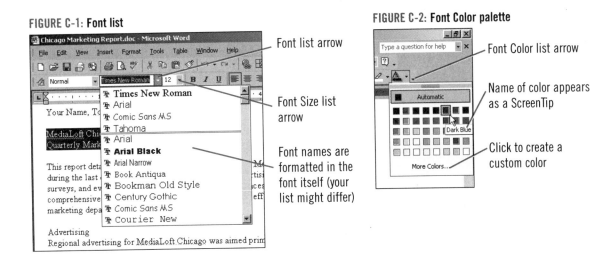

FIGURE C-1: Font list

- Font list arrow
- Font Size list arrow
- Font names are formatted in the font itself (your list might differ)

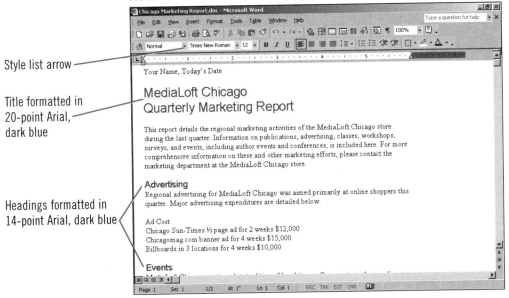

FIGURE C-2: Font Color palette

- Font Color list arrow
- Name of color appears as a ScreenTip
- Click to create a custom color

FIGURE C-3: Document formatted with fonts

- Style list arrow
- Title formatted in 20-point Arial, dark blue
- Headings formatted in 14-point Arial, dark blue

Word 2002

CLUES TO USE

Clearing text formatting

If you are unhappy with the way text is formatted, you can use the Clear Formats command to return the text to the default format settings. By default, text is formatted in 12-point Times New Roman and paragraphs are left-aligned and single-spaced. To clear formatting from text, select the text you want to clear, point to Clear on the Edit menu, then click Formats. Alternately, click the Styles list arrow on the Formatting toolbar, then click Clear Formatting. Clearing formatting from text does not delete or change the text itself; it simply formats the text with the default format settings.

Word 2002

Changing Font Styles and Effects

You can dramatically change the appearance of text by applying different font styles, font effects, and character-spacing effects. For example, you can use the buttons on the Formatting toolbar to make text darker by applying **bold**, or to slant text by applying *italic*. You can also use the Font command on the Format menu to apply font effects and character-spacing effects to text. Isaac spices up the appearance of the text in his document by applying different font styles and effects.

Steps

> **QuickTip**

Click the Underline button
U on the Formatting tool-
bar to underline text.

1. Select **MediaLoft Chicago Quarterly Marketing Report**, then click the **Bold button** B on the Formatting toolbar
   Applying bold makes the characters darker and thicker.

2. Select the **paragraph** under the title, then click the **Italic button** *I* on the Formatting toolbar
   The paragraph is formatted in italic.

> **QuickTip**

To quickly apply bold to multiple headings, press and hold
[Ctrl] as you select each
heading, then click B.

3. Scroll down and apply bold to each dark blue heading
   The headings all have a darker, thicker appearance.

4. Scroll up until the subheading Author Events is at the top of your screen, select **Author Events**, click **Format** on the menu bar, then click **Font**
   The Font dialog box opens, as shown in Figure C-4. You can use the Font tab to change the font, font style, size, and color of text, and to add an underline and apply font effects to the selected text.

5. Scroll up the Font list, click **Arial**, click **Bold Italic** in the Font style list box, select the **Small caps check box**, then click **OK**
   The subheading is formatted in Arial, bold, italic, and small caps. When you change text to small caps, the lowercase letters are changed to uppercase letters in a smaller font size.

> **QuickTip**

If you apply formats one by
one, then pressing [F4]
repeats only the last format
you applied.

6. Select **Travel Writers & Photographers Conference**, then press **[F4]**
   Pressing [F4] repeats the last action you took. Because you last applied Arial, bold, italic, and small caps together in one action (using the Font dialog box), the subheading is formatted in Arial, bold, italic, and small caps.

7. Under Author Events, select the book title **Just H20 Please: Tales of True Adventure on the Environmental Frontline**, click *I*, select **2** in the book title, click **Format** on the menu bar, click **Font**, click the **Subscript check box**, click **OK**, then deselect the text
   As shown in Figure C-5, the book title is formatted in italic and the character 2 is subscript.

> **QuickTip**

To animate the selected text,
click the Text Effects tab in
the Font dialog box, then
select an animation style. The
animation appears only when
a document is viewed in
Word; animation effects do
not print.

8. Press **[Ctrl][Home]**, select the **report title**, click **Format** on the menu bar, click **Font**, then click the **Character Spacing tab** in the Font dialog box
   You use the Character Spacing tab to change the scale, or width, of the selected characters, to alter the spacing between characters, or to raise or lower the position of the characters.

9. Click the **Scale list arrow**, click **150%**, click **OK**, deselect the text, then click the **Save button** on the Standard toolbar
   Increasing the scale of the characters makes them wider and gives the text a shorter, squat appearance, as shown in Figure C-6.

FIGURE C-4: Font tab in Font dialog box

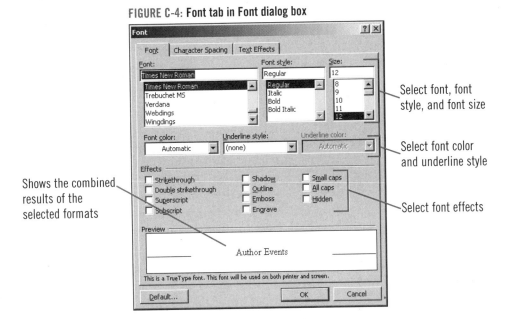

Shows the combined results of the selected formats

Select font, font style, and font size

Select font color and underline style

Select font effects

FIGURE C-5: Font effects applied to text

Subhead formatted in 12-point Arial, bold, italic, and small caps

Subscript text

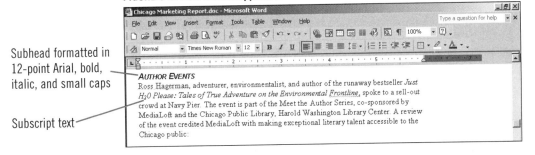

FIGURE C-6: Character-spacing effects applied to text

Report title formatted in bold with a character scale of 150%

Paragraph formatted in italic

Headings formatted in bold

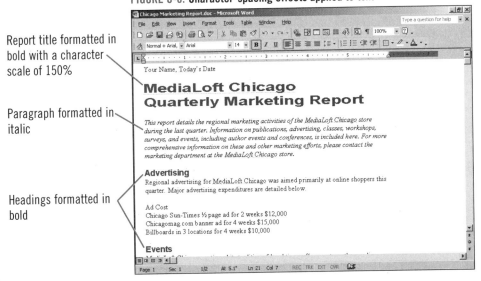

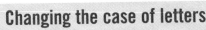

Changing the case of letters

The Change Case command on the Format menu allows you to quickly change letters from uppercase to lowercase—and vice versa—saving you the time it takes to retype text you want to change. To change the case of selected text, use the Change Case command to open the Change Case dialog box, then select the case style you want to use. Sentence case capitalizes the first letter of a sentence, title case capitalizes the first letter of each word, and toggle case switches all letters to the opposite case.

Changing Line and Paragraph Spacing

Word 2002

Increasing the amount of space between lines adds more white space to a document and can make it easier to read. Adding space between paragraphs can also open up a document and improve its appearance. You can change line and paragraph spacing using the Paragraph command on the Format menu. You can also use the Line Spacing button to quickly change line spacing. ✒ Isaac increases the line spacing of several paragraphs and adds extra space under each heading to give the report a more open feel.

Steps

QuickTip

The checkmark on the Line Spacing list indicates the current line spacing.

1. Place the insertion point in the italicized paragraph under the report title, then click the **Line Spacing list arrow** 📄 on the Formatting toolbar

   The Line Spacing list opens. This list includes options for increasing the space between lines.

2. Click **1.5**

   The space between the lines in the paragraph increases to 1.5 lines. Notice that you do not need to select an entire paragraph to change its paragraph formatting; simply place the insertion point in the paragraph you want to format.

QuickTip

Word recognizes any string of text that ends with a paragraph mark as a paragraph, including titles, headings, and single lines in a list.

3. Scroll down until the heading Advertising is at the top of your screen, select the **four-line list** that begins with Ad Cost, click 📄, then click **1.5**

   The line spacing between the selected paragraphs changes to 1.5. To change the paragraph-formatting features of more than one paragraph, you must select the paragraphs.

4. Place the insertion point in the heading **Advertising**, click **Format** on the menu bar, then click **Paragraph**

   The Paragraph dialog box opens, as shown in Figure C-7. You can use the Indents and Spacing tab to change line spacing and the spacing above and below paragraphs. Spacing between paragraphs is measured in points.

QuickTip

Adjusting the space between paragraphs is a more precise way to add white space to a document than inserting blank lines.

5. Click the **After up arrow** in the Spacing section so that 6 pt appears, then click **OK**

   Six points of space are added below the paragraph—the Advertising heading.

6. Select **Advertising**, then click the **Format Painter button** 🖌 on the Standard toolbar

   The pointer changes to 🖌. The **Format Painter** is a powerful Word feature that allows you to copy all the format settings applied to the selected text to other text that you want to format the same way. The Format Painter is especially useful when you want to copy multiple format settings, but you can also use it to copy individual formats.

QuickTip

Using the Format Painter is not the same as using [F4]. Pressing [F4] repeats only the last action you took. You can use the Format Painter at any time to copy multiple format settings.

7. Select **Events** with the 🖌 pointer, then deselect the text

   Six points of space are added below the Events heading paragraph and the pointer changes back to the I-beam pointer. Compare your document with Figure C-8.

8. Select **Events**, then double-click 🖌

   Double-clicking the Format Painter button allows the Format Painter to remain active until you turn it off. By keeping the Format Painter turned on you can apply formatting to multiple items.

9. Scroll down, select the headings **Classes & Workshops**, **Publications**, and **Surveys** with the 🖌 pointer, then click 🖌 to turn off the Format Painter

   Six points of space are added below each heading paragraph.

10. Press **[Ctrl][Home]**, then click the **Save button** 💾 on the Standard toolbar

FIGURE C-7: Indents and Spacing tab in Paragraph dialog box

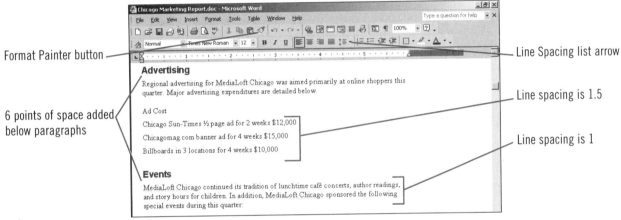

Change the spacing above and below paragraphs

Spacing After up arrow

Change the line spacing

Preview of selected settings

FIGURE C-8: Line and paragraph spacing applied to document

Format Painter button

6 points of space added below paragraphs

Line Spacing list arrow

Line spacing is 1.5

Line spacing is 1

Formatting with styles

You can also apply multiple format settings to text in one step by applying a style. A **style** is a set of formats, such as font, font size, and paragraph alignment, that are named and stored together. To work with styles, click the Styles and Formatting button 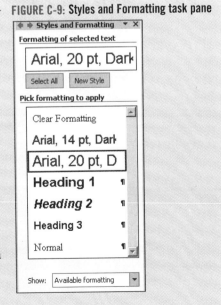 on the Formatting toolbar to open the Styles and Formatting task pane, shown in Figure C-9. The task pane displays the list of available styles and the formats you have created for the current document, if any. To view all the styles available in Word, click the Show list arrow at the bottom of the task pane, then click All Styles.

A **character style**, indicated by a ⟨a⟩ character in the list of styles, includes character format settings, such as font and font size. A **paragraph style**, indicated by a ¶ character in the list, is a combination of character and paragraph formats, such as font, font size, paragraph alignment, and paragraph spacing. To apply a style, select the text or paragraph you want to format, then click the style name in the Pick formatting to apply list box.

FIGURE C-9: Styles and Formatting task pane

Aligning Paragraphs

Changing paragraph alignment is another way to enhance a document's appearance. Paragraphs are aligned relative to the left and right margins in a document. By default, text is **left-aligned**, which means it is flush with the left margin and has a ragged right edge. Using the alignment buttons on the Formatting toolbar, you can **right-align** a paragraph—make it flush with the right margin—or **center** a paragraph so that it is positioned evenly between the left and right margins. You can also **justify** a paragraph so that both the left and right edges of the paragraph are flush with the left and right margins. ✐ Isaac changes the alignment of several paragraphs at the beginning of the report to make it visually more interesting.

Steps

1. Replace **Your Name, Today's Date** with your name, a comma, and the date

2. Select your name and the date, then click the **Align Right button** 📄 on the Formatting toolbar

   The text is aligned with the right margin. In Normal view, the junction of the white and shaded sections of the horizontal ruler indicates the location of the right margin. The left end of the ruler indicates the left margin.

3. Place the insertion point between your name and the comma, press **[Delete]** to delete the comma, then press **[Enter]**

   The new paragraph containing the date is also right-aligned. Pressing [Enter] in the middle of a paragraph creates a new paragraph with the same text and paragraph formatting as the original paragraph.

4. Select the **report title**, then click the **Center button** 📄 on the Formatting toolbar

   The two paragraphs that make up the title are centered between the left and right margins.

5. Place the insertion point in the **Advertising** heading, then click 📄

   The Advertising heading is centered.

6. Place the insertion point in the italicized paragraph under the report title, then click the **Justify button** 📄

   The paragraph is aligned with both the left and right margins, as shown in Figure C-10. When you justify a paragraph, Word adjusts the spacing between words so that each line in the paragraph is flush with the left and the right margins.

7. Place the insertion point in **MediaLoft** in the report title, click **Format** on the menu bar, then click **Reveal Formatting**

   The Reveal Formatting task pane opens in the Word program window, as shown in Figure C-11. The task pane shows the formatting applied to the text and paragraph where the insertion point is located. You can use the Reveal Formatting task pane to check or change the formatting of any character, word, paragraph, or other aspect of a document.

8. Select **Advertising**, then click the **Alignment** hyperlink in the Reveal Formatting task pane

   The Paragraph dialog box opens with the Indents and Spacing tab displayed. It shows the settings for the selected text.

9. Click the **Alignment list arrow**, click **Left**, click **OK**, then deselect the text

   The Advertising heading is left-aligned.

10. Close the Reveal Formatting task pane, then click the **Save button** 📄 on the Standard toolbar

FIGURE C-10: Modified paragraph alignment

Right margin in Normal view

Right-aligned

Center-aligned

Justified

Left-aligned

FIGURE C-11: Reveal Formatting task pane

Reveal Formatting task pane

Format settings for the selected text

Click hyperlinks to change format settings

Click - to hide information

Click + to display information

Select to show underlying style

Select to show formatting marks in document

CLUES TO USE

Working with Click and Type

Word's Click and Type feature allows you to automatically apply the paragraph formatting necessary to insert text (or graphics or tables) in a blank area of a document in Print Layout or Web Layout view. As you move the pointer around in a blank area of a document, the pointer changes depending on its location. Double-clicking with a click and type pointer in a blank area of a document automatically applies the appropriate alignment and indentation for that location, so that when you begin typing, the text is already formatted.

The pointer shape indicates which formatting will be applied at each location when you double-click. For example, if you click with the ⬇ pointer, the text you type will be center-aligned. Clicking with I⁼ creates a left tab stop at the location of the insertion point so that the text you type is left-aligned at the tab stop. Clicking with ⁼I right-aligns the text you type. The I⁼ pointer creates left-aligned text with a first line indent. The best way to learn how to use Click and Type is to experiment in a blank document.

Word 2002

Working with Tabs

Tabs allow you to align text vertically at a specific location in a document. A **tab stop** is a point on the horizontal ruler that indicates the location at which to align text. By default, tab stops are located every ½" from the left margin, but you can also set custom tab stops. Using tabs, you can align text to the left, right, or center of a tab stop, or you can align text at a decimal point or bar character. You set tabs using the horizontal ruler or the Tabs command on the Format menu. Isaac uses tabs to format the information on advertising expenditures so it is easy to read.

1. **Scroll down until the heading Advertising is at the top of your screen, then select the four-line list beginning with Ad Cost**
   Before you set tab stops for existing text, you must select the paragraphs for which you want to set tabs.

Trouble?
If the horizontal ruler is not visible, click Ruler on the View menu.

2. **Point to the tab indicator at the left end of the horizontal ruler**
   The icon that appears in the tab indicator indicates the active type of tab; pointing to the tab indicator displays a ScreenTip with the name of the active tab type. By default, left tab is the active tab type. Clicking the tab indicator scrolls through the types of tabs.

3. **Click the tab indicator to see each of the available tab types, make left tab the active tab type, then click the 1" mark on the horizontal ruler**
   A left tab stop is inserted at the 1" mark on the horizontal ruler. Clicking the horizontal ruler inserts a tab stop of the active type for the selected paragraph or paragraphs.

4. **Click the tab indicator twice so the Right Tab icon is active, then click the 4½" mark on the horizontal ruler**
   A right tab stop is inserted at the 4½" mark on the horizontal ruler, as shown in Figure C-12.

QuickTip
Don't use the Spacebar to vertically align text in columns; always use tabs or a table.

5. **Place the insertion point before Ad in the first line in the list, press [Tab], place the insertion point before Cost, then press [Tab]**
   Inserting a tab before Ad left-aligns the text at the 1" mark. Inserting a tab before Cost right-aligns Cost at the 4½" mark.

6. **Insert a tab at the beginning of each remaining line in the list, then insert a tab before each $ in the list.**
   The paragraphs left-align at the 1" mark. The prices right-align at the 4½" mark.

7. **Select the four lines of tabbed text, drag the right tab stop to the 5" mark on the horizontal ruler, then deselect the text**
   Dragging the tab stop moves it to a new location. The prices right-align at the 5" mark.

QuickTip
Place the insertion point in a paragraph to see the tab stops for that paragraph on the horizontal ruler.

8. **Select the last three lines of tabbed text, click Format on the menu bar, then click Tabs**
   The Tabs dialog box opens, as shown in Figure C-13. You can use the Tabs dialog box to set tab stops, change the position or alignment of existing tab stops, clear tab stops, and apply tab leaders to tabs. **Tab leaders** are lines that appear in front of tabbed text.

9. **Click 5" in the Tab stop position list box, click the 2 option button in the Leader section, click OK, deselect the text, then click the Save button on the Standard toolbar**
   A dotted tab leader is added before each 5" tab stop, as shown in Figure C-14.

FIGURE C-12: **Left and right tab stops on the horizontal ruler**

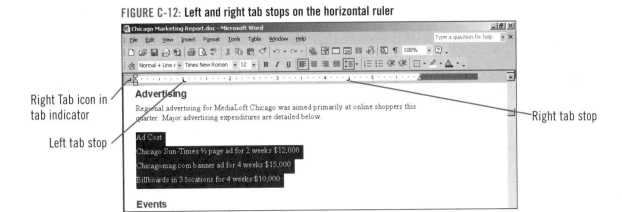

Right Tab icon in tab indicator

Left tab stop

Right tab stop

FIGURE C-13: **Tabs dialog box**

Select the tab stop you want to modify

FIGURE C-14: **Tab leaders**

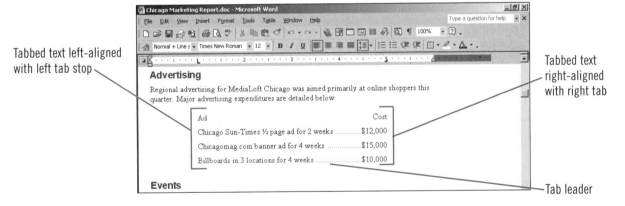

Tabbed text left-aligned with left tab stop

Tabbed text right-aligned with right tab

Tab leader

 CLUES TO USE

Creating a table

In addition to using tabs to organize text in rows and columns, you can create a table and then enter the text in rows and columns. To create a simple table, place the insertion point where you want to insert the table, click the Insert Table button on the Standard toolbar, then, on the grid that appears, drag to select the number of columns and rows you want for the table. When you release the mouse button, an empty table is inserted in the document. To enter or edit text in the table, place the insertion point in a table cell, then type. To move the insertion point from cell to cell, press [Tab] or click in a cell. To format text in a table, select the text, then use the buttons on the Formatting toolbar. The Table menu also includes commands for modifying and formatting tables.

Working with Indents

When you **indent** a paragraph, you move its edge in from the left or right margin. You can indent the entire left or right edge of a paragraph or just the first line. The **indent markers** on the horizontal ruler indicate the indent settings for the paragraph in which the insertion point is located. Dragging the indent markers to a new location on the ruler is one way to change the indentation of a paragraph; using the indent buttons on the Formatting toolbar is another. You can also use the Paragraph command on the Format menu to indent paragraphs. Table C-1 describes different types of indents and the methods for creating each. ◆ Isaac indents several paragraphs in the report.

Steps 1 2 3 4

1. Press **[Ctrl][Home]**, click the **Print Layout View button** 🔳 on the horizontal scroll bar, click the **Zoom list arrow** on the Standard toolbar, then click **Page Width**
   The document is displayed in Print Layout view, making it easier to see the document margins.

QuickTip

Press [Tab] at the beginning of a paragraph to indent the first line ½". You can also set a custom indent using the Indents and Spacing tab in the Paragraph dialog box.

2. Place the insertion point in the italicized paragraph under the title, then click the **Increase Indent button** 📰 on the Formatting toolbar
   The entire paragraph is indented ½" from the left margin, as shown in Figure C-15. The indent marker 🔺 also moves to the ½" mark on the horizontal ruler. Each time you click the Increase Indent button, the left edge of a paragraph moves another ½" to the right.

3. Click the **Decrease Indent button** 📰 on the Formatting toolbar
   The left edge of the paragraph moves ½" to the left, and the indent marker moves back to the left margin.

Trouble?

Take care to drag only the First Line Indent marker. If you make a mistake, click the Undo button 🔙, then try again.

4. Drag the **First Line Indent marker** ▽ to the ¼" mark on the horizontal ruler as shown in Figure C-16
   The first line of the paragraph is indented ¼". Dragging the first line indent marker indents only the first line of a paragraph.

5. Scroll to the bottom of page 1, place the insertion point in the **quote** (the last paragraph), then drag the **Left Indent marker** 🔲 to the ½" mark on the horizontal ruler
   When you drag the Left Indent marker, the First Line and Hanging Indent markers move as well. The left edge of the paragraph is indented ½" from the left margin.

6. Drag the **Right Indent marker** 🔺 to the 5½" mark on the horizontal ruler
   The right edge of the paragraph is indented ½" from the right margin, as shown in Figure C-17.

7. Click the **Save button** 💾 on the Standard toolbar

TABLE C-1: Types of indents

indent type	description	to create
Left indent	The left edge of a paragraph is moved in from the left margin	Drag the Left Indent marker 🔲 right to the position where you want the left edge of the paragraph to align, or click the Increase Indent button 📰 to indent the paragraph in ½" increments
Right indent	The right edge of a paragraph is moved in from the right margin	Drag the Right Indent marker 🔺 left to the position where you want the right edge of the paragraph to end
First-line indent	The first line of a paragraph is indented more than the subsequent lines	Drag the First Line Indent marker ▽ right to the position where you want the first line of the paragraph to start
Hanging indent	The subsequent lines of a paragraph are indented more than the first line	Drag the Hanging Indent marker 🔺 right to the position where you want the hanging indent to start
Negative indent (or Outdent)	The left edge of a paragraph is moved to the left of the left margin	Drag the Left Indent marker 🔲 left to the position where you want the negative indent to start

FIGURE C-15: Indented paragraph

First Line
Indent marker

Hanging Indent
marker

Left Indent
marker

Indented
paragraph

Decrease Indent
button

Increase Indent
button

Right Indent
marker

FIGURE C-16: First Line Indent marker being dragged

First Line
Indent marker
being dragged
to the ¼" mark

FIGURE C-17: Paragraph indented from the left and right

Paragraph
indented ½"
from left

Paragraph indented
½" from right

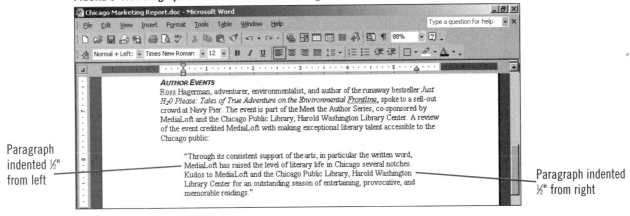

Adding Bullets and Numbering

Word 2002

Formatting a list with bullets or numbering can help to organize the ideas in a document. A **bullet** is a character, often a small circle, that appears before the items in a list to add emphasis. Formatting a list as a numbered list helps illustrate sequences and priorities. You can quickly format a list with bullets or numbering by using the Bullets and Numbering buttons on the Formatting toolbar. You can also use the Bullets and Numbering command on the Format menu to change or customize bullet and numbering styles. ✎ Isaac formats the lists in his report with numbers and bullets.

1. Scroll down until the first paragraph on the second page (Authors on our...) is at the top of your screen

2. Select the **three-line list of names** under the paragraph, then click the **Numbering button** 📋 on the Formatting toolbar
   The paragraphs are formatted as a numbered list.

> **QuickTip**
>
> To change the numbers to letters, Roman numerals, or another numbering style, right-click the list, click Bullets and Numbering, then select a new numbering style on the Numbered tab.

3. Place the insertion point after **Jack Seneschal**, press **[Enter]**, then type **Polly Flanagan**
   Pressing [Enter] in the middle of the numbered list creates a new numbered paragraph and automatically renumbers the remainder of the list. Similarly, if you delete a paragraph from a numbered list, Word automatically renumbers the remaining paragraphs.

4. Click 1 in the list
   Clicking a number in a list selects all the numbers, as shown in Figure C-18.

5. Click the **Bold button** 🅱 on the Formatting toolbar
   The numbers are all formatted in bold. Notice that the formatting of the items in the list does not change when you change the formatting of the numbers. You can also use this technique to change the formatting of bullets in a bulleted list.

> **QuickTip**
>
> To remove a bullet or number, select the paragraph(s), then click 📋 or 📋.

6. Select the **list of classes and workshops** under the Classes & Workshops heading, scrolling down if necessary, then click the **Bullets button** 📋 on the Formatting toolbar
   The five paragraphs are formatted as a bulleted list.

7. With the list still selected, click **Format** on the menu bar, then click **Bullets and Numbering**
   The Bullets and Numbering dialog box opens with the Bulleted tab displayed, as shown in Figure C-19. You use this dialog box to apply bullets and numbering to paragraphs, or to change the style of bullets or numbers.

8. Click the **Square bullets box** or select another style if square bullets are not available to you, click **OK**, then deselect the text
   The bullet character changes to a small square, as shown in Figure C-20.

9. Click the **Save button** 💾 on the Standard toolbar

FIGURE C-18: **Numbered list**

Numbers selected in numbered list

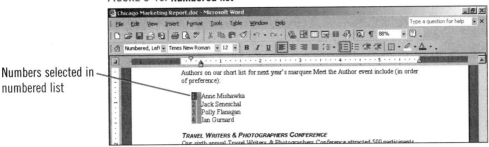

FIGURE C-19: **Bulleted tab in the Bullets and Numbering dialog box**

Numbered tab contains options for numbered lists

Square bullets (your bullet styles might differ)

Outline Numbered tab contains options for outlines

Click to select different characters and pictures to use as bullets

FIGURE C-20: **Square bullets applied to list**

Numbers are bold

Square bullets applied to list

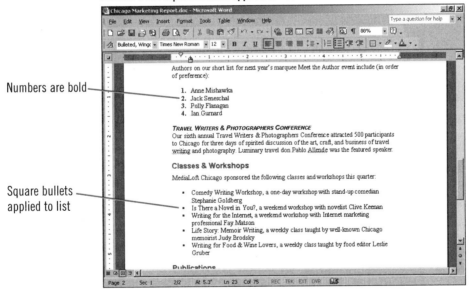

Creating outlines

You can create lists with hierarchical structures by applying an outline numbering style to a list. To create an outline, begin by applying an outline numbering style from the Outline Numbered tab in the Bullets and Numbering dialog box, then type your outline, pressing [Enter] after each item. To demote items to a lower level of importance in the outline, place the insertion point in the item, then click the Increase Indent button on the Formatting toolbar. Each time you indent a paragraph, the item is demoted to a lower lever in the outline. Similarly, you can use the Decrease Indent button to promote an item to a higher level in the outline. You can also create a hierarchical structure in any bulleted or numbered list by using and to demote and promote items in the list. To change the outline numbering style applied to a list, select a new style from the Outline Numbered tab in the Bullets and Numbering dialog box.

Adding Borders and Shading

Borders and shading can add color and splash to a document. **Borders** are lines you add above, below, to the side, or around words or a paragraph. You can format borders using different line styles, colors, and widths. **Shading** is a color or pattern you apply behind words or paragraphs to make them stand out on a page. You apply borders and shading using the Borders and Shading command on the Format menu. Isaac enhances the advertising expenses table by adding shading to it. He also applies a border under every heading to visually punctuate the sections of the report.

Steps

1. Scroll up until the heading Advertising is at the top of your screen

2. Select the **four paragraphs** of tabbed text under the Advertising heading, click **Format** on the menu bar, click **Borders and Shading**, then click the **Shading tab**
   The Shading tab in the Borders and Shading dialog box is shown in Figure C-21. You use this tab to apply shading to words and paragraphs.

3. Click the **Pale Blue box** in the bottom row of the Fill section, click **OK**, then deselect the text
   Pale blue shading is applied to the four paragraphs. Notice that the shading is applied to the entire width of the paragraphs, despite the tab settings.

4. Select the **four paragraphs**, drag the **Left Indent marker** ▢ to the ¾" mark on the horizontal ruler, drag the **Right Indent marker** △ to the 5¼" mark, then deselect the text
   The paragraphs are indented from the left and right, making the shading look more attractive.

5. Select **Advertising**, click **Format** on the menu bar, click **Borders and Shading**, then click the **Borders tab**
   The Borders tab is shown in Figure C-22. You use this tab to add boxes and lines to words or paragraphs.

6. Click the **Custom box** in the Setting section, click the **Width list arrow**, click ¾ pt, click the **Bottom Border button** ▣ in the Preview section, click **OK**, then deselect the text
   A ¾-point black border is added below the Advertising paragraph.

7. Click **Events**, press **[F4]**, then scroll down and use **[F4]** to add a border under each blue heading
   The completed document is shown in Figure C-23.

8. Click the **Save button** 🖫 on the Standard toolbar, click the **Print button** 🖨, close the document, then exit Word
   A copy of the report prints. Depending on your printer, colors might appear differently when you print. If you are using a black and white printer, colors will print in shades of gray.

Highlighting text in a document

You can mark important text in a document with highlighting. **Highlighting** is transparent color that is applied to text using the Highlight pointer ⫟. To highlight text, click the Highlight list arrow 🖉▾ on the Formatting toolbar, select a color, then use the I-beam part of the ⫟ pointer to select the text. Click 🖉 to turn off the Highlight pointer. To remove highlighting, select the highlighted text, click 🖉▾, then click None. Highlighting prints, but it is used most effectively when a document is viewed online.

FIGURE C-21: Shading tab in Borders and Shading dialog box

Name of active color appears here

Pale Blue

Click to select a shading pattern

Preview of shading settings

Click to choose to apply the settings to the paragraph or to the selected text

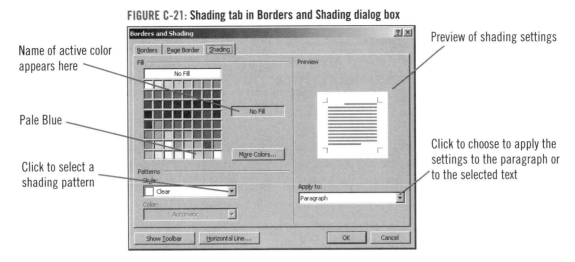

FIGURE C-22: Borders tab in Borders and Shading dialog box

Select border formats before applying them in the Preview section

Select Custom to add a single border

Preview of border settings

Bottom border button

Click buttons or edges of preview to apply individual borders

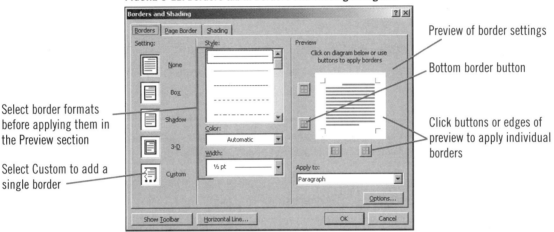

FIGURE C-23: Borders and shading applied to the document

Border under headings

Shading applied to paragraphs

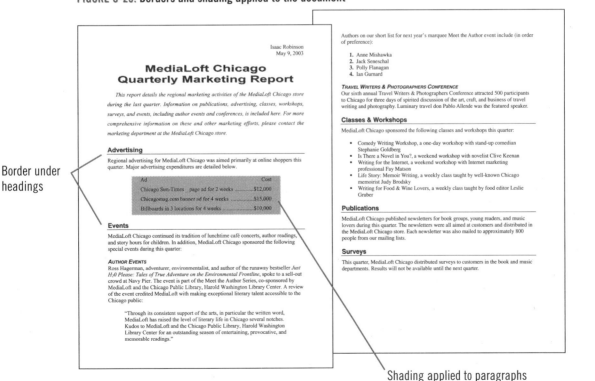

Practice

► Concepts Review

Label each element of the Word program window shown in Figure C-24.

FIGURE C-24

Match each term with the statement that best describes it.

8. Italic
9. Bullet
10. Style
11. Bold
12. Point
13. Highlight
14. Shading
15. Border

a. A character that appears at the beginning of a paragraph to add emphasis
b. Transparent color that is applied to text to mark it in a document
c. A text style in which characters are slanted
d. Color or a pattern that is applied behind text to make it look attractive
e. A set of format settings
f. A unit of measurement equal to ½ of an inch
g. A line that can be applied above, below, or to the sides of a paragraph
h. A text style in which characters are darker and thicker

Select the best answer from the list of choices.

16. Which button is used to align a paragraph with both the left and right margins?
   a. ▤
   b. ▤
   c. ▤
   d. ▤

17. **What is Times New Roman?**
   a. A character format
   b. A font
   c. A style
   d. A text effect

18. **What is the most precise way to increase the amount of white space between two paragraphs?**
   a. Indent the paragraphs.
   b. Insert an extra blank line between the paragraphs.
   c. Use the Paragraph command to change the spacing below the first paragraph.
   d. Change the line spacing of the paragraphs.

19. **What element of the Word program window can be used to check the font effects applied to text?**
   a. Standard toolbar
   b. Formatting toolbar
   c. Styles and Formatting task pane
   d. Reveal Formatting task pane

20. **Which command would you use to apply color behind a paragraph?**
   a. Borders and Shading
   b. Background
   c. Paragraph
   d. Styles and Formatting

▶ Skills Review

1. **Format with fonts.**
   a. Start Word, open the file WD C-2 from the drive and folder where your Project Files are located, save it as **EDA Report**, then scroll through the document to get a feel for its contents.
   b. Press [Ctrl][Home], format the report title **Concord Springs Economic Development Report Executive Summary** in 22-point Tahoma. Choose a different font if Tahoma is not available to you.
   c. Change the font color of the report title to Blue-Gray.
   d. Format each of the following headings in 14-point Tahoma with the Blue-Gray font color: **Mission Statement, Guiding Principles, Issues, Proposed Actions.**
   e. Press [Ctrl][Home], then save your changes to the report.

2. **Change font styles and effects.**
   a. Apply bold to the report title and to each heading in the report.
   b. Format the paragraph under the Mission Statement heading in italic.
   c. Format the third paragraph under the Issues heading, **Years Population Growth**, in bold small caps, with a Blue-Gray font color.
   d. Change the font color of the two paragraphs under Years Population Growth to Blue-Gray.
   e. Format the paragraph **Source: Office of State Planning** in italic.
   f. Scroll to the top of the report, change the character scale of **Concord Springs Economic Development Report** to 80%, then save your changes.

3. **Change line and paragraph spacing.**
   a. Change the line spacing of the three-line list under the first body paragraph to 1.5 lines.
   b. Add 12 points of space before the Executive Summary paragraph.
   c. Add 12 points of space after each heading in the report.
   d. Add 6 points of space after each paragraph in the list under the Guiding Principles heading.
   e. Add 6 points of space after each paragraph under the Proposed Actions heading.
   f. Press [Ctrl][Home], then save your changes to the report.

4. Align paragraphs.

   a. Press [Ctrl][A] to select the entire document, then justify all the paragraphs.

   b. Center the two-paragraph report title.

   c. Press [Ctrl][End], type your name, press [Enter], type the current date, then right-align your name and the date.

   d. Save your changes to the report.

5. Work with tabs.

   a. Scroll up and select the four-line list of blue-gray population information.

   b. Set left tab stops at the 1¾"-mark and the 3" mark.

   c. Insert a tab at the beginning of each paragraph in the list.

   d. In the first paragraph, insert a tab before Population. In the second paragraph, insert a tab before 4.5%. In the third paragraph, insert a tab before 53%.

   e. Select the first three paragraphs, then drag the second tab stop to the 2¾" mark on the horizontal ruler.

   f. Press [Ctrl][Home], then save your changes to the report.

6. Work with indents.

   a. Indent the first line of the first body paragraph ½".

   b. Indent the paragraph under the Mission Statement heading ½" from the left and ½" from the right.

   c. Indent the first line of the paragraph under the Guiding Principles heading ½".

   d. Indent the first line of the three body paragraphs under the Issues heading ½".

   e. Press [Ctrl][Home], then save your changes to the report.

7. Add bullets and numbering.

   a. Apply bullets to the three-line list under the first body paragraph.

   b. Change the bullet style to small circles (or choose another bullet style if small circles are not available to you).

   c. Change the font color of the bullets to Blue-Gray.

   d. Scroll down until the Guiding Principles heading is at the top of your screen.

   e. Format the five-paragraph list under Guiding Principles as a numbered list.

   f. Format the numbers in 12-point Tahoma bold, then change the font color to Blue-Gray.

   g. Scroll down until the Proposed Actions heading is at the top of your screen, then format the paragraphs under the heading as a bulleted list using checkmarks as the bullet style (or choose another bullet style).

   h. Change the font color of the bullets to Blue-Gray, press [Ctrl][Home], then save your changes to the report.

8. Add borders and shading.

   a. Change the font color of the report title to Light Yellow, then apply Blue-Gray shading.

   b. Apply Light Yellow shading to the Mission Statement heading, then add a 1-point Blue-Gray border below the Mission Statement heading.

   c. Use the Format Painter to copy the formatting of the Mission Statement heading to the other headings in the report.

   d. Under the Issues heading, select the first three lines of tabbed text, which are formatted in Blue-Gray.

   e. Apply Light Yellow shading to the paragraphs, then add a 1-point Blue-Gray box border around the paragraphs.

   f. Indent the paragraphs 1½" from the left and 1½" from the right.

   g. Press [Ctrl][Home], save your changes to the report, view the report in Print Preview, then print a copy. The formatted report is shown in Figure C-25.

   h. Close the file and exit Word.

FIGURE C-25

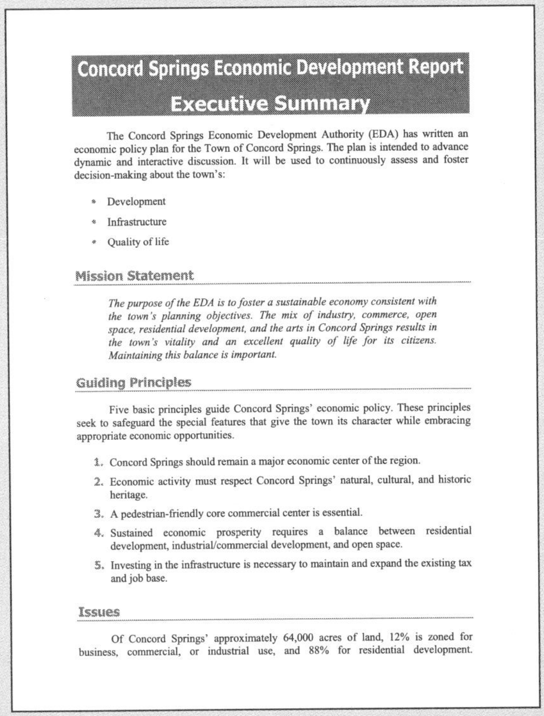

Concord Springs Economic Development Report

Executive Summary

The Concord Springs Economic Development Authority (EDA) has written an economic policy plan for the Town of Concord Springs. The plan is intended to advance dynamic and interactive discussion. It will be used to continuously assess and foster decision-making about the town's:

- Development
- Infrastructure
- Quality of life

Mission Statement

The purpose of the EDA is to foster a sustainable economy consistent with the town's planning objectives. The mix of industry, commerce, open space, residential development, and the arts in Concord Springs results in the town's vitality and an excellent quality of life for its citizens. Maintaining this balance is important.

Guiding Principles

Five basic principles guide Concord Springs' economic policy. These principles seek to safeguard the special features that give the town its character while embracing appropriate economic opportunities.

1. Concord Springs should remain a major economic center of the region.
2. Economic activity must respect Concord Springs' natural, cultural, and historic heritage.
3. A pedestrian-friendly core commercial center is essential.
4. Sustained economic prosperity requires a balance between residential development, industrial/commercial development, and open space.
5. Investing in the infrastructure is necessary to maintain and expand the existing tax and job base.

Issues

Of Concord Springs' approximately 64,000 acres of land, 12% is zoned for business, commercial, or industrial use, and 88% for residential development.

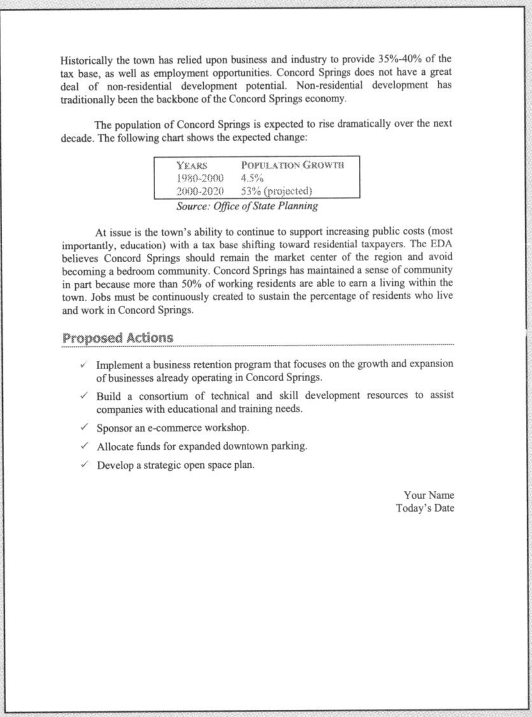

Historically the town has relied upon business and industry to provide 35%-40% of the tax base, as well as employment opportunities. Concord Springs does not have a great deal of non-residential development potential. Non-residential development has traditionally been the backbone of the Concord Springs economy.

The population of Concord Springs is expected to rise dramatically over the next decade. The following chart shows the expected change:

YEARS	POPULATION GROWTH
1980-2000	4.5%
2000-2020	53% (projected)

Source: Office of State Planning

At issue is the town's ability to continue to support increasing public costs (most importantly, education) with a tax base shifting toward residential taxpayers. The EDA believes Concord Springs should remain the market center of the region and avoid becoming a bedroom community. Concord Springs has maintained a sense of community in part because more than 50% of working residents are able to earn a living within the town. Jobs must be continuously created to sustain the percentage of residents who live and work in Concord Springs.

Proposed Actions

- ✓ Implement a business retention program that focuses on the growth and expansion of businesses already operating in Concord Springs.
- ✓ Build a consortium of technical and skill development resources to assist companies with educational and training needs.
- ✓ Sponsor an e-commerce workshop.
- ✓ Allocate funds for expanded downtown parking.
- ✓ Develop a strategic open space plan.

Your Name
Today's Date

▶ Independent Challenge 1

You are an estimator for Zakia Construction in the Australian city of Wollongong. You have drafted an estimate for a home renovation job, and need to format it. It's important that your estimate have a clean, striking design, and reflect your company's professionalism.

FIGURE C-26

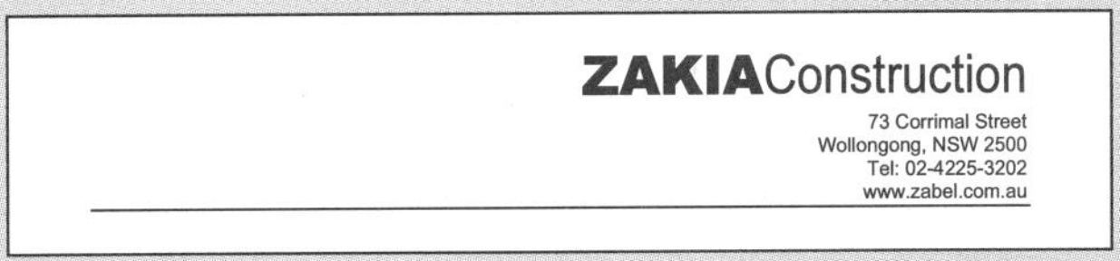

ZAKIAConstruction
73 Corrimal Street
Wollongong, NSW 2500
Tel: 02-4225-3202
www.zabel.com.au

a. Start Word, open the file WD C-3 from the drive and folder where your Project Files are located, save it as **Zakia Construction**, then read the document to get a feel for its contents. Figure C-26 shows how you will format the letterhead.

b. In the first paragraph, format **ZAKIA** in 24-point Arial Black. (*Hint*: Select a similar font if Arial Black is not available to you.)

c. Format **Construction** in 24-point Arial, then change the character scale to 90%.

d. Format the next four lines in 9-point Arial, right-align them, then add a 1-point border below the last line.

e. In the body of the document, format the title **Proposal of Renovation** in 16-point Arial Black, then center the title.

f. Format the following headings (including the colons) in 12-point Arial Black: **Date**, **Work to be performed for and at**, **Scope of work**, **Payment schedule** and **Agreement**.

g. Format the 14-paragraph list under Scope of work as a numbered list, then apply bold to the numbers.

h. Change the paragraph spacing to add 4 points of space after each paragraph in the list.

i. With the list selected, set a right tab stop at the 5¾" mark, then insert tabs before every price in the list.

j. Apply bold to the two paragraphs—**Total estimated job cost** and **Approximate job time**—below the list.

k. Replace Your Name with your name in the signature block, select the signature block, set a left tab stop at the 3½" mark, then indent the signature block.

l. Examine the document carefully for formatting errors and make any necessary adjustments.

m. Save and print the document, then close the file and exit Word.

▶ Independent Challenge 2

Your employer, The Lange Center for Contemporary Arts in Halifax, Nova Scotia, is launching a membership drive. Your boss has written the text for a flyer advertising Lange membership, and asks you to format it so that it is eye-catching and attractive.

a. Open the file WD C-4 from the drive and folder where your Project Files are located, save it as **Membership Flyer**, then read the document. Figure C-27 shows how you will format the first several paragraphs of the flyer.

FIGURE C-27

> **MEMBERSHIP DRIVE**
> **2003**
>
> **What we do for ARTISTS**
> Since 1982, the artist residency program at the Lange Center for Contemporary Arts has supported the work of more than 1500 artists from all over Canada and from 40 other nations. The residency awards include studio and living space, a monthly stipend to help artists with their expenses, and use of specialized equipment for all types of visual and performance art. Each artist gives a public lecture or performance at the Lange.

b. Select the entire document and format it in 10-point Arial Narrow.

c. Format the first paragraph, **Membership Drive**, in 26-point Arial Narrow, bold, with a white font color. Expand the character spacing by 7 points. Center the paragraph and apply plum shading to the paragraph.

d. Format the second paragraph, **2003**, in 36-point Arial Black, 80% gray font color, with a shadow effect. Expand the character spacing by 25 points and change the character scale to 200%. Center the paragraph.

e. Format each **What we do for**... heading in 12-point Arial, bold, with a plum font color. Add a single line ½-point border under each heading.

f. Format each subheading (**Gallery, Lectures, Library, All members**..., and **Membership Levels**) in 10-point Arial, bold. Add 3 points of spacing before each paragraph.

g. Indent each body paragraph ¼", except for the paragraphs under the What we do for YOU heading.

h. Format the four paragraphs under the All members... subheading as a bulleted list. Use a bullet symbol of your choice and format the bullets in the plum color.

i. Indent the five paragraphs under the Membership Levels heading ¼". For these five paragraphs, set left tab stops at the 1¼" mark and the 2" mark on the horizontal ruler. Insert tabs before the price and before the word **All** in each of the five paragraphs.

j. Format the name of each membership level (**Artistic, Conceptual**, etc.) in 10-point Arial, bold, italic, with a plum font color.

k. Format the **For more information** paragraph in 14-point Arial, bold, with a plum font color. Center the paragraph and add a 6-point dotted black border above the paragraph.

l. Format the last two paragraphs in 11-point Arial Narrow, and center the paragraphs. In the contact information, replace **Your Name** with your name, then apply bold to your name.

m. Examine the document carefully for formatting errors and make any necessary adjustments.

n. Save and print the flyer, then close the file and exit Word.

▶ Independent Challenge 3

One of your responsibilities as program coordinator at Solstice Mountain Sports is to develop a program of winter outdoor learning and adventure workshops. You have written a memo to your boss to update her on your progress. You need to format the memo so it is professional-looking and easy to read.

a. Start Word, open the file WD C-5 from the drive and folder where your Project Files are located, then save it as **Solstice Memo**.

b. Format the heading **Solstice Mountain Sports Memorandum** in 26-point Impact, then center it.

c. In the memo header, replace Today's Date and Your Name with the current date and your name.

d. Select the four-line memo header, set a left tab stop at the ¾" mark, then insert tabs before the date, the recipient's name, your name, and the subject of the memo.

e. Select **Date:**, then apply the character style Strong to it. FIGURE C-28
(*Hint*: Open the Styles and Formatting task pane, click the Show list arrow, click All Styles if necessary, scroll through the alphabetical list of styles to locate the style Strong, then click Strong.)

f. Apply the Strong style to **To:**, **From:**, and **Re:**, then double-space the four lines in the memo header.

g. Apply a 3-point dotted border below the blank line under the memo header. (*Hint*: Turn on formatting marks, select the paragraph symbol below the memo header, then apply a border below it.)

h. Apply the paragraph style Heading 3 to the headings **Overview**, **Workshops**, **Accommodation**, **Fees**, and **Proposed winter programming**.

i. Under the Fees heading, format the words **Workshop fees** and **Accommodation fees** using the Strong style.

j. Add 6 points of space after the Workshop fees paragraph.

k. In the Fees section, apply green highlighting to these sentences: **Workshop fees include materials and equipment.** and **This is a discounted rate.**

l. On the second page of the document, format the list under the Proposed winter programming heading as an outline. Figure C-28 shows the hierarchical structure of the outline. (*Hint*: Format the list as an outline numbered list, then use the Increase Indent and Decrease Indent buttons to change the level of importance of each item.)

m. Change the outline numbering style to the bullet numbering style shown in Figure C-28, if necessary.

n. Save and print the document, then close the file and exit Word.

Proposed winter programming
- ❖ Skiing, Snowboarding, and Snowshoeing
  - ➤ Skiing and Snowboarding
    - ▪ Cross-country skiing
      - • Cross-country skiing for beginners
      - • Intermediate cross-country skiing
      - • Inn-to-inn ski touring
      - • Moonlight cross-country skiing
    - ▪ Telemarking
      - • Basic telemark skiing
      - • Introduction to backcountry skiing
      - • Exploring on skis
    - ▪ Snowboarding
      - • Backcountry snowboarding
  - ➤ Snowshoeing
    - ▪ Beginner
      - • Snowshoeing for beginners
      - • Snowshoeing and winter ecology
    - ▪ Intermediate and Advanced
      - • Intermediate snowshoeing
      - • Guided snowshoe trek
      - • Above tree line snowshoeing
- ❖ Winter Hiking, Camping, and Survival
  - ➤ Hiking
    - ▪ Beginner
      - • Long-distance hiking
      - • Winter summits
      - • Hiking for women
  - ➤ Winter camping and survival
    - ▪ Beginner
      - • Introduction to winter camping
      - • Basic winter mountain skills
      - • Building snow shelters
    - ▪ Intermediate
      - • Basic winter mountain skills II
      - • Ice climbing
      - • Avalanche awareness and rescue

Independent Challenge 4

The fonts you choose for a document can have a major effect on the document's tone. Not all fonts are appropriate for use in a business document, and some fonts, especially those with a definite theme, are appropriate only for specific purposes. The World Wide Web includes hundreds of Web sites devoted to fonts and text design. Some Web sites sell fonts, others allow you to download fonts for free and install them on your computer. In this independent challenge, you will research Web sites related to fonts and find examples of fonts you could use in your work.

a. Start Word, open the file WD C-6 from the drive and folder where your Project Files are located, and save it as **Fonts**. This document contains the questions you will answer about the fonts you find.

b. Use your favorite search engine to search the Web for Web sites related to fonts. Use the keyword **font** to conduct your search. If your search does not result in appropriate links, try looking at the following Web sites: www.1001freefonts.com, www.fontsnthings.com, and www.fontfreak.com.

c. Explore the fonts available for downloading. As you examine the fonts, notice that fonts fall into two general categories: serif fonts, which have a small stroke, called a serif, at the ends of characters, and sans serif fonts, which do not have a serif. Times New Roman is an example of a serif font and Arial is an example of a sans serif font.

d. Type your answers in the Fonts document, save it, print a copy, then close the file and exit Word.

Visual Workshop

Using the file WD C-7 found in the drive and folder where your Project Files are located, create the menu shown in Figure C-29. (*Hints*: Use Georgia for the font. Change the font size of the heading to 72 points, scale the font to 66%, and expand the spacing by 2 points. For the rest of the text, change the font size to 11 points. Indent all the text ½" from the left and the right. Use paragraph spacing to adjust the spacing between paragraphs so that all the text fits on one page. If the Georgia font is not available to you, choose a different font.) Save the menu as **Rosebud Specials**, then print a copy.

FIGURE C-29

Rosebud Café

••

DAILY SPECIALS

MONDAY
Veggie Chili
Hearty veggie chili with melted cheddar in our peasant French bread bowl. Topped with sour cream & scallions.
$5.95

TUESDAY
Greek Salad
Our large garden salad with kalamata olives, feta cheese, and garlic vinaigrette. Served with an assortment of rolls.
$5.95

WEDNESDAY
French Dip
Lean roast beef topped with melted cheddar on our roasted garlic roll. Served with a side of au jus and red bliss mashed potatoes.
$6.95

THURSDAY
Chicken Cajun Bleu
Cajun chicken, chunky blue cheese, cucumbers, leaf lettuce, and tomato on our roasted garlic roll.
$6.50

FRIDAY
Clam Chowder
Classic New England thick, rich, clam chowder in our peasant French bread bowl. Served with a garden salad.
$5.95

SATURDAY
Hot Chicken and Gravy
Delicious chicken and savory gravy served on a thick slice of toasted honest white. Served with red bliss mashed potatoes.
$6.95

SUNDAY
Turkey-Bacon Club
Double-decker roasted turkey, crisp bacon, leaf lettuce, tomato, and sun-dried tomato mayo on toasted triple seed.
$6.50

Your Name

••

Word 2002

Unit **D**

Formatting
Documents

Word's page formatting features allow you to creatively lay out and design the pages of your documents. In this unit, you learn how to change the document margins, determine the page orientation of a document, add page numbers, and insert headers and footers. You also learn how to format text in columns and how to illustrate your documents with clip art. ✐ Alice Wegman has written and formatted the text for a quarterly newsletter for the MediaLoft marketing staff. She is now ready to lay out and design the pages of the newsletter. She plans to organize the articles in columns and to illustrate the newsletter with clip art. You will work with Alice as she formats the newsletter.

Setting Document Margins

Changing a document's margins is one way to change the appearance of a document and control the amount of text that fits on a page. The **margins** of a document are the blank areas between the edge of the text and the edge of the page. When you create a document in Word, the default margins are 1" at the top and bottom of the page, and 1.25" on the left and right sides of the page. You can adjust the size of a document's margins using the Page Setup command on the File menu, or using the rulers. Alice plans the newsletter to be a four-page document when finished. She reduces the size of the document margins so that more text fits on each page.

Steps

1. Start **Word**, open the file **WD D-1** from the drive and folder where your Project Files are located, then save it as **MediaLoft Buzz**
   The newsletter opens in Print Layout view.

2. Scroll through the newsletter to get a feel for its contents, then press **[Ctrl][Home]**
   The newsletter is currently six pages long. Notice the status bar indicates the page where the insertion point is located and the total number of pages in the document.

3. Click **File** on the menu bar, click **Page Setup**, then click the **Margins tab** in the Page Setup dialog box if necessary
   The Margins tab in the Page Setup dialog box is shown in Figure D-1. You can use the Margins tab to change the width of the top, bottom, left, or right document margins, to change the orientation of the pages from portrait to landscape, and to alter other page layout settings. **Portrait orientation** means a page is taller than it is wide; **landscape orientation** means a page is wider than it is tall. This newsletter uses portrait orientation.

4. Click the **Top down arrow** three times until 0.7" appears, then click the **Bottom down arrow** until 0.7" appears
   The top and bottom margins of the newsletter will be .7". Notice that the margins in the Preview section of the dialog box change as you adjust the margin settings.

5. Press **[Tab]**, type **.7** in the Left text box, press **[Tab]**, then type **.7** in the Right text box
   The left and right margins of the newsletter will also be .7". You can change the margin settings by using the arrows or by typing a value in the appropriate text box.

6. Click **OK**
   The document margins change to .7", as shown in Figure D-2. The bar at the intersection of the white and gray areas on the horizontal and vertical rulers indicates the location of the margin. You can also change a document's margins by dragging the bar to a new location. Notice that the status bar indicates the total number of pages in the document is now five.

7. Click the **Zoom list arrow** on the Standard toolbar, then click **Two Pages**
   The first two pages of the document appear in the document window.

8. Scroll down to view all five pages of the newsletter, press **[Ctrl][Home]**, click the **Zoom list arrow**, click **Page Width**, then click the **Save button** on the Standard toolbar to save the document

FIGURE D-1: Margins tab in Page Setup dialog box

Default margin settings

Set gutter margin

Select page orientation

Select part of document
to apply settings to

Select gutter position

Set mirror margins and
other page layout options

Preview of margin settings

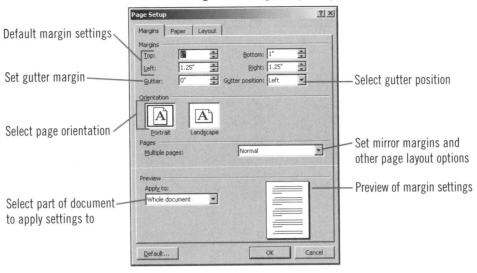

FIGURE D-2: Newsletter with smaller margins

Ruler shows location
of left margin

Ruler shows location
of top margin

Document margins
are narrower

Page 1 is the
active page

Zoom list arrow

Ruler shows location
of right margin

After adjusting
margins, document
is five pages long

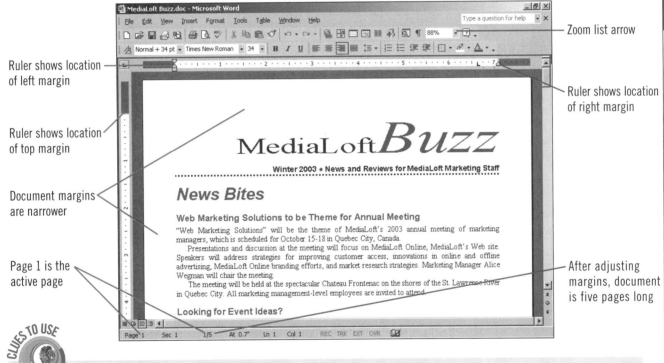

Changing paper size, orientation, and margin settings

By default, the documents you create in Word use an 8½" x 11" paper size in portrait orientation with the default margin settings, but you can adjust these settings in the Page Setup dialog box to create documents of any size, shape, and layout. On the Margins tab, change the orientation of the pages by selecting Portrait or Landscape. To change the layout of multiple pages, use the Multiple pages list arrow to create pages that use mirror margins, include two pages per sheet of paper, or are formatted like a folded booklet. **Mirror margins** are used in documents with facing pages, such as a magazine, where the margins on the left page of the document are a mirror image of the margins on

the right. Documents with mirror margins have inside and outside margins, rather than right and left margins. Another type of margin is a gutter margin, which is used in documents that are bound, such as books. A **gutter** adds extra space to the left or top margin so that the binding does not obscure text. Add a gutter to a document by adjusting the setting in the Gutter text box on the Margins tab. If you want to change the size of the paper used in a document, use the Paper tab in the Page Setup dialog box. Use the Paper size list arrow to select a standard paper size, or enter custom measurements in the Width and Height text boxes.

Dividing a Document into Sections

Dividing a document into sections allows you to format each section of the document with different page layout settings. A **section** is a portion of a document that is separated from the rest of the document by section breaks. **Section breaks** are formatting marks that you insert in a document to show the end of a section. Once you have divided a document into sections, you can format each section with different column, margin, page orientation, header and footer, and other page layout settings. By default, a document is formatted as a single section, but you can divide a document into as many sections as you like. ✐ Alice wants to format the body of the newsletter in two columns, but leave the masthead and the headline "News Bites" as a single column. She inserts a section break before the body of the newsletter to divide the document into two sections, then she changes the number of columns in the second section to two.

Steps

1. Click the **Show/Hide ¶ button** ¶ on the Standard toolbar to display formatting marks if they are not visible
   Turning on formatting marks allows you to see the section breaks you insert in a document.

QuickTip

When you insert a section break at the beginning of a paragraph, Word inserts the break at the end of the previous paragraph. A section break stores the formatting information for the preceding section.

2. Place the insertion point before the headline **Web Marketing Solutions to be...**, click **Insert** on the menu bar, then click **Break**
   The Break dialog box opens, as shown in Figure D-3. You use this dialog box to insert different types of section breaks. Table D-1 describes the different types of section breaks.

3. Click the **Continuous option button**, then click **OK**
   Word inserts a continuous section break, shown as a dotted double line, above the headline. A continuous section break begins a new section of the document on the same page. The document now has two sections. Notice that the status bar indicates that the insertion point is in section 2.

4. With the insertion point in section 2, click the **Columns button** ▦ on the Standard toolbar
   A grid showing four columns opens below the button. You use the grid to select the number of columns you want to create.

QuickTip

To change the margins or page orientation of a section, place the insertion point in the section, change the margin or page orientation settings on the Margins tab in the Page Setup dialog box, click the Apply to list arrow on the Margins tab, click This section, then click OK.

5. Point to the second column on the grid, then click
   Section 2 is formatted in two columns, as shown in Figure D-4. The text in section 1 remains formatted in a single column. Notice the status bar now indicates the document is four pages long. Formatting text in columns is another way to increase the amount of text that fits on a page. You'll learn more about columns in a later lesson.

6. Click the **Zoom list arrow** on the Standard toolbar, click **Two Pages**, then scroll down to examine all four pages of the document
   The text in section 2—all the text below the continuous section break—is formatted in two columns. Text in columns flows automatically from the bottom of one column to the top of the next.

7. Press **[Ctrl][Home]**, click the **Zoom list arrow**, click **Page Width**, then save the document

TABLE D-1: Types of section breaks

section break	function
Next page	Begins a new a section and moves the text following the break to the top of the next page
Continuous	Begins a new section on the same page
Even page	Begins a new section and moves the text following the break to the top of the next even-numbered page
Odd page	Begins a new section and moves the text following the break to the top of the next odd-numbered page

FIGURE D-3: Break dialog box

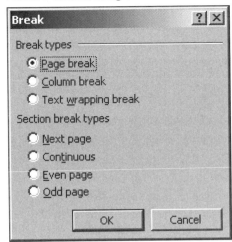

FIGURE D-4: Continuous section break and columns

Text in section 1 is formatted in one column

Insertion point is in section 2

Text in section 2 is formatted in two columns

Section 2 is the active section

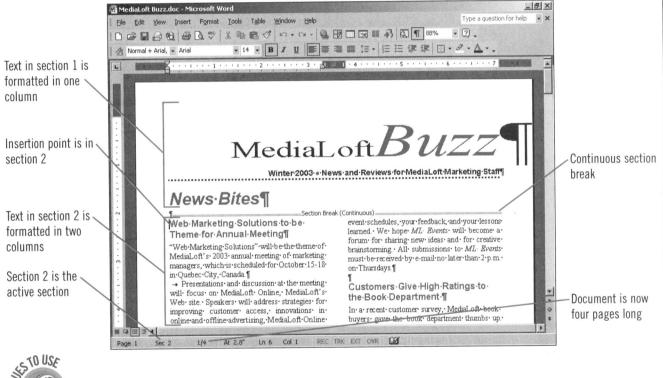

Continuous section break

Document is now four pages long

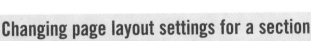

Changing page layout settings for a section

Dividing a document into sections allows you to vary the layout of a document. In addition to applying different column settings to sections, you can apply different margins, page orientation, paper size, vertical alignment, header and footer, page numbering, and other page layout settings. For example, if you are formatting a report that includes a table with many columns, you might want to change the table's page orientation to landscape so that it is easier to read. To do this, you would insert a section break before and after the table to create a section that contains only the table. Then you would use the Margins tab in the Page Setup dialog box to change the page orientation of the table section to landscape.

To change the page layout settings for an individual section, place the insertion point in the section, open the Page Setup (or Columns) dialog box, select the options you want to change, click the Apply to list arrow, click This section, then click OK. When you select This section in the Apply to list box, the settings are applied to the current section only. If you select Whole document in the Apply to list box, the settings are applied to all the sections in the document.

Word 2002

Adding Page Breaks

As you type text in a document, Word automatically inserts a **soft page break** when you reach the bottom of a page, allowing you to continue typing on the next page. You can also force text onto the next page of a document by using the Break command to insert a **hard page break**. ✐ Alice inserts hard page breaks where she knows she wants to begin each new page of the newsletter.

Steps 1 2 3 4

1. **Scroll down to the bottom of page 1, place the insertion point before the headline Career Corner, click Insert on the menu bar, then click Break**
   The Break dialog box opens. You also use this dialog box to insert page, column, and text-wrapping breaks. Table D-2 describes these types of breaks.

QuickTip

Hard and soft page breaks are always visible in Normal view.

2. **Make sure the Page break option button is selected, then click OK**
   Word inserts a hard page break before "Career Corner" and moves all the text following the page break to the beginning of the next page, as shown in Figure D-5. The page break appears as a dotted line in Print Layout view. Page break marks are visible on the screen but do not print.

3. **Scroll down to the bottom of page 2, place the insertion point before the headline Webcasts Slated for May, press and hold [Ctrl], then press [Enter]**
   Pressing [Ctrl][Enter] is a fast way to insert a hard page break. The headline is forced to the top of the third page.

4. **Scroll down to the bottom of page 3, place the insertion point before the headline Staff News, then press [Ctrl][Enter]**
   The headline is forced to the top of the fourth page.

5. **Press [Ctrl][Home], click the Zoom list arrow on the Standard toolbar, then click Two Pages**
   The first two pages of the document are displayed, as shown in Figure D-6.

6. **Scroll down to view pages 3 and 4, click the Zoom list arrow, click Page Width, then save the document**

CLUES TO USE

Vertically aligning text on a page

By default, text is vertically aligned with the top margin of a page, but you can change the vertical alignment of text so that it is centered between the top and bottom margins, justified between the top and bottom margins, or aligned with the bottom margin of the page. You would vertically align text on a page only when the text does not fill the page; for example, if you are creating a flyer or a title page for a report. To change the vertical alignment of text in a section (or a document), place the insertion point in the section you want to align, open the Page Setup dialog box, use the Vertical alignment list arrow on the Layout tab to select the alignment you want—top, center, justified, or bottom—use the Apply to list arrow to select the part of the document you want to align, then click OK.

FIGURE D-5: **Hard page break in document**

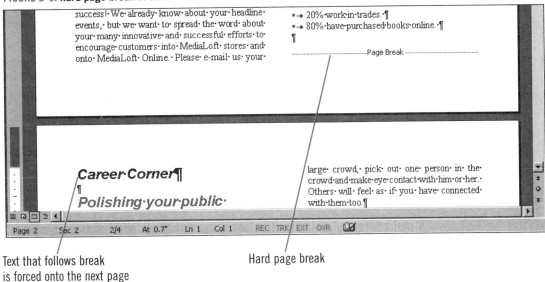

Text that follows break
is forced onto the next page

Hard page break

FIGURE D-6: **Pages 1 and 2**

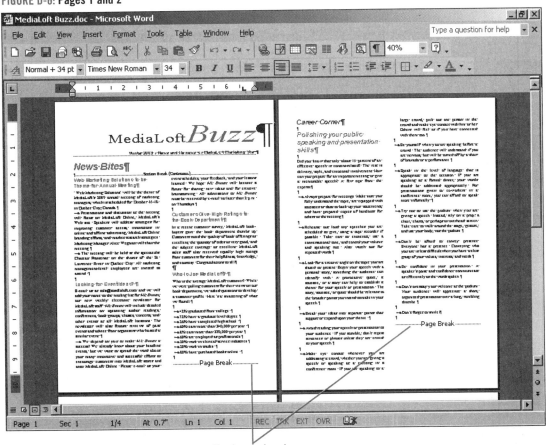

Hard page breaks

TABLE D-2: **Types of breaks**

break	function
Page break	Forces the text following the break to begin at the top of the next page
Column break	Forces the text following the break to begin at the top of the next column
Text wrapping break	Forces the text following the break to begin at the beginning of the next line

Word 2002

Adding Page Numbers

If you want to number the pages of a multi-page document, you can insert a page number field at the top or bottom of each page. A **field** is a code that serves as a placeholder for data that changes in a document, such as a page number or the current date. When you use the Page Numbers command on the Insert menu to add page numbers to a document, Word automatically numbers the pages for you.  Alice adds page numbers to the bottom of each page in the document.

1. Click **Insert** on the menu bar, then click **Page Numbers**
   The Page Numbers dialog box opens, as shown in Figure D-7. You use this dialog box to specify the position—top or bottom of the page—and the alignment for the page numbers. Bottom of page (Footer) is the default position.

QuickTip
You can also align page numbers with the left, right, inside, or outside margins of a document.

2. Click the **Alignment list arrow**, then click **Center**
   The page numbers will be centered between the left and right margins at the bottom of each page.

3. Click **OK**, then scroll to the bottom of the first page
   The page number 1 appears in gray at the bottom of the first page, as shown in Figure D-8. The number is gray, or dimmed, because it is located in the Footer area. When the document is printed, the page numbers appear as normal text. You will learn more about headers and footers in the next lesson.

4. Click the **Print Preview button** 🔍 on the Standard toolbar, then click the **One Page button** 🔲 on the Print Preview toolbar if necessary
   The first page of the newsletter appears in Print Preview. Notice the page number.

5. Click the **page number** with the ⊕ pointer to zoom in on the page
   The page number is centered at the bottom of the page, as shown in Figure D-9.

6. Scroll down the document to see the page number at the bottom of each page
   Word automatically numbered the pages of the newsletter.

QuickTip
To display more than six pages of a document in Print Preview, drag to expand the Multiple Pages grid.

7. Click the **Multiple Pages button** 🔳 on the Print Preview toolbar, point to the second box in the bottom row on the grid to select **2 x 2 pages**, then click
   All four pages of the newsletter appear in the Print Preview window.

8. Click **Close** on the Print Preview toolbar, then save the document

Inserting date and time fields

Using the Date and Time command on the Insert menu, you can add a field for the current date or the current time into a document. To insert the current date or time at the location of the insertion point, click Date and Time on the Insert menu, then select the date or time format you want to use from the list of available formats in the Date and Time dialog box. To insert the date or time as a field that will be updated automatically each time you open or print the document, select the Update automatically check box, then click OK. If you want to insert the current date or time as static text that does not change each time you open or print the document, deselect the Update automatically check box, then click OK. Word uses the clock on your computer to compute the current date and time.

Once you have inserted a date or time field, you can modify the format by changing the field code: right-click the field, click Edit Field on the shortcut menu, then select a new format in the Field properties list in the Field dialog box. You can edit static text just as you would any other text in Word.

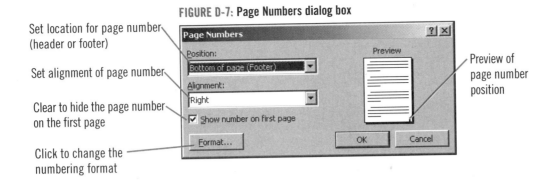

FIGURE D-7: Page Numbers dialog box

Set location for page number (header or footer)

Set alignment of page number

Clear to hide the page number on the first page

Click to change the numbering format

Preview of page number position

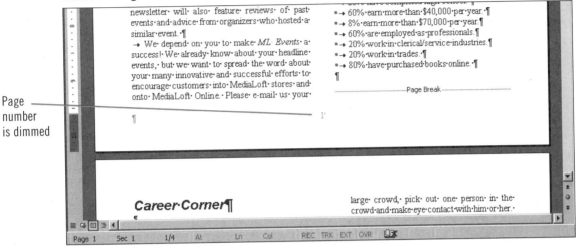

FIGURE D-8: Page number in document

Page number is dimmed

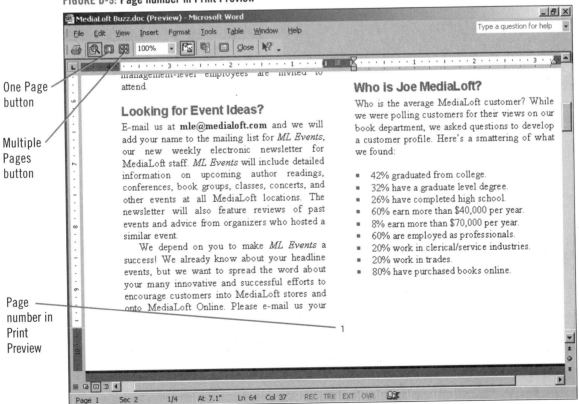

FIGURE D-9: Page number in Print Preview

One Page button

Multiple Pages button

Page number in Print Preview

Inserting Headers and Footers

A **header** is text or graphics that appears at the top of every page of a document. A **footer** is text or graphics that appears at the bottom of every page. In longer documents, headers and footers often contain information such as the title of the publication, the title of the chapter, the name of the author, the date, or a page number. You can add headers and footers to a document by using the Header and Footer command on the View menu to open the Header and Footer areas, and then inserting text and graphics in them. Alice creates a header that includes the name of the newsletter and the current date.

Steps

1. Click View on the menu bar, then click Header and Footer

The Header and Footer areas open and the document text is dimmed, as shown in Figure D-10. When the document text is dimmed, it cannot be edited. The Header and Footer toolbar also opens. It includes buttons for inserting standard text into headers and footers and for navigating between headers and footers. See Table D-3. The Header and Footer areas of a document are independent of the document itself and must be formatted separately. For example, if you select all the text in a document and then change the font, the header and footer font does not change.

2. Type Buzz in the Header area, press [Spacebar] twice, then click the Insert Date button 🗓 **on the Header and Footer toolbar**

Clicking the Insert Date button inserts a date field into the header. The date is inserted using the default date format (usually month/date/year, although your default date format might be different). The word "Buzz" and the current date will appear at the top of every page in the document.

3. Select Buzz and the date, then click the Center button 🖿 **on the Formatting toolbar**

The text is centered in the Header area. You can also use tabs to center and right-align text in the Header and Footer areas. Notice that the center and right tab stops shown on the ruler do not align with the current margin settings. The tab stops are the default tab stops for the Header and Footer areas, based on the default margin settings. If you change the margins in a document, you need to adjust the tab stops in the Header or Footer area to align with the new margin settings.

4. With the text still selected, click the Font list arrow on the Formatting toolbar, click Arial, click the Bold button 🅱 **, then click in the Header area to deselect the text**

The header text is formatted in 12-point Arial bold, as shown in Figure D-11.

5. Click the Switch Between Header and Footer button 🗐 **on the Header and Footer toolbar**

The insertion point moves to the Footer area. A page number field already appears centered in the Footer area.

6. Double-click the page number to select the field, click the Font list arrow, click Arial, click 🅱 **, then click in the Footer area to deselect the field**

The page number is formatted in 12-point Arial bold.

7. Click Close on the Header and Footer toolbar, save the document, then scroll down until the bottom of page 1 and the top of page 2 appear in the document window

The Header and Footer areas close and the header and footer text is dimmed, as shown in Figure D-12. The header text—"Buzz" and the current date—appear at the top of every page in the document, and a page number appears at the bottom of each page.

FIGURE D-10: Header area

Header and Footer toolbar

Insert Date button

Header area is open

Document text is dimmed

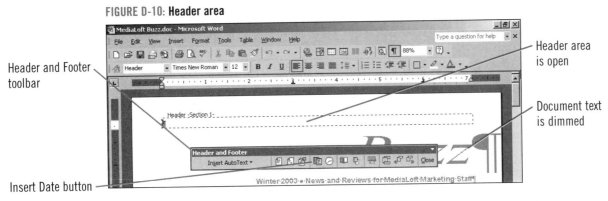

FIGURE D-11: Formatted header text

Information in Header area for section 1 appears on every page

Formatted text is centered in the Header area

Tab stops for the header are set for the default document margins

Switch Between Header and Footer button

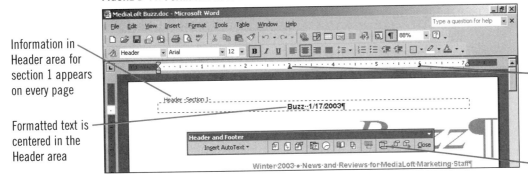

FIGURE D-12: Header and footer in the document

Page number appears in footer on every page

Header text appears in header on every page (your date will differ)

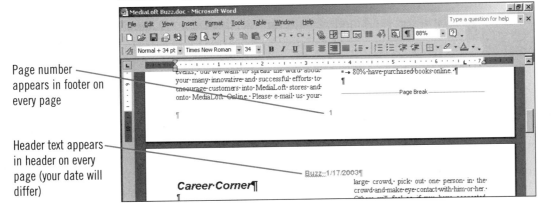

TABLE D-3: Buttons on the Header and Footer toolbar

button	function
Insert AutoText ▾	Inserts an AutoText entry, such as a field for the filename, or the author's name
# Insert Page Number	Inserts a field for the page number so that the pages are numbered automatically
Insert Number of Pages	Inserts a field for the total number of pages in the document
Format Page Number	Opens the Page Number Format dialog box; use to change the numbering format or to begin automatic page numbering with a specific number
Insert Date	Inserts a field for the current date
Insert Time	Inserts a field for the current time
Page Setup	Opens the Page Setup dialog box
Switch Between Header and Footer	Moves the insertion point between the Header and Footer areas

Editing Headers and Footers

Word 2002

To change header and footer text or to alter the formatting of headers and footers you must first open the Header and Footer areas. You can open headers and footers using the Header and Footer command on the View menu, or by double-clicking a header or footer in Print Layout view. Alice modifies the header by adding a small circle symbol between "Buzz" and the date. She also adds a border under the header text to set it off from the rest of the page. Finally, she removes the header and footer text from the first page of the document.

Trouble?

If the Header and Footer toolbar is in the way, click its title bar and drag it to a new location.

1. **Place the insertion point at the top of page 2, position the ▷ pointer over the header text at the top of page 2, then double-click**
The Header and Footer areas open.

2. **Place the insertion point between the two spaces after Buzz, click Insert on the menu bar, then click Symbol**
The Symbol dialog box opens and is similar to Figure D-13. **Symbols** are special characters, such as graphics, shapes, and foreign language characters, that you can insert into a document. The symbols shown in Figure D-13 are the symbols included with the (normal text) font. You can use the Font list arrow on the Symbols tab to view the symbols included with each font on your computer.

Trouble?

If you cannot locate the symbol, type 25CF in the Character code text box.

3. **Scroll the list of symbols if necessary to locate the black circle symbol shown in Figure D-13, select the black circle symbol, click Insert, then click Close**
A circle symbol is added at the location of the insertion point.

4. **With the insertion point in the header text, click Format on the menu bar, then click Borders and Shading**
The Borders and Shading dialog box opens.

5. **Click the Borders tab, click Custom in the Setting section, click the dotted line in the Style scroll box (the second line style), click the Width list arrow, click 2¼ pt, click the Bottom border button in the Preview section, make sure Paragraph is selected in the Apply to list box, click OK, then click Close on the Header and Footer toolbar**
A dotted line border is added below the header text, as shown in Figure D-14.

6. **Press [Ctrl][Home] to move the insertion point to the beginning of the document**
The newsletter already includes the name of the document at the top of the first page, making the header information redundant. You can modify headers and footers so that the header and footer text does not appear on the first page of a document or a section.

7. **Click File on the menu bar, click Page Setup then click the Layout tab**
The Layout tab of the Page Setup dialog box includes options for creating a different header and footer for the first page of a document or a section, and for creating different headers and footers for odd- and even-numbered pages in a document or a section. For example, in a document with facing pages, such as a magazine, you might want the publication title to appear in the left-page header and the publication date to appear in the right-page header.

QuickTip

You can enter different text in the First Page Header and First Page Footer areas.

8. **Click the Different first page check box to select it, click the Apply to list arrow, click Whole document, then click OK**
The header and footer text is removed from the Header and Footer areas on the first page.

9. **Scroll to see the header and footer on pages 2, 3, and 4, then save the document**

FIGURE D-13: Symbol dialog box

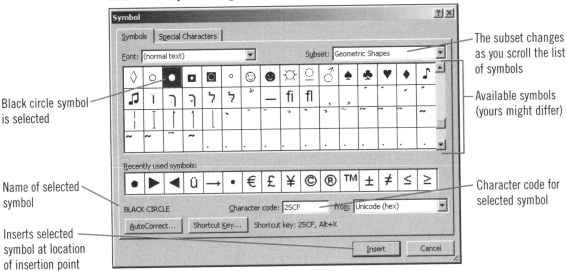

Black circle symbol is selected

Name of selected symbol

Inserts selected symbol at location of insertion point

The subset changes as you scroll the list of symbols

Available symbols (yours might differ)

Character code for selected symbol

FIGURE D-14: Symbol and border added to header

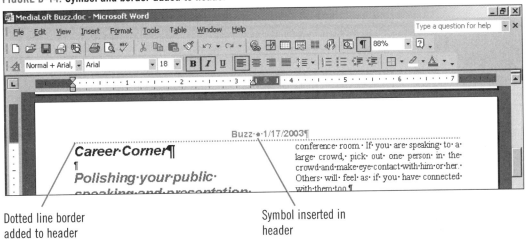

Dotted line border added to header

Symbol inserted in header

CLUES TO USE

Inserting and creating AutoText entries

Word includes a number of built-in AutoText entries, including salutations and closings for letters, as well as information for headers and footers. To insert a built-in AutoText entry at the location of the insertion point, point to AutoText on the Insert menu, point to a category on the AutoText menu, then click the AutoText entry you want to insert. You can also use the Insert AutoText button on the Header and Footer toolbar to insert an AutoText entry from the Header/Footer category into a header or footer.

Word's AutoText feature also allows you to store text and graphics that you use frequently so that you can

easily insert them in a document. To create a custom AutoText entry, enter the text or graphic you want to store—such as a company name or logo—in a document, select it, point to AutoText on the Insert menu, and then click New. In the Create AutoText dialog box, type a name for your AutoText entry, then click OK. The text or graphic is saved as a custom AutoText entry. To insert a custom AutoText entry in a document, point to AutoText on the Insert menu, click AutoText, select the entry name on the AutoText tab in the AutoCorrect dialog box, click Insert, then click OK.

Formatting Columns

Formatting text in columns often makes it easier to read. You can apply column formatting to a whole document, to a section, or to selected text. The Columns button on the Standard toolbar allows you to quickly create columns of equal width. In addition, you can use the Columns command on the Format menu to create columns and to customize the width and spacing of columns. To control the way text flows between columns, you can insert a **column break**, which forces the text following the break to move to the top of the next column. You can also balance columns of unequal length by inserting a continuous section break at the end of the last column in a section. *Alice formats the Staff News page in three columns, then she adjusts the flow of text.*

Steps

1. Scroll to the top of page 4, place the insertion point before **Boston**, click **Insert** on the menu bar, click **Break**, select the **Continuous option button**, then click **OK**
   A continuous section break is inserted before Boston. The newsletter now contains three sections.

2. Refer to the status bar to confirm that the insertion point is in section 3, click **Format** on the menu bar, then click **Columns**
   The Columns dialog box opens, as shown in Figure D-15.

3. Select **Three** in the Presets section, click the **Spacing down arrow** twice until 0.3" appears, select the **Line between check box**, then click **OK**
   All the text in section 3 is formatted in three columns of equal width with a line between the columns, as shown in Figure D-16.

4. Click the **Zoom list arrow** on the Standard toolbar, then click **Whole Page**
   Notice that the third column of text is much shorter than the first two columns. Page 4 would look better if the three columns were balanced—each the same length.

5. Place the insertion point at the end of the third column, click **Insert** on the menu bar, click **Break**, select the **Continuous option button**, then click **OK**
   The columns in section 3 adjust to become roughly the same length.

6. Scroll up to page 3
   The two columns on page 3 are also uneven. The page would look better if the information about the third webcast did not break across the two columns.

7. Click the **Zoom list arrow**, click **Page Width**, scroll to the bottom of page 3, place the insertion point before **Tuesday, June 10**, click **Insert** on the menu bar, click **Break**, click the **Column break option button**, then click **OK**
   The text following the column break is forced to the top of the next column.

8. Click the **Zoom list arrow**, click **Two Pages**, then save the document
   The columns on pages 3 and 4 are displayed, as shown in Figure D-17.

QuickTip

To change the width and spacing of existing columns, you can use the Columns dialog box or drag the column markers on the horizontal ruler.

QuickTip

To create a banner headline that spans the width of a page, select the headline text, click the Columns button, then click 1 Column.

QuickTip

If a section contains a column break, you cannot balance the columns by inserting a continuous section break.

Clues to Use

Hyphenating text in a document

Hyphenating a document is another way to control the flow of text in columns. Hyphens are small dashes that break words that fall at the end of a line. Hyphenation diminishes the gaps between words in justified text and reduces ragged right edges in left-aligned text. If a document includes narrow columns, hyphenating the text can help give the pages a cleaner look. To hyphenate a document automatically, point to Language on the Tools menu, click Hyphenation, select the Automatically hyphenate document check box in the Hyphenation dialog box, and then click OK. You can also use the Hyphenation dialog box to change the hyphenation zone—the distance between the margin and the end of the last word in the line. A smaller hyphenation zone results in a greater number of hyphenated words and a cleaner look to columns of text.

FIGURE D-15: **Columns dialog box**

Select a preset format for columns

Change the number of columns

Select to add a line between columns

Preview of current settings

Set custom widths and spacing for columns

Select to create columns of equal width

Select part of document to apply format to

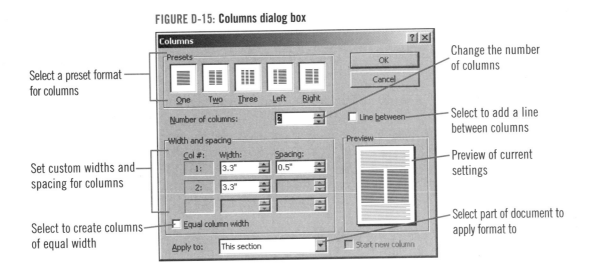

FIGURE D-16: **Text formatted in three columns**

Column markers show the width and spacing of columns

Text in section 3 is formatted in 3 columns

Section break is at end of section 2

Line added between columns

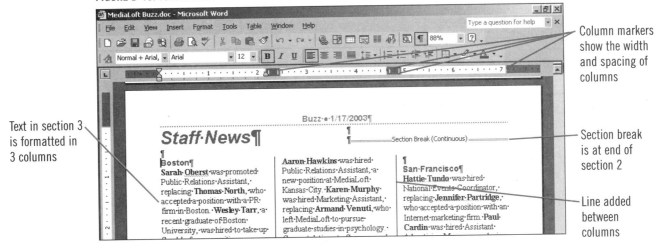

FIGURE D-17: **Completed pages 3 and 4 of newsletter**

Text following column break is forced to top of next column

Column break

Continuous section break

Columns in section are balanced

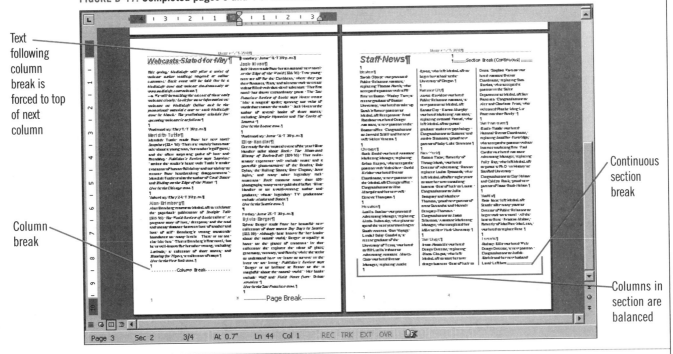

Word 2002

Inserting Clip Art

Illustrating a document with clip art images can give it visual appeal and help to communicate your ideas. **Clip art** is a collection of graphic images that you can insert into a document. Clip art images are stored in the Clip Organizer, a library of the **clips**—media files, including graphics, photographs, sounds, movies, and animations—that come with Word. Clips are organized in collections in the Clip Organizer. You can add a clip to a document using the Clip Art command on the Insert menu. Once you insert a clip art image, you can wrap text around it, resize it, and move it to a different location. ⬛ Alice illustrates the second page of the newsletter with a clip art image. After she inserts the image, she wraps text around it, enlarges it, and then moves it so that it is centered between the two columns of text.

Steps 1 2 3 4

1. Click the **Zoom list arrow** on the Standard toolbar, click **Page Width**, scroll to the top of page 2, then place the insertion point before the first body paragraph, which begins **Did you know...**
   You will insert the clip art graphic at the location of the insertion point.

Trouble?
If the Add Clips to Organizer message box opens, click Later.

2. Click **Insert** on the menu bar, point to **Picture**, then click **Clip Art**
   The Insert Clip Art task pane opens, as shown in Figure D-18. You can use this task pane to search for clips related to a keyword.

3. Select the text in the Search text text box if necessary, type **communication**, then click **Search**
   Clips with the keyword "communication" appear in the Insert Clip Art task pane, as shown in Figure D-19. When you point to a clip, a ScreenTip showing the first few keywords applied to the clip, the width and height of the clip in pixels, and the file size and file type for the clip appears.

Trouble?
Select a different clip if the clip shown in Figure D-19 is not available to you.

4. Point to the **clip** shown in Figure D-19, click the **list arrow** that appears next to the clip, click **Insert** on the menu, then close the Insert Clip Art task pane
   The clip is inserted at the location of the insertion point. You want to center the graphic on the page. Until you apply text wrapping to a graphic, it is part of the line of text in which it was inserted (an **inline graphic**). To move a graphic independently of text, you must wrap the text around it to make it a **floating graphic**, which can be moved anywhere on a page.

5. Double-click the **clip art image**, click the **Layout tab** in the Format Picture dialog box, click **Tight**, then click **OK**
   The text in the first body paragraph wraps around the irregular shape of the clip art image. The white circles that appear on the square edges of the graphic are the **sizing handles**, which appear when a graphic is selected. You can drag a sizing handle to change the size of the image.

QuickTip
To verify the size of a graphic or to set precise measurements, double-click the graphic to open the Format Picture dialog box, then adjust the Height and Width settings on the Size tab.

6. Position the pointer over the **lower-right sizing handle**, when the pointer changes to ↖ drag down and to the right until the graphic is about 2½" wide and 2½" tall
   As you drag a sizing handle, the dotted lines show the outline of the graphic. Refer to the dotted lines and the rulers as you resize the graphic. When you release the mouse button, the image is enlarged.

7. With the graphic still selected, position the pointer over the graphic, when the pointer changes to ⊹ drag the graphic down and to the right so it is centered on the page as shown in Figure D-20, release the mouse button, then deselect the graphic
   The graphic is now centered between the two columns of text.

Trouble?
If page 3 is a blank page or contains text continued from page 2, reduce the size of the graphic on page 2.

8. Click the **Zoom list arrow**, then click **Two Pages**
   The completed pages 1 and 2 are displayed, as shown in Figure D-21.

9. Press **[Ctrl][End]**, press **[Enter]**, type your name, save your changes, print the document, then close the document and exit Word

FIGURE D-18: Insert Clip Art task pane

Type search keyword here

Select collections in which to search for clips

Select type of clips

Click to open the Clip Organizer

Click to search for clips online

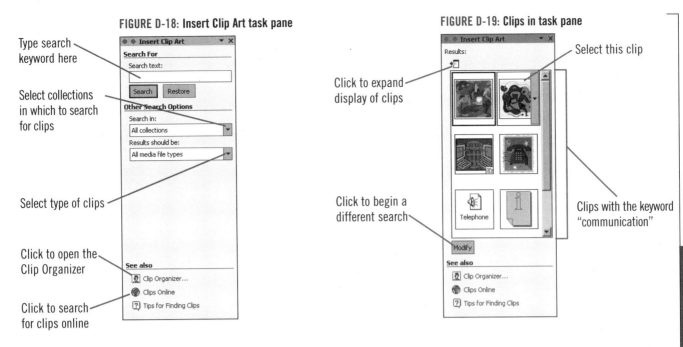

FIGURE D-19: Clips in task pane

Select this clip

Click to expand display of clips

Click to begin a different search

Clips with the keyword "communication"

FIGURE D-20: Graphic being moved to a new location

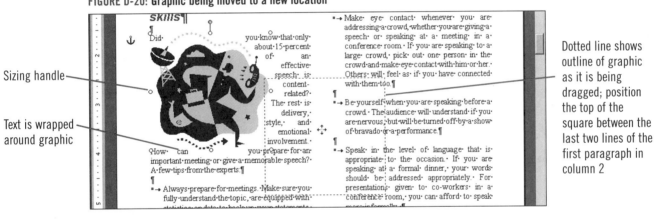

Sizing handle

Text is wrapped around graphic

Dotted line shows outline of graphic as it is being dragged; position the top of the square between the last two lines of the first paragraph in column 2

FIGURE D-21: Completed pages 1 and 2 of newsletter

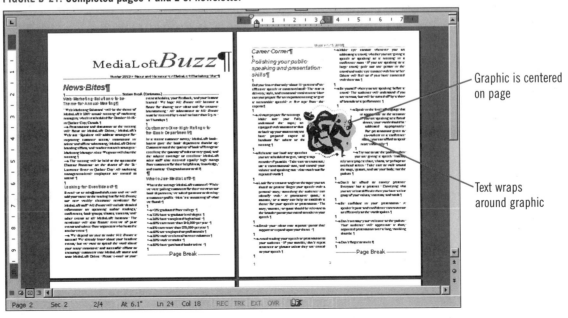

Graphic is centered on page

Text wraps around graphic

Practice

▶ Concepts Review

Label each element shown in Figure D-22.

FIGURE D-22

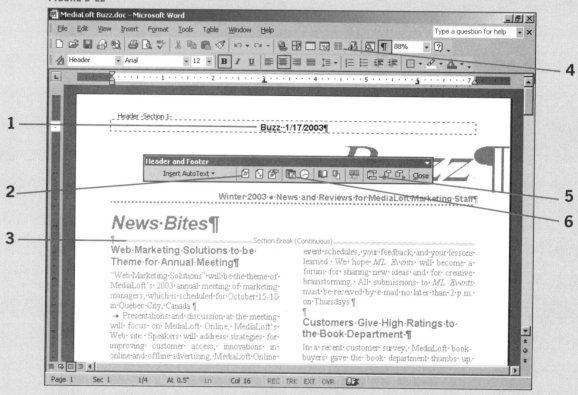

Match each term with the statement that best describes it.

7. Section break
8. Header
9. Footer
10. Field
11. Hard page break
12. Margin
13. Inline graphic
14. Floating graphic

a. A formatting mark that forces the text following the mark to begin at the top of the next page
b. The blank area between the edge of the text and the edge of the page
c. A placeholder for information that changes
d. Text or graphics that appears at the top of every page in a document
e. An image to which text wrapping has been applied
f. A formatting mark that divides a document into parts that can be formatted differently
g. An image that is inserted as part of a line of text
h. Text or graphics that appears at the bottom of every page in a document

Select the best answer from the list of choices.

15. **Which of the following do documents with mirror margins always have?**
    a. Landscape orientation
    b. Inside and outside margins
    c. Gutters
    d. Different first page headers and footers

16. **Which button is used to insert a field into a header or footer?**
    a.
    b.
    c.
    d.

17. **Which type of break do you insert if you want to force text to begin on the next page?**
    a. Continuous section break
    b. Soft page break
    c. Hard page break
    d. Text wrapping break

18. **Which type of break do you insert if you want to balance the columns in a section?**
    a. Continuous section break
    b. Soft page break
    c. Column break
    d. Text wrapping break

19. **What must you do to change an inline graphic to a floating graphic?**
    a. Resize the graphic
    b. Move the graphic
    c. Apply text wrapping to the graphic
    d. Anchor the graphic

20. **Pressing [Ctrl][Enter] does which of the following?**
    a. Inserts a soft page break
    b. Inserts a continuous section break
    c. Moves the insertion point to the beginning of the document
    d. Inserts a hard page break

► Skills Review

1. **Set document margins.**
   a. Start Word, open the file WD D-2 from the drive and folder where your Project Files are located, then save it as **Amherst Fitness**.
   b. Change the top and bottom margins to 1.2" and the left and right margins to 1".
   c. Save your changes to the document.

2. **Divide a document into sections.**
   a. Scroll down, then insert a continuous section break before the **Facilities** heading.
   b. Format the text in Section 2 in two columns, then save your changes to the document.

3. **Add page breaks.**
   a. Insert a hard page break before the heading **Welcome to the Amherst Fitness Center!**, scrolling up if necessary.
   b. Scroll down and insert a hard page break before the heading **Services**.
   c. Scroll down and insert a hard page break before the heading **Membership**.
   d. Press [Ctrl][Home], then save your changes to the document.

4. **Add page numbers.**
   a. Insert page numbers in the document. Center the page numbers at the bottom of the page.
   b. View the page numbers on each page in Print Preview, then save your changes to the document.

5. **Insert headers and footers.**
   a. Open the Header and Footer areas, then type your name in the Header area.
   b. Press [Tab] twice, then use the Insert Date button on the Header and Footer toolbar to insert the current date.
   c. On the horizontal ruler, drag the right tab stop from the 6" mark to the 6½" mark so that the date aligns with the right margin of the document.
   d. Move the insertion point to the Footer area.
   e. Double-click the page number to select it, then format the page number in bold italic.
   f. Close headers and footers, preview the header and footer on each page in Print Preview, close Print Preview, then save your changes to the document.

6. Edit headers and footers.

   a. Open headers and footers, then apply italic to the text in the header.

   b. Move the insertion point to the Footer area, double-click the page number to select it, then press [Delete].

   c. Click the Align Right button on the Formatting toolbar.

   d. Use the Symbol command on the Insert menu to open the Symbol dialog box.

   e. Insert a black right-pointing triangle symbol, then close the Symbol dialog box.

   f. Use the Insert Page Number button on the Header and Footer toolbar to insert a page number.

   g. Use the Page Setup button on the Header and Footer toolbar to open the Page Setup dialog box.

   h. Use the Layout tab to create a different header and footer for the first page of the document.

   i. Scroll to the beginning of the document. If you want your name on the first page of the document, type your name in the First Page Header area, then apply italic to your name.

   j. Close headers and footers, preview the header and footer on each page in Print Preview, close Print Preview, then save your changes to the document.

7. Format columns.

   a. On page 2, select **Facilities** and the paragraph mark below it, use the Columns button to format the selected text as one column, then center **Facilities** on the page.

   b. Balance the columns on page 2 by inserting a continuous section break at the bottom of the second column.

   c. On page 3, select **Services** and the paragraph mark below it, format the selected text as one column, then center the text.

   d. Balance the columns on page 3.

   e. On page 4, select **Membership** and the paragraph mark below it, format the selected text as one column, then center the text.

   f. Insert a column break before the **Membership Cards** heading, then save your changes to the document.

8. Insert clip art.

   a. On page 1, place the insertion point in the second blank paragraph below **A Rehabilitation and Exercise Facility**. (*Hint*: Place the insertion point to the left of the paragraph mark.)

   b. Open the Insert Clip Art task pane. Search for clips related to the keyword **Victories**.

   c. Insert the clip shown in Figure D-23. Select a different clip if this one is not available to you.

   d. Select the graphic, then drag the lower-right sizing handle up and to the left so that the graphic is about 2" wide and 3" tall. Size the graphic so that all the text and the hard page break fit on page 1. (*Hint*: The sizing handles on inline graphics are black squares.)

   e. Scroll to page 3, then place the insertion point before the **Personal Training** heading.

   f. In the Insert Clip Art task pane, search for an appropriate clip to illustrate this page. You might try searching using the keywords **sports**, **health**, or **heart**.

   g. When you find an appropriate clip, insert it in the document, then close the Insert Clip Art task pane.

   h. Double-click the graphic to open the Format Picture dialog box, then click the Layout tab. Apply the Tight text wrapping style to the graphic.

   i. Move the graphic so that it is centered below the text at the bottom of the page (below the page break mark). Adjust the size and position of the graphic so that the page looks attractive.

   j. Save your changes to the document. Preview the document, print a copy, then close the document and exit Word.

FIGURE D-23

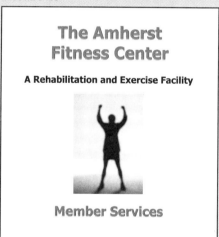

The Amherst
Fitness Center

A Rehabilitation and Exercise Facility

Member Services

Independent Challenge 1

You are the owner of a small catering business in Latona, Ontario called Bon Appetit Catering Services. You have begun work on the text for a brochure advertising your business and are now ready to lay out the pages and prepare the final copy. The brochure will be printed on both sides of an 8½" × 11" sheet of paper, and folded in thirds.

FIGURE D-24

Bon Appetit

◇

Catering Services

Complete catering services available for all types of events. Menus and estimates provided upon request.

a. Start Word, open the file WD D-3 from the drive and folder where your Project Files are located, then save it as **Bon Appetit**. Read the document to get a feel for its contents.

b. Change the page orientation to landscape, and change all four margins to .6".

c. Format the document in three columns of equal width.

d. Insert a hard page break before the heading **Catering Services**.

e. On page 1, insert column breaks before the headings **Sample Indian Banquet Menu** and **Sample Tuscan Banquet Menu**.

f. On page 1, insert a continuous section break at the end of the third column.

g. Add lines between the columns on the first page, then center the text in the columns.

h. Create a different header and footer for the first page. Type **Call for custom menus designed to your taste and budget** in the First Page Footer area.

i. Center the text in the footer area, format it in 20-point Comic Sans MS, all caps, with a plum font color, then close headers and footers.

j. On page 2, insert a column break before Your Name. Press [Enter] as many times as necessary to move the contact information to the bottom of the second column. Be sure all five lines of the contact information are in column 2 and do not flow to the next column.

k. Replace Your Name with your name, then center the contact information in the column.

l. Insert a column break at the bottom of the second column. Then, type the text shown in Figure D-24 in the third column. Refer to the figure as you follow the instructions for formatting the text in the third column.

m. Format **Bon Appetit Catering Services** in 28-point Comic Sans MS, bold, with a plum font color.

n. Format the remaining text in 12-point Comic Sans MS, with a plum font color. Center the text in the third column.

o. Below Bon Appetit, insert the symbol shown in Figure D-24. (*Hint*: Type the character code 25CA in the Character code text box in the Symbol dialog box to find the symbol.) Change the font color of the symbol to gold.

p. Insert the clip art graphic shown in Figure D-24 or another appropriate clip art graphic. Do not wrap text around the graphic.

q. Add and remove blank paragraphs in the third column of your brochure so that the spacing between elements roughly matches the spacing shown in Figure D-24.

r. Save your changes, preview the brochure in Print Preview, then print a copy. If possible, print the two pages of the brochure back to back so that the brochure can be folded in thirds. Close the document and exit Word.

▶ Independent Challenge 2

You work in the Campus Safety Department at Miller State College. You have written the text for an informational flyer about parking regulations on campus and now you need to format the flyer so it is attractive and readable.

a. Start Word, open the file WD D-4 from the drive and folder where your Project Files are located, then save it as **Parking FAQ**. Read the document to get a feel for its contents.

b. Change all four margins to .7".

c. Insert a continuous section break before **1. May I bring a car to school?** (*Hint:* Place the insertion point before "May.")

d. Scroll down and insert a next page section break before **Sample Parking Permit**.

e. Format the text in section 2 in three columns of equal width with .3" of space between the columns.

f. Hyphenate the document using the automatic hyphenation feature. (*Hint:* If the Hyphenation feature is not installed on your computer, skip this step.)

g. Add a 3-pt dotted line bottom border to the blank paragraph under Miller State College. (*Hint:* Place the insertion point before the paragraph mark under Miller State College, then apply a bottom border to the paragraph.)

h. Add your name to the header. Right-align your name and format it in 10-point Arial.

i. Add the following text to the footer, inserting symbols between words as indicated: **Parking and Shuttle Service Office • 54 Buckley Street • Miller State College • 942-555-2227**.

j. Format the footer text in 10-point Arial Black and center it in the footer. Use a different font if Arial Black is not available to you. If necessary adjust the font and font size so that the entire address fits on one line.

k. Apply a 3-pt dotted line border above the footer text. Make sure to apply the border to the paragraph.

l. Balance the columns in section 2.

m. Add an appropriate clip art image to the upper-right corner of the document, above the border. Make sure the graphic does not obscure the border.

n. Place the insertion point on page 2 (which is section 4). Change the left and right margins in section 4 to 1". Also change the page orientation of section 4 to landscape.

o. Change the vertical alignment of section 4 to Center.

p. Save your changes, preview the flyer in Print Preview, then print a copy. If possible, print the two pages of the flyer back to back. Close the document and exit Word.

▶ Independent Challenge 3

A book publisher would like to publish an article you wrote on stormwater pollution in Australia as a chapter in a forth-coming book called *Environmental Issues for the New Millennium*. The publisher has requested that you format your article like a book chapter before submitting it for publication, and has provided you with a style sheet.

a. Start Word, open the file WD D-5 from the drive and folder where your Project Files are located, then save it as **Stormwater**.

b. Change the font of the entire document to 11-point Book Antiqua. If this font is not available to you, select a different font suitable for the pages of a book. Change the alignment to justified.

c. Change the paper size to 6" × 9".

d. Create mirror margins. (*Hint:* Use the Multiple Pages list arrow.) Change the top and bottom margins to .8", change the inside margin to .4", change the outside margin to .6", and create a .3" gutter to allow room for the book's binding.

e. Change the Zoom level to Two Pages. Create different headers and footers for odd- and even- numbered pages.

f. Change the Zoom level to Page Width. In the odd page header, type **Chapter 7**, insert a symbol of your choice, then type **Stormwater Pollution in the Fairy Creek Catchment**.

g. Format the header text in 9-point Book Antiqua italic, then right-align the text.

h. In the even page header, type your name, insert a symbol of your choice, then insert the current date. (*Hint*: Scroll down or use the Show Next button to move the insertion point to the even page header.)

i. Change the format of the date to include just the month and the year. (*Hint*: Right-click the date field, then click Edit Field.)

j. Format the header text in 9-point Book Antiqua italic. The even page header should be left-aligned.

k. Insert page numbers that are centered in the footer. Format the page number in 10-point Book Antiqua. Make sure to insert a page number field in both the odd and even page footer areas.

l. Format the page numbers so that the first page of Chapter 7 begins on page 53. (*Hint*: Select a page number field, then use the Format Page Number button.)

m.Go to the beginning of the document, press [Enter] 10 times, type **Chapter 7: Stormwater Pollution in the Fairy Creek Catchment**, press [Enter] twice, type your name, then press [Enter] twice.

n. Format the chapter title in 16-point Book Antiqua bold, format your name in 14-point Book Antiqua using small caps, then left-align the text.

o. Save your changes, preview the chapter in Print Preview, print the first three pages of the chapter, then close the document and exit Word.

Independent Challenge 4

One of the most common opportunities to use Word's page layout features is when formatting a research paper. The format recommended by the *MLA Handbook for Writers of Research Papers*, a style guide that includes information on preparing, writing, and formatting research papers, is the standard format used by many schools, colleges, and universities. In this independent challenge, you will research the MLA (Modern Language Association) guidelines for formatting a research paper and use the guidelines you find to prepare a sample first page of a research report.

a. Start Word, open the file WD D-6 from the drive and folder where your Project Files are located, then save it as **MLA Style**. This document contains the questions you will answer about MLA style guidelines.

b. Use your favorite search engine to search the Web for information on the MLA guidelines for formatting a research report. Use the keywords **MLA Style** and **research paper format**, to conduct your search. If your search does not result in links to appropriate sources, try the following Web sites: http://webster.commnet.edu/mla.htm or www.mla.org.

c. Look for information on the proper formatting for the following aspects of a research paper: paper size, margins, title page or first page of the report, line spacing, paragraph indentation, page numbers, and works cited.

d. Type your answers to the questions in the MLA Style document, save it, print a copy, then close the document.

e. Using the information you learned, start a new document and create a sample first page of a research report. Use **MLA Format for Research Papers** as the title for your sample report, and make up information about the course and instructor, if necessary. For the body of the report, type several sentences about MLA style. Make sure to format the page exactly as the MLA style dictates.

f. Save the document as **MLA Sample Format** to the drive and folder where your Project Files are located, print a copy, close the document, then exit Word.

▶ Visual Workshop

Use the file WD D-7, found on the drive and folder where your Project Files are located, to create the article shown in Figure D-25. (*Hint*: Change all four margins to .6". Make the width of the first column 2.2" and the width of the second column 4.8". Format the second column with borders and shading, but take care not to apply shading to the blank paragraph before the Clean Up heading. Select a different clip if the clip shown in the figure is not available to you.) Save the document with the filename **Gardener's Corner**, then print a copy.

FIGURE D-25

GARDENER'S CORNER

Putting a Perennial Garden to Bed

By Your Name

A certain sense of peace descends when a perennial garden is put to bed for the season. The plants are safely tucked in against the elements, and the garden is ready to welcome the first signs of life. When the work is done, you can sit back and anticipate the bright blooms of spring. Many gardeners are uncertain of how to close a perennial garden. This week's column demystifies the process.

Clean up

Debris that is left on top of soil invites garden pests to lay their eggs and spend the winter. Garden clean up can be a gradual process—plants will deteriorate at different rates, allowing you to do a little bit each week.

1. Edge beds and borders and remove stakes and other plant supports.
2. Dig and divide irises, daylilies, and other early bloomers.
3. Cut back plants when foliage starts to deteriorate.
4. Rake all debris out of the garden and pull any weeds that remain.

Plant perennials

Fall is the perfect time to plant perennials! The warm, sunny days and cool nights provide optimal conditions for new root growth.

1. Dig deeply and enhance soil with organic matter.
2. Use a good starter fertilizer to speed up new root growth.
3. Untangle the roots of new plants before planting them.
4. Water deeply after planting as the weather dictates.

Add compost

Organic matter is the key ingredient to healthy soil. If you take care of the soil, your plants will become strong and disease resistant.

1. Use an iron rake to loosen the top few inches of soil.
2. Spread a one to two inch layer of compost over the entire garden.
3. Refrain from stepping on the area and compacting the soil.

To mulch or not to mulch?

Winter protection for perennial beds can only help plants survive the winter. Here's what works and what doesn't:

1. Always apply mulch after the ground is frozen.
2. Never apply generic hay because is contains billions of weed seeds. Also, whole leaves and bark mulch hold too much moisture.
3. Straw and salt marsh hay are excellent choices for mulch.

Creating
and Formatting Tables

Tables are commonly used to display information for quick reference and analysis. In this unit, you learn how to create and modify a table in Word, how to sort table data and perform calculations, and how to format a table with borders and shading. You also learn how to use a table to structure the layout of a page. ◆ Alice Wegman is preparing a summary budget for an advertising campaign aimed at the Boston market. The goal of the ad campaign is to promote MediaLoft Online, the MediaLoft Web site. Alice decides to format the budget information as a table so that it is easy to read and analyze. You will work with Alice as she creates the table.

Word 2002

Inserting a Table

A **table** is a grid made up of rows and columns of cells that you can fill with text and graphics. A **cell** is the box formed by the intersection of a column and a row. The lines that divide the columns and rows and help you see the grid-like structure of a table are called **borders**. You can create a table in a document by using the Insert Table button on the Standard toolbar or the Insert command on the Table menu. Once you have created a table, you can add text and graphics to it. Alice begins by inserting a blank table into the document and then adding text to it.

Steps

1. Start **Word**, close the **New Document task pane**, click the **Print Layout View button** on the horizontal scroll bar if necessary, click the **Zoom list arrow** on the Standard toolbar, then click **Page Width**
   A blank document appears in Print Layout view.

QuickTip

To convert tabbed text to a table, select the tabbed text, click Table on the menu bar, point to Convert, then click Text to Table.

2. Click the **Insert Table button** on the Standard toolbar
   A grid opens below the button. You move the pointer across this grid to select the number of columns and rows you want the table to contain. To expand the grid, drag the lower-right corner.

3. Point to the **second box** in the fourth row to select 4 × 2 Table, then click
   A table with two columns and four rows is inserted in the document, as shown in Figure E-1. The insertion point is in the first cell in the first row.

4. Type **Location**, then press **[Tab]**
   Pressing [Tab] moves the insertion point to the next cell in the row.

5. Type **Cost**, press **[Tab]**, then type **Boston Sunday Globe**
   Pressing [Tab] at the end of a row moves the insertion point to the first cell in the next row.

6. Press **[Tab]**, type **27,600**, then type the following text in the table, pressing **[Tab]** to move from cell to cell
   | Boston.com | 25,000 |
   | Taxi tops | 18,000 |

7. Press **[Tab]**
   Pressing [Tab] at the end of the last cell of a table creates a new row at the bottom of the table, as shown in Figure E-2. The insertion point is located in the first cell in the new row.

Trouble?

If you pressed [Tab] after the last row, click the Undo button on the Standard toolbar to remove the new blank row.

8. Type the following, pressing **[Tab]** to move from cell to cell and to create new rows
Boston Herald	18,760
Townonline.com	3,250
Bus stops	12,000
Boston Magazine	12,400

9. Click the **Save button** on the Standard toolbar, then save the document with the file-name **Boston Ad Budget** to the drive and folder where your Project Files are located
   The table is shown in Figure E-3.

FIGURE E-1: Blank table

Insert Table button

Column

Row

Cell

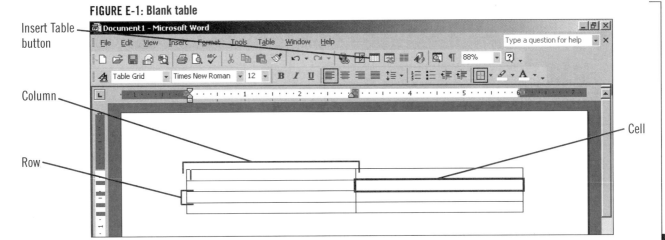

FIGURE E-2: New row in table

New row

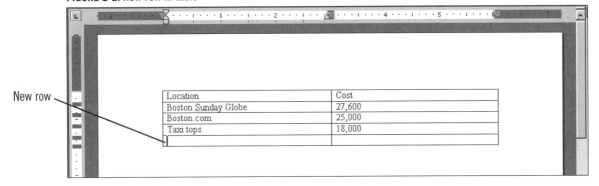

FIGURE E-3: Text in the table

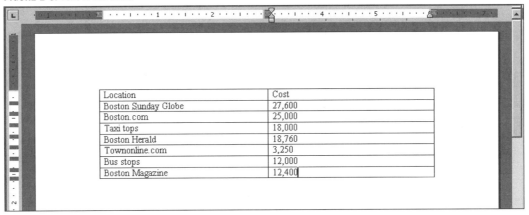

Creating a formatted blank table

When you use the Insert command on the Table menu to create a table, you have the option of formatting the table before you create it. To create a formatted blank table, point to Insert on the Table menu, then click Table to open the Insert Table dialog box. In the dialog box, first select the number of columns and rows you want your table to include. Next, in the AutoFit behavior area, choose an option for sizing the width of the columns in your table: set a specific fixed width, automatically size the columns to fit the text, or resize columns according to the width of the window. Finally, click AutoFormat to open the AutoFormat dialog box. In the AutoFormat dialog box, select a format for the table, then click OK. Click OK in the Insert Table dialog box to insert a table formatted with the options you specified.

Inserting and Deleting Rows and Columns

You can easily modify the structure of a table by adding and removing rows and columns. First, you must select an existing row or column in the table to indicate where you want to insert or delete information. You can select any element of a table using the Select command on the Table menu, but it is often easier to select rows and columns using the mouse: click in the margin to the left of a row to select the row; click the top border of a column to select the column. Alternatively, you can drag across a row or down a column to select it. To insert rows and columns, use the Insert command on the Table menu or the Insert Rows and Insert Columns button on the Standard toolbar. To delete rows and columns, use the Delete command on the Table menu. Alice adds a new row to the table and deletes an unnecessary row. She also adds new columns to the table to provide more detailed information.

1. Click the **Show/Hide/¶ button** ¶ on the Standard toolbar to display formatting marks
   An end of cell mark appears at the end of each cell and an end of row mark appears at the end of each row.

2. Place the pointer in the margin to the left of the **Townonline.com row** until the pointer changes to ⤢ , then click
   The entire row is selected, including the end of row mark. If the end of row mark is not selected, you have selected only the text in a row, not the row itself. When a row is selected, the Insert Table button changes to the Insert Rows button.

3. Click the **Insert Rows button** on the Standard toolbar
   A new row is inserted above the Townonline.com row, as shown in Figure E-4.

4. Click in the **first cell** of the new row, type **Boston Phoenix**, press **[Tab]**, then type **15,300**
   Clicking in a cell moves the insertion point to that cell.

5. Select the **Boston Herald row**, right-click, then click **Delete Rows** on the shortcut menu
   The selected row is deleted. If you select a row and press [Delete], you delete only the contents of the row, not the row itself.

6. Place the pointer over the top border of the **Location column** until the pointer changes to ↓, then click
   The entire column is selected. When a column is selected, the Insert Table button changes to the Insert Columns button.

7. Click the **Insert Columns button** on the Standard toolbar, then type **Type**
   A new column is inserted to the left of the Location column, as shown in Figure E-5.

8. Click in the **Location column**, click **Table** on the menu bar, point to **Insert**, click **Columns to the Right**, then type **Details** in the first cell of the new column
   A new column is added to the right of the Location column. You can also use the Insert command to add columns to the left of the active column or to insert rows above or below the active row.

9. Press **[↓]** to move the insertion point to the next cell in the Details column, enter the text shown in Figure E-6 in each cell in the Details and Type columns, click ¶ to turn off the display of formatting marks, then save your changes
   You can use the arrow keys to move the insertion point from cell to cell. Notice that text wraps to the next line in the cell as you type. Compare your table to Figure E-6.

FIGURE E-4: Inserted row

Insert Rows button

End of cell mark

End of row mark

New row is inserted and selected by default

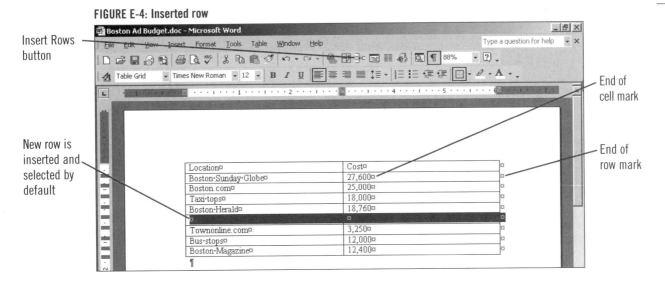

Location¤	Cost¤	¤
Boston·Sunday·Globe¤	27,600¤	¤
Boston.com¤	25,000¤	¤
Taxi·tops¤	18,000¤	¤
Boston·Herald¤	18,760¤	¤
¤	¤	¤
Townonline.com¤	3,250¤	¤
Bus·stops¤	12,000¤	¤
Boston·Magazine¤	12,400¤	¤

FIGURE E-5: Inserted column

New column

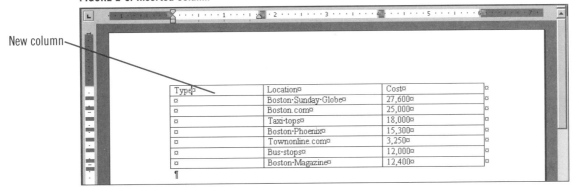

Type¤	Location¤	Cost¤	¤
¤	Boston·Sunday·Globe¤	27,600¤	¤
¤	Boston.com¤	25,000¤	¤
¤	Taxi·tops¤	18,000¤	¤
¤	Boston·Phoenix¤	15,300¤	¤
¤	Townonline.com¤	3,250¤	¤
¤	Bus·stops¤	12,000¤	¤
¤	Boston·Magazine¤	12,400¤	¤

FIGURE E-6: Text in Type and Details columns

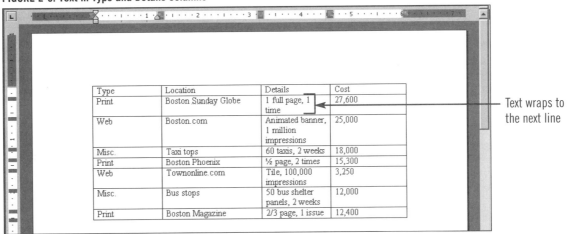

Text wraps to the next line

Type	Location	Details	Cost
Print	Boston Sunday Globe	1 full page, 1 time	27,600
Web	Boston.com	Animated banner, 1 million impressions	25,000
Misc.	Taxi tops	60 taxis, 2 weeks	18,000
Print	Boston Phoenix	½ page, 2 times	15,300
Web	Townonline.com	Tile, 100,000 impressions	3,250
Misc.	Bus stops	50 bus shelter panels, 2 weeks	12,000
Print	Boston Magazine	2/3 page, 1 issue	12,400

CLUES TO USE

Copying and moving rows and columns

You can copy and move rows and columns within a table in the same manner you copy and move text. Select the row or column you want to move, then use the Copy or Cut button to place the selection on the Clipboard. Place the insertion point in the location you want to insert the row or column, then click the Paste button to paste the selection. Rows are inserted above the row containing the insertion point; columns are inserted to the left of the column containing the insertion point. You can also copy or move columns and rows by selecting them and using the 🔖 pointer to drag them to a new location in the table.

 **Word 2002**

Modifying Table Rows and Columns

Once you create a table, you can easily adjust the size of columns and rows to make the table easier to read. You can change the size of columns and rows by dragging a border, by using the AutoFit command on the Table menu, or by setting exact measurements for column width and row height using the Table Properties dialog box. ____ Alice adjusts the size of the columns and rows to make the table more attractive and easier to read. She also centers the text vertically in each table cell.

Steps

QuickTip

Press [Alt] as you drag a column or row border to display the column width or row height measurements on the ruler.

1. Position the pointer over the **border** between the first and second columns until the pointer changes to +‖+, then drag the border to approximately the ½" **mark** on the horizontal ruler
   The dotted line that appears as you drag represents the border. Dragging the column border changes the width of the first and second columns: the first column is narrower and the second column is wider. When dragging a border to change the width of an entire column, make sure no cells are selected in the column. You can also drag a row border to change the width of the row above it.

2. Position the pointer over the **right border** of the Location column until the pointer changes to +‖+, then double-click
   Double-clicking a column border automatically resizes the column to fit the text.

3. Use +‖+ to double-click the **right border** of the Details column, then use +‖+ to double-click the **right border** of the Cost column
   The widths of the Details and Cost columns are adjusted.

QuickTip

To move a table, drag the table move handle to a new location.

4. Move the pointer over the table, then click the **table move handle** ⊞ that appears outside the upper-left corner of the table
   Clicking the table move handle selects the entire table. You can also use the Select command on the Table menu to select an entire table.

QuickTip

Quickly resize an entire table by dragging the table resize handle to a new location.

5. Click **Table** on the menu bar, point to **AutoFit**, click **Distribute Rows Evenly**, then deselect the table
   All the rows in the table become the same height, as shown in Figure E-7. You can also use the commands on the AutoFit menu to make all the columns the same width, to make the width of the columns fit the text, and to adjust the width of the columns so the table is justified between the margins.

QuickTip

To change the margins in all the cells in a table, click Options on the Table tab, then enter new margin settings in the Table Options dialog box.

6. Click in the **Details column**, click **Table** on the menu bar, click **Table Properties**, then click the **Column tab** in the Table Properties dialog box
   The Column tab, shown in Figure E-8, allows you to set an exact width for columns. You can specify an exact height for rows and an exact size for cells using the Row and Cell tabs. You can also use the Table tab to set a precise size for the table, to change the alignment of the table on a page, and to wrap text around a table.

7. Select the measurement in the Preferred width text box, type **3**, then click **OK**
   The width of the Details column changes to 3".

QuickTip

Quickly center a table on a page by selecting the table and clicking the Center button ▦ on the Formatting toolbar.

8. Click ⊞ to select the table, click **Table** on the menu bar, click **Table Properties**, click the **Cell tab**, click the **Center box** in the Vertical Alignment section, click **OK**, deselect the table, then save your changes
   The text is centered vertically in each table cell, as shown in Figure E-9.

FIGURE E-7: Resized columns and rows

Table move handle: click to select the table; drag to move the table

Rows are all the same height

Table resize handle; drag to change the size of all the rows and columns

Type	Location	Details	Cost
Print	Boston Sunday Globe	1 full page, 1 time	27,600
Web	Boston.com	Animated banner, 1 million impressions	25,000
Misc.	Taxi tops	60 taxis, 2 weeks	18,000
Print	Boston Phoenix	½ page, 2 times	15,300
Web	Townonline.com	Tile, 100,000 impressions	3,250
Misc.	Bus stops	50 bus shelter panels, 2 weeks	12,000
Print	Boston Magazine	2/3 page, 1 issue	12,400

FIGURE E-8: Table Properties dialog box

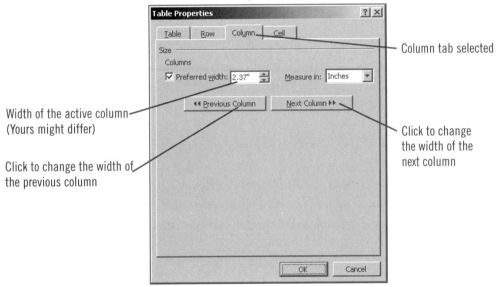

Column tab selected

Width of the active column (Yours might differ)

Click to change the width of the previous column

Click to change the width of the next column

FIGURE E-9: Text centered vertically in cells

Column is widened

Text is centered vertically in the cell

Type	Location	Details	Cost
Print	Boston Sunday Globe	1 full page, 1 time	27,600
Web	Boston.com	Animated banner, 1 million impressions	25,000
Misc.	Taxi tops	60 taxis, 2 weeks	18,000
Print	Boston Phoenix	½ page, 2 times	15,300
Web	Townonline.com	Tile, 100,000 impressions	3,250
Misc.	Bus stops	50 bus shelter panels, 2 weeks	12,000
Print	Boston Magazine	2/3 page, 1 issue	12,400

Word 2002

Sorting Table Data

Tables are often easier to interpret and analyze when the data is **sorted**, which means the rows are organized in alphabetical or sequential order based on the data in one or more columns. When you sort a table, Word arranges all the table data according to the criteria you set. You set sort criteria by specifying the column (or columns) by which you want to sort, and indicating the sort order—ascending or descending—you want to use. **Ascending order** lists data alphabetically or sequentially (from A to Z, 0 to 9, or earliest to latest). **Descending order** lists data in reverse alphabetical or sequential order (from Z to A, 9 to 0, or latest to earliest). You can sort using the data in one column or multiple columns. When you sort by multiple columns you must select primary, secondary, and tertiary sort criteria. You can use the Sort command on the Table menu to sort a table. Alice sorts the table so that all ads of the same type are listed together. She also adds secondary criteria so that the ads within each type are listed in descending order by cost.

QuickTip

To quickly sort a table by a single column, click in the column, then click the Sort Ascending ⬆ or Sort Descending ⬇ button on the Tables and Borders toolbar. When you use these buttons, Word does not include the header row in the sort.

1. **Place the insertion point anywhere in the table**
   To sort an entire table, you simply need to place the insertion point anywhere in the table. If you want to sort specific rows only you must select the rows you want to sort.

2. **Click Table on the menu bar, then click Sort**
   The Sort dialog box opens, as shown in Figure E-10. You use this dialog box to specify the column or columns by which you want to sort, the type of information you are sorting (text, numbers, or dates), and the sort order (ascending or descending). Column 1 is selected by default in the Sort by list box. You want to sort your table first by the information in the first column—the type of ad (Print, Web, or Misc.)—so you won't change the Sort by criteria.

3. **Click the Descending option button in the Sort by area**
   The ad type information will be sorted in descending—or reverse alphabetical—order, so that the "Web" ads will be listed first, followed by the "Print" ads, and then the "Misc." ads.

4. **In the Then by section click the Then by list arrow, click Column 4, click the Type list arrow, click Number, then click the Descending option button**
   Within the Web, Print, and Misc. groups, the rows will be sorted by the cost of the ad—the information contained in the fourth column. The data in the fourth column is numbers, not dates or text. The rows will appear in descending order within each group, with the most expensive ad listed first.

5. **Click the Header row option button in the My list has section to select it**
   The table includes a header row that you do not want included in the sort.

6. **Click OK, then deselect the table**
   The rows in the table are sorted first by the information in the Type column and second by the information in the Cost column, as shown in Figure E-11. The first row of the table, which is the Header row, is not included in the sort.

7. **Save your changes to the document**

FIGURE E-10: Sort dialog box

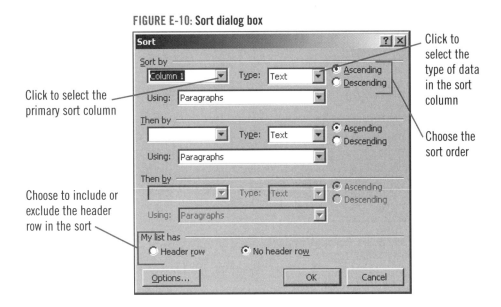

Click to select the primary sort column

Click to select the type of data in the sort column

Choose the sort order

Choose to include or exclude the header row in the sort

FIGURE E-11: Sorted table

Header row is not included in the sort

First, rows are sorted by type in descending order

Second, within each type, rows are sorted by cost in descending order

Type	Location	Details	Cost
Web	Boston.com	Animated banner, 1 million impressions	25,000
Web	Townonline.com	Tile, 100,000 impressions	3,250
Print	Boston Sunday Globe	1 full page, 1 time	27,600
Print	Boston Phoenix	½ page, 2 times	15,300
Print	Boston Magazine	2/3 page, 1 issue	12,400
Misc.	Taxi tops	60 taxis, 2 weeks	18,000
Misc.	Bus stops	50 bus shelter panels, 2 weeks	12,000

Sorting lists and paragraphs

In addition to sorting table data, you can use the Sort command on the Table menu to sort lists and paragraphs. For example, you might want to sort a list of names alphabetically. To sort lists and paragraphs, select the items you want included in the sort, click Table on the menu bar, and then click Sort. In the Sort Text dialog box, use the Sort by list arrow to select the sort by criteria (paragraphs or fields), use the Type list arrow to select the type of data (text, numbers, or dates), and then click the Ascending or Descending option button to choose a sort order.

When sorting text information in a document, "fields" refers to text or numbers that are separated by a character, such as tabs or commas. For example, if the names are listed in "Lastname, Firstname" order, the last names and first names are each considered a field, and you can choose to sort the list in alphabetical order by last name or by first name. Use the Options button in the Sort Text dialog box to specify the character that separates the fields in your lists or paragraphs, along with other sort options.

Word 2002

Splitting and Merging Cells

A convenient way to change the format and structure of a table is to merge and split the table cells. When you **merge** cells, you combine adjacent cells into a single larger cell. When you **split** a cell, you divide an existing cell into multiple cells. You can merge and split cells using the Merge Cells and Split Cells commands on the Table menu, or the Merge Cells and Split Cells buttons on the Tables and Borders toolbar. Alice merges cells in the first column to create a single cell for each ad type—Web, Print, and Misc. She also adds a new row to the bottom of the table, and splits the cells in the row to create three new rows with a different structure.

Trouble?

To move the Tables and Borders toolbar, click its title bar and drag it to a new location.

1. **Click the Tables and Borders button** 🔳 **on the Standard toolbar, then click the Draw Table button** 🖉 **on the Tables and Borders toolbar to turn off the Draw pointer** ✏ **if necessary**
   The Tables and Borders toolbar, which includes buttons for formatting and working with tables, opens. See Table E-1.

2. **Select the two Web cells in the first column of the table, click the Merge Cells button** 🔲 **on the Tables and Borders toolbar, then deselect the text**
   The two Web cells merge to become a single cell. When you merge cells, Word converts the text in each cell into a separate paragraph in the merged cell.

3. **Select the first Web in the cell, then press [Delete]**

4. **Select the three Print cells in the first column, click** 🔲**, type Print, select the two Misc. cells, click** 🔲**, then type Misc.**
   The three Print cells merge to become one cell and the two Misc. cells merge to become one cell.

5. **Click in the Bus stops cell, click the Insert Table list arrow** 🔳 **on the Tables and Borders toolbar, then click Insert Rows Below**
   A row is added to the bottom of the table. The Insert Table button on the Tables and Borders toolbar also changes to the Insert Rows Below button. The active buttons on the Tables and Borders toolbar reflect the most recently used commands. You can see a menu of related commands by clicking the list arrow next to a button.

QuickTip

To split a table in two, click the row you want to be the first row in the second table, click Table on the menu bar, then click Split Table.

6. **Select the first three cells in the new last row of the table, click** 🔲**, then deselect the cell**
   The three cells in the row merge to become a single cell.

7. **Click in the first cell in the last row, then click the Split Cells button** 🔳 **on the Tables and Borders toolbar**
   The Split Cells dialog box opens, as shown in Figure E-12. You use this dialog box to split the selected cell or cells into a specific number of columns and rows.

8. **Type 1 in the Number of columns text box, press [Tab], type 3 in the Number of rows text box, click OK, then deselect the cells**
   The single cell is divided into three rows of equal height. When you split a cell into multiple rows and/or columns, the width of the original column does not change. If the cell you split contains text, all the text will appear in the upper left-most cell.

9. **Click in the last cell in the Cost column, click** 🔳**, repeat step 8, then save your changes**
   The cell is split into three rows, as shown in Figure E-13. The last three rows of the table now have only two columns.

FIGURE E-12: **Split Cells dialog box**

Tables and Borders button

Insert Rows Below button

Cells created by merging other cells

Draw Table button

Split Cells button

Merge Cells button

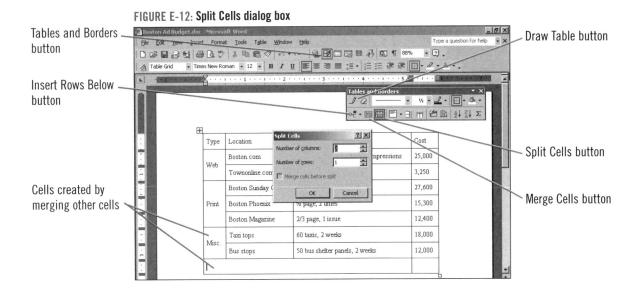

FIGURE E-13: **Cells split into three rows**

Cells are split into three rows

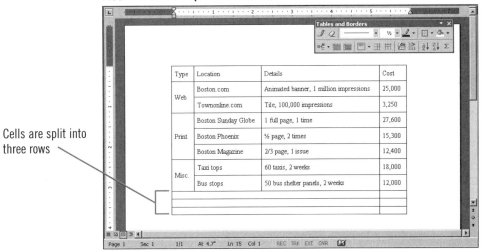

TABLE E-1: **Buttons on the Tables and Borders toolbar**

button	use to	button	use to
	Draw a table or cells		Divide a cell into multiple cells
	Remove a border between cells		Change the alignment of text in cells
	Change border line style		Make rows the same height
½	Change the thickness of borders		Make columns the same width
	Change the border color		AutoFormat the table
	Add or remove individual borders		Change the orientation of text
	Change shading color of cells		Sort rows in ascending order
	Insert rows, columns, cells, or a table, and AutoFit columns		Sort rows in descending order
	Combine selected cells into a single cell	Σ	Calculate sum of values above or to the left of the active cell

Performing Calculations in Tables

If your table includes numerical information, you can perform simple calculations in the table. Word's AutoSum feature allows you to quickly total the numbers in a column or row. In addition, you can use the Formula command to perform other standard calculations, such as averages. When you calculate data in a table using formulas, you use cell references to refer to the cells in the table. Each cell has a unique **cell reference** composed of a letter and a number; the letter represents its column and the number represents its row. For example, the cell in the third row of the second column is cell B3. Figure E-14 shows the cell references in a simple table. Alice uses the AutoSum feature to calculate the total cost of the Boston ad campaign. She also adds information about the budgeted cost and creates a formula to calculate the difference between the actual and budgeted costs.

Steps

1. Click in the first blank cell in column 1, type Total Cost, press [Tab], then click the AutoSum button 🔢 on the Tables and Borders toolbar

> **QuickTip**
> If a column or row contains blank cells, you must type a zero in any blank cell before using AutoSum.

Word totals the numbers in the cells above the active cell and inserts the sum. You can use the AutoSum button to quickly total the numbers in a column or a row. If the cell you select is at the bottom of a column of numbers, AutoSum totals the column. If the cell is at the right end of a row of numbers, AutoSum totals the row.

2. Select 12,000 in the cell above the total, then type 13,500

If you change a number that is part of a calculation, you must recalculate the result.

3. Press [↓], then press [F9]

> **QuickTip**
> When the insertion point is in the cell that contains a formula, pressing [F9] updates the calculation.

4. Press [Tab], type Budgeted, press [Tab], type 113,780, press [Tab], type Difference, then press [Tab]

The insertion point is in the last cell of the table.

5. Click Table on the menu bar, then click Formula

The Formula dialog box opens, as shown in Figure E-15. The SUM formula appears in the Formula text box. Word proposes to sum the numbers above the active cell, but you want to insert a formula that calculates the difference between the actual and budgeted costs.

6. Select =SUM(ABOVE) in the Formula text box, then type =B9-B10

> **Trouble?**
> Cell references are determined by the number of columns in each row, not by the number of columns in the table. Therefore, rows 9 and 10 have only two columns.

You must type an equal sign ("=") to indicate that the text following it is a formula. You want to subtract the budgeted cost in the second column of row 10 from the actual cost in the second column of row 9; therefore, you type a formula to subtract the value in cell B10 from the value in cell B9.

7. Click OK, then save your changes

The difference appears in the cell, as shown in Figure E-16.

Working with formulas

In addition to the sum function, Word includes formulas for averaging, counting, and rounding data, to name a few. To use a Word formula, click the Paste function list arrow in the Formula dialog box, select a function, then insert the cell references of the cells you want included in the calculation in parentheses after the name of the function. When entering formulas, you must separate cell references by a comma. For example, if you want to average the values in cells A1, B3, and C4, enter the formula =AVERAGE(A1,B3,C4). You must also separate cell ranges by a colon. For example, to total the values in cells A1 through A9, enter the formula =SUM(A1:A9). You can also type simple custom formulas using a plus sign (+) for addition, a minus sign (-) for subtraction, an asterisk (*) for multiplication, and a slash (/) for division. All Word formulas begin with an equal sign.

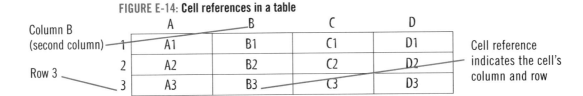

FIGURE E-14: Cell references in a table

Column B (second column) →

	A	B	C	D
1	A1	B1	C1	D1
2	A2	B2	C2	D2
3	A3	B3	C3	D3

Row 3 →

Cell reference indicates the cell's column and row

FIGURE E-15: Formula dialog box

Suggested formula

Suggested range of cells

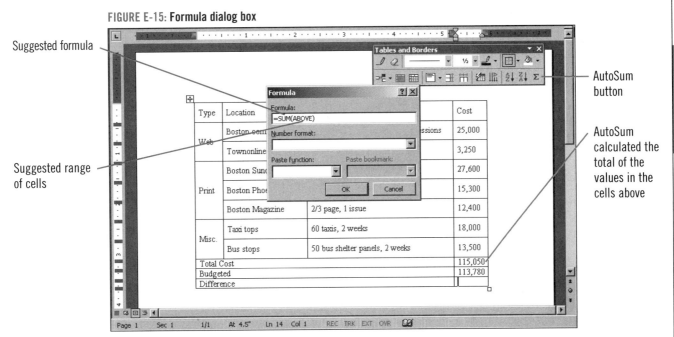

AutoSum button

AutoSum calculated the total of the values in the cells above

FIGURE E-16: Difference calculated in table

Cell A9

Cell A10

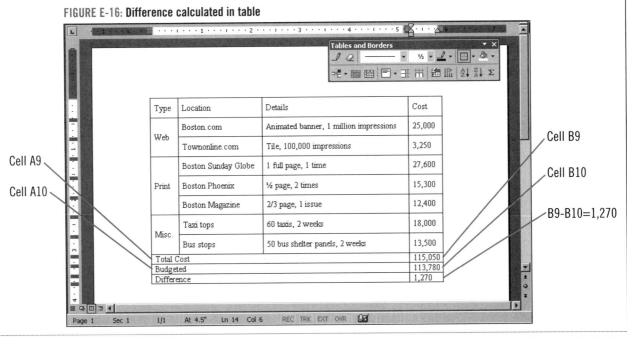

Cell B9

Cell B10

B9-B10=1,270

Using Table AutoFormat

Adding shading and other design elements to a table can help give it a polished appearance and make the data easier to read. Word's Table AutoFormat feature allows you to quickly apply a professional table design to a table. Table format styles include borders, shading, fonts, alignment, colors, and other formatting effects. You can apply a table format style to a table using the Table AutoFormat command on the Table menu or the Table AutoFormat button on the Tables and Borders toolbar. Alice wants to enhance the appearance of the table with shading, borders, and other formats. She uses the Table AutoFormat feature to quickly apply a table format style to the table.

Steps

1. Click **Table** on the menu bar, then click **Table AutoFormat**
The Table AutoFormat dialog box opens, as shown in Figure E-17.

2. Scroll down the list of table styles, then click **Table List 7**
A preview of the Table List 7 style appears in the Preview area.

3. Clear the **Last row** and **Last column check boxes** in the Apply special formats to area
The Preview area shows that the formatting of the last row and column of the table now match the formatting of the other rows and columns in the table.

4. Click **Apply**
The Table List 7 style is applied to the table, as shown in Figure E-18. Because of the structure of the table, this style neither enhances the table nor helps make the data more readable.

> **QuickTip**
> Use the Reveal Formatting task pane to view the format settings applied to tables and cells.

5. With the insertion point in the table, click the **Table AutoFormat button** 📋 on the Tables and Borders toolbar, scroll down the list of table styles in the Table AutoFormat dialog box, click **Table Professional**, then click **Apply**
The Table Professional style is applied to the table. This style works with the structure of the table.

6. Select the **Type column**, click the **Center button** 📄 on the Formatting toolbar, select the **Cost column**, then click the **Align Right button** 📄 on the Formatting toolbar
The data in the Type column is centered, and the data in the Cost column is right-aligned.

7. Select the **last three rows** of the table, click 📄, then click the **Bold button** 🅱 on the Formatting toolbar

8. Select the **first row** of the table, click 📄, click the **Font Size list arrow** on the Formatting toolbar, click **16**, click 🅱, deselect the row, then save your changes
The text in the header row is centered, enlarged, and bold, as shown in Figure E-19.

Using tables to lay out a page

Tables are often used to display information for quick reference and analysis, but you can also use tables to structure the layout of a page. You can insert any kind of information in the cell of a table—including graphics, bulleted lists, charts, and other tables (called nested tables). For example, you might use a table to lay out a resume, a newsletter, or a Web page. When you use a table to lay out a page, you generally remove the table borders to hide the table structure from the reader. When you remove a border, a gridline appears on the screen. Gridlines are light gray lines that show the edges of cells, but do not print. If your document will be viewed online—for example, if you are planning to e-mail your resume to potential employers—you should turn off the display of gridlines so that the document looks the same online as it would look if printed. To turn gridlines off or on, click the Hide Gridlines or Show Gridlines command on the Table menu.

FIGURE E-17: Table AutoFormat dialog box

List of table styles

Preview of the selected style

Options for customizing the application of style settings

Click to create a new table format style

Click to modify an existing style

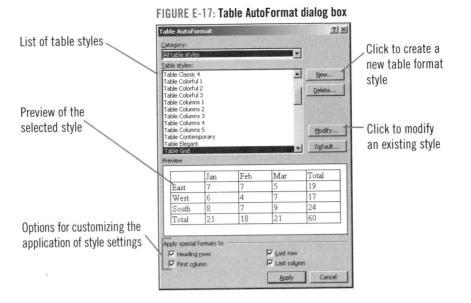

FIGURE E-18: List 7 style applied to table

The shading applied to the merged cells is confusing

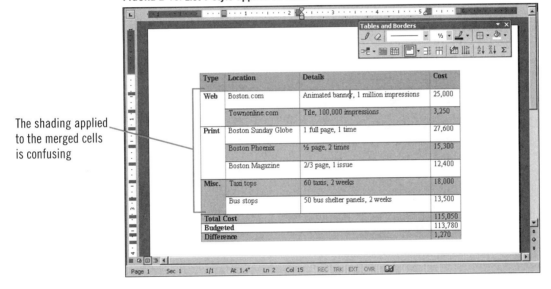

FIGURE E-19: Professional style applied to table

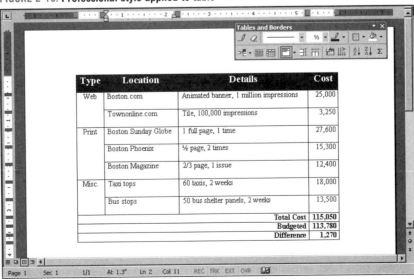

Creating a Custom Format for a Table

You can also use the buttons on the Tables and Borders toolbar to create your own table designs. For example, you can add or remove borders and shading, vary the line style, thickness, and color of borders, change the orientation of text from horizontal to vertical, and change the alignment of text in cells. Alice adjusts the text direction, shading, and borders in the table to make it easier to understand at a glance.

Steps

1. Select the **Type and Location cells** in the first row, click the **Merge Cells button** on the Tables and Borders toolbar, then type **Ad Location**
   The two cells are combined into a single cell containing the text "Ad Location."

2. Select the **Web, Print, and Misc. cells** in the first column, click the **Change Text Direction button** on the Tables and Borders toolbar twice, then deselect the cells
   The text is rotated 270 degrees.

   QuickTip
   In cells with vertical text, the I-beam pointer is rotated 90 degrees.

3. Position the pointer over the **right border** of the Web cell until the pointer changes to ◄‖►, then drag the border to approximately the ¼" **mark** on the horizontal ruler
   The width of the column containing the vertical text narrows.

4. Place the insertion point in the **Web cell**, then click the **Shading Color list arrow** on the Tables and Borders toolbar
   The Shading Color palette opens, as shown in Figure E-20.

5. Click **Gold** on the palette, click the **Print cell**, click , click **Aqua**, click the **Misc. cell**, click , then click **Orange**
   Shading is applied to each cell.

6. Drag to select the **six white cells** in the Web rows (rows 2 and 3), click , then click **Light Yellow**

7. Repeat step 6 to apply **Light Turquoise** shading to the Print rows and **Tan** shading to the Misc. rows
   Shading is applied to all the cells in rows 1-8.

   QuickTip
   On the Borders button menu, click the button that corresponds to the border you want to add or remove.

8. Select the **last three rows** of the table, click the **Border list arrow** on the Tables and Borders toolbar, click the **No Border button** on the menu that appears, then deselect the rows
   The top, bottom, left, and right borders are removed from each cell in the selected rows.

9. Select the **Total Cost row**, click the **Border list arrow** , click the **Top Border button** , click the **113,780 cell**, click **the Border list arrow** , click the **Bottom Border button** , click **Table** on the menu bar, then click **Hide Gridlines**
   A top border is added to each cell in the Total Cost row, and a bottom border is added below 113,780. Hiding the gridlines allows you to see the table as it will appear when printed. The completed table is shown in Figure E-21.

10. Press **[Ctrl][Home]**, press **[Enter]**, type your name, save your changes, print a copy of the document, close the document, then exit Word
   Press [Enter] at the beginning of a table to move the table down one line in a document.

FIGURE E-20: Shading Color palette

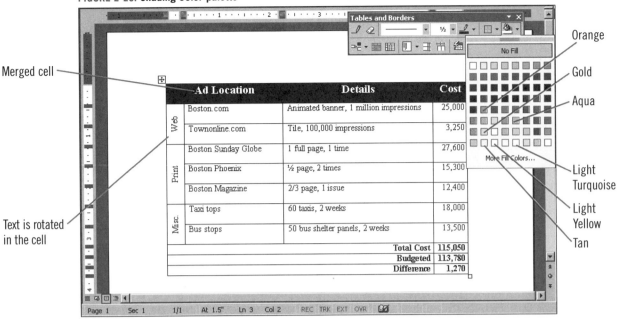

Merged cell

Text is rotated in the cell

Orange
Gold
Aqua
Light Turquoise
Light Yellow
Tan

FIGURE E-21: Completed table

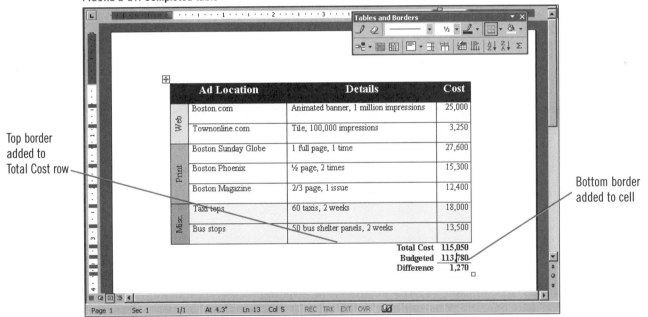

Top border added to Total Cost row

Bottom border added to cell

Drawing a table

Word's Draw Table feature allows you to draw table cells exactly where you want them. To draw a table, click the Draw Table button on the Tables and Borders toolbar to turn on the Draw pointer , then click and drag to draw a cell. Using the same method, draw borders within the cell to create columns and rows, or draw additional cells attached to the first cell. If you want to remove a border from a table, click the Eraser button on the Tables and Borders toolbar to activate the Eraser pointer , then click the border you want to remove. You can use the Draw pointer and the Eraser pointer to change the structure of any table. Click the Draw Table button or the Eraser button again to turn off the draw or erase feature.

Practice

▶ Concepts Review

Label each element of the Tables and Borders toolbar shown in Figure E-22.

FIGURE E-22

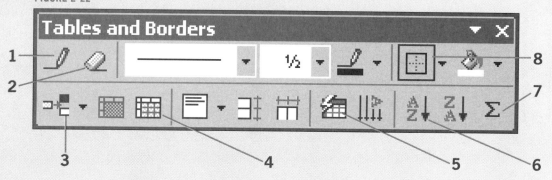

Match each term with the statement that best describes it.

9. Cell
10. Nested table
11. Ascending order
12. Descending order
13. Borders
14. Gridlines
15. Cell reference

a. An object inserted in a table cell
b. Sort order that organizes text from A to Z
c. The box formed by the intersection of a column and a row
d. Lines that show columns and rows in a table, but do not print
e. Lines that separate columns and rows in a table
f. A cell address composed of a column letter and a row number
g. Sort order that organizes text from Z to A

Select the best answer from the list of choices.

16. Which of the following is the cell reference for the third cell in the fourth column?
    a. C4
    b. 4C
    c. 3D
    d. D3

17. Which of the following is *not* a valid way to add a new row to the bottom of a table?
    a. Click in the bottom row, then click the Insert Rows button on the Standard toolbar
    b. Click in the bottom row, then click the Insert Rows Below button on the Tables and Borders toolbar
    c. Click in the bottom row, point to Insert on the Table menu, then click Rows Below
    d. Place the insertion point in the last cell of the last row, then press [Tab]

18. Which button would you use to change the orientation of text in a cell?
    a. ▦
    b. ▭
    c. ▦
    d. ▦

19. Which of the following is *not* a correct formula for adding the values in cells A1, A2, and A3?
- **a.** =SUM(A1~A3)
- **b.** =A1+A2+A3
- **c.** =SUM(A1:A3)
- **d.** =SUM(A1, A2, A3)

20. What happens when you double-click a column border?
- **a.** The columns in the table are distributed evenly.
- **b.** A new column is added to the right.
- **c.** A new column is added to the left.
- **d.** The column width is adjusted to fit the text.

▶ Skills Review

1. Insert a table.
- **a.** Start Word, open a new blank document, then save it as **Mutual Funds** to the drive and folder where your Project Files are located.
- **b.** Type your name, press [Enter] twice, type **Mutual Fund Performance**, then press [Enter].
- **c.** Insert a table that contains four columns and four rows.
- **d.** Type the information shown in Table E-2, pressing [Tab] to add rows as necessary.
- **e.** Save your changes.

TABLE E-2

Fund Name	1 Year	5 Year	10 Year
Computers	16.47	25.56	27.09
Europe	-6.15	13.89	10.61
Natural Resources	19.47	12.30	15.38
Health Care	32.45	24.26	23.25
Financial Services	22.18	21.07	24.44
500 Index	9.13	15.34	13.69

2. Insert and delete rows and columns.
- **a.** Insert a row above the Health Care row, then type the following text in the new row:
  Canada   8.24   8.12   8.56
- **b.** Delete the Europe row.
- **c.** Insert a column to the right of the 10 Year column, type **Date Purchased** in the header row, then enter a date in each cell in the column using the format MM/DD/YY (for example, 11/27/91).
- **d.** Move the Date Purchased column to the right of the Fund Name column, then save your changes.

3. Modify table rows and columns.
- **a.** Double-click the border between the first and second columns to resize the columns.
- **b.** Drag the border between the second and third columns to the 2¼" mark on the horizontal ruler.
- **c.** Double-click the right border of the 1 Year, 5 Year, and 10 Year columns, select the three columns, then distribute the columns evenly.
- **d.** Select rows 2-7, use the Table Properties dialog box to set the row height to exactly .3", then save your changes.

4. Sort table data.
- **a.** Sort the table rows in descending order by the information in the 1 Year column.
- **b.** Sort the rows in ascending order by date purchased.
- **c.** Alphabetize the table by fund name, then save your changes.

5. Split and merge cells.
- **a.** Insert a row above the header row.
- **b.** Merge the first cell in the new row with the Fund Name cell.
- **c.** Merge the second cell in the new row with the Date Purchased cell.

d. Merge the three remaining blank cells in the first row into a single cell, then type **Average Annual Returns** in the merged cell.

e. Add a new row to the bottom of the table.

f. Merge the first two cells in the new row, then type **Average Return** in the merged cell.

g. Select the first seven cells in the first column (from Fund Name to Natural Resources), open the Split Cells dialog box, clear the Merge cells before split check box, then split the cells into two columns.

h. Type **Trading Symbol** as the heading for the new column, then enter the following text in the remaining cells in the column: **FINX, CAND, COMP, FINS, HCRX, NARS.**

i. Double-click the right border of the first column to resize the column, double-click the right border of the last column, then save your changes.

6. Perform calculations in tables.

a. Place the insertion point in the last cell in the 1 Year column, then open the Formula dialog box.

b. Delete the text in the Formula text box, type **=average(above)**, click the Number Format list arrow, click 0.00%, then click OK.

c. Repeat step b to insert the average return in the last cell in the 5 Year and 10 Year columns.

d. Change the value of the 1-year average return for the Natural Resources fund to **10.35.**

e. Use [F9] to recalculate the average return for 1 year, then save your changes.

7. Use Table AutoFormat.

a. Open the AutoFormat dialog box, select an appropriate table style for the table, then apply the style to the table. Was the style you chose effective?

b. Using AutoFormat, apply the Table List 3 style to the table.

c. Change the font of all the text in the table to 10-point Arial.

d. Apply bold to the 1 Year, 5 Year, and 10 Year column headings, and to the bottom row of the table.

e. Center the table between the margins, center the table title **Mutual Funds Performance**, format the title in 14-point Arial bold, then save your changes.

8. Create a custom format for a table.

a. Select the entire table, then use the Align Center button on the Tables and Borders toolbar to center the text in every cell vertically and horizontally.

b. Right-align the dates and the numbers in columns 3-6.

c. Left-align the fund names and trading symbols in columns 1 and 2.

d. Right-align the text in the bottom row. Make sure the text in the header row is still centered.

e. Select all the cells in the header row, including the 1 Year, 5 Year, and 10 Year column headings, change the shading color to indigo, then change the font color to white.

f. Apply light yellow shading to the cells containing the fund names and trading symbols.

g. Apply pale blue, tan, and lavender shading to the cells containing the 1 Year, 5 Year, and 10 Year data, respectively. Do not apply shading to the bottom row of the table.

h. Remove all the borders in the table.

i. Add a ½ pt white bottom border to the Average Annual Returns cell.

j. Add a 2¼ pt black border around the outside of the table. Also add a top border to the last row of the table.

k. Examine the table, make any necessary adjustments, then save your changes.

l. Preview the table in Print Preview, print a copy, close the file, then exit Word.

Independent Challenge 1

You are organizing a series of canoe races on the Murray River in southeastern Australia as part of a river festival. For each race, you need to create a flyer that describes the race for the participants. In this exercise, you will format one flyer.

a. Start Word, open the file WD E-1, then save it as **40K Relay** to the drive and folder where your Project Files are located.

b. In the second blank paragraph below the Relay Details heading, insert a table with 5 columns and 3 rows.

c. Enter the text shown in Table E-3, adding rows as necessary.

d. Resize the columns to fit the text.

e. Add a column between the Start Location and Distance columns. Type **Portages** in the header row, then enter the following information in the Portages column: **0**; **0**; **2 @ 300m**; **1 @ 800m**; **2 @ 200m each and 1 @ 500m**.

f. Resize the Portages column to fit the text, then distribute the table rows evenly.

g. Using AutoFormat, apply a table style to the table. Select a style that makes the table attractive and easy to read.

h. Center the text in each cell in the table both horizontally and vertically. (*Hint*: Use the Align Center button.)

i. Scroll up, then select the six paragraphs of tabbed text under the Race Details heading.

j. Convert the text to a 2-column table. (*Hint*: Point to Convert on the Table menu, click Text to Table, then click OK.)

k. Remove all the borders from the table, then enhance the flyer with font and paragraph formatting.

l. Press [Ctrl][End], type your name, save your changes, preview the flyer, print it, close the file, then exit Word.

TABLE E-3

Leg	Km	Check-in	Start Location	Distance
1	0	8:30	Echuca Wharf	8 km
2	8	10:00	Rosemount Homestead	8 km
3	16	11:00	Mungo Billabong	4 km
4	20	11:30	Kingfisher Park	9 km
5	29	12:30	Yarrawonga Winery	11 km

 Independent Challenge 2

You need new business cards with a fresh design that expresses your personality or the character of your business. In this exercise, you will create a page of business cards using a table to lay out the page. The standard size for business cards is 2"33.5". Figure E-23 shows sample business cards.

a. Start Word, open a new blank document, then save it as **Business Cards** to the drive and folder where your Project Files are located.

b. Change the top, bottom, left and right margins to .4".

c. At the top of the document, insert a table with 2 columns and 5 rows.

d. Select the table, then change the height of the rows to exactly 2" and the width of the columns to exactly 3.5".

e. Center the table on the page.

f. In one cell, enter the information you want to include on your business card. Include your name, address, phone and fax numbers, e-mail address, and Web site, if appropriate. Also include your title and the name of your

FIGURE E-23

Top End Web
Web Site Design & Hosting

Luís Vouzikas
General Manager

550 Knuckey Street, Darwin NT 0801
Phone: 08-8555-7634; Fax: 08-8555-3445
www.topendweb.com.au

Vouzikas Construction
Carpentry · Construction · Remodeling

Luís Vouzikas
Owner

300 Yorkshire Street North, Guelph, Ontario N1H 5B7
Tel: 519-555-8229; vouzikas@yahoo.com

company if appropriate. (*Hint*: If Word automatically formats your e-mail or Web site address as a hyperlink, right click the underlined text, then click Remove Hyperlink.)

g. Use fonts, paragraph alignment, paragraph spacing, colors, clip art, borders, shading, symbols, and other formatting features to create an attractive design for your business card.

h. When you are satisfied with your design, double-check to make sure the row height is still 2" and the column width is still 3.5". Make any necessary adjustments.

i. Select the cell containing the business card, then copy the cell contents to each cell in the table. Once the contents are copied, check your column and row measurements again and make any necessary adjustments.

j. Remove all the table borders, save your changes, preview the business cards in Print Preview, print a copy of the document, close the file, then exit Word.

▶ Independent Challenge 3

You work in the advertising department at a magazine. Your boss has asked you to create a fact sheet on the ad dimensions for the magazine. The fact sheet should include the dimensions for each type of ad as well as a visual representation of the different ad shapes and sizes, shown in Figure E-24. You'll use tables to lay out the fact sheet, present the dimension information, and illustrate the ad shapes and sizes.

a. Start Word, open the file WD E-2 from the drive and folder where your Project Files are located, then save it as **Ad Dimensions**. Read the document to get a feel for its contents.

b. Drag the border between the first and second column to approximately the 2¾" mark on the horizontal ruler, resize the second and third columns to fit the text, then use the Table Properties dialog box to make each row in the table at least .5".

c. Change the alignment of the text in the first column to Center Left, then change the alignment of the text in the Width and Height columns to Center Right.

d. Remove all the borders from the table, then apply a 2¼ point, dark blue, dotted line, inside horizontal border to the entire table.

e. In the second blank paragraph under the table heading, insert a new table with three columns and four rows, then merge the cells in the third column of the new blank table.

f. Drag the border between the first and second columns of the new blank table to the 1¼" mark on the horizontal ruler. Drag the border between the second and third columns to the 1½" mark.

FIGURE E-24

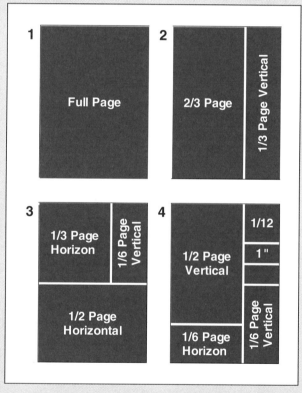

g. Select the table that contains text, cut it to the Clipboard, then paste it in the merged cell in the blank table. The table with text is now a nested table in the main table.

h. Split the nested table above the Unit Size (Bleed) row. (*Hint*: Use the Split Table command on the Table menu.)

i. Merge the cells in the first column of the main table, then merge the cells in the second column.

j. Split the first column into one column and seven rows.

k. Using the Row tab in the Table Properties dialog box, change the row height of each cell in the first column so that the rows alternate between exactly 1.8" and .25" in height. Make the height of the first, third, fifth, and seventh rows 1.8".

l. Add dark blue shading to the first, third, fifth, and seventh cells in the first column, then remove all the borders from the main table.

m. In the first blue cell, type **Full Page**, then center it vertically in the cell.

n. On the Tables and Borders toolbar, change the Line Style to a single line, change the Line Weight to 1, then change the Border Color to white.

o. Activate the Draw Table pointer, then, referring to Figure E-24, draw a vertical border that divides the second blue cell into 2/3 and 1/3. (*Hint*: You can also divide the cell using the Split Cells and Merge Cells buttons.)

p. Label the cells and align the text as shown in the figure. (*Hint*: Change the text direction and alignment before typing text. Take care not to change the size of the cells when you type. If necessary, press [Enter] to start a new line of text in a cell, or reduce the font size of the text.)

q. Referring to Figure E-24, divide the third and fourth blue cells, then label the cells as shown in the figure.

r. Hide the gridlines in the document, examine it for errors, then make any necessary adjustments.

s. Press [Ctrl][End], type your name, save your changes to the document, preview it, print a copy, close the file, then exit Word.

Independent Challenge 4

A well-written and well-formatted resume gives you a leg up on getting a job interview. In a winning resume, the content and format support your career objective and effectively present your background and qualifications. One simple way to create a resume is to lay out the page using a table. In this exercise you will research guidelines for writing and formatting resumes. You will then create your own resume using a table for its layout.

a. Use your favorite search engine to search the Web for information on writing and formatting resumes. Use the keywords resume templates. If your search does not result in links to appropriate sources, try the following Web sites: www.jobsonline.com or www.career.vt.edu.

b. Print helpful advice on writing and formatting resumes from at least two Web sites.

c. Think about the information you want to include in your resume. The header should include your name, address, telephone number, and e-mail address. The body should include your career objective and information on your education, work experience, and skills. You may want to add additional information.

d. Sketch a layout for your resume using a table as the underlying grid. Include the table rows and columns in your sketch.

e. Start Word, open a new blank document, then save it as **My Resume** to the drive and folder where your Project Files are located.

f. Set appropriate margins, then insert a table to serve as the underlying grid for your resume. Split and merge cells and adjust the size of the table columns as necessary.

g. Type your resume in the table cells. Take care to use a professional tone and keep your language to the point.

h. Format your resume with fonts, bullets, and other formatting features. Adjust the spacing between sections by resizing the table columns and rows.

i. When you are satisfied with the content and format of your resume, remove the borders from the table, then hide the gridlines.

j. Check your resume for spelling and grammar errors.

k. Save your changes, preview your resume, print a copy, close the file, then exit Word.

▶ Visual Workshop

Create the calendar shown in Figure E-25 using a table to lay out the entire page. (*Hints*: The clip art image is inserted in the table. The top and bottom margins are .5", the left and right margins are .7", the font is Century Gothic, and the clip art image uses the keyword "carnival," but you can use a different clip art image or font if necessary.) Type your name in the last table cell, save the calendar with the filename **March 2003** to the drive and folder where your Project Files are located, then print a copy.

FIGURE E-25

March 2003

Sunday	Monday	Tuesday	Wednesday	Thursday	Friday	Saturday
						1
2	3	4	5	6	7	8
9	10	11	12	13	14	15
16	17	18	19	20	21	22
23	24	25	26	27	28	29
30	31					

Illustrating
Documents with Graphics

Objectives

- MOUS ▶ **Add graphics**
- MOUS ▶ **Resize graphics**
- MOUS ▶ **Position graphics**
- MOUS ▶ **Create text boxes**
- MOUS ▶ **Create AutoShapes**
- MOUS ▶ **Use the drawing canvas**
- MOUS ▶ **Create WordArt**
- MOUS ▶ **Create charts**

Graphics can help illustrate the ideas in your documents, provide visual interest on a page, and give your documents punch and flair. In addition to clip art, you can add graphics created in other programs to a document, or you can use Word's drawing features to create your own images. In this unit, you learn how to insert, modify, and position graphics, how to draw your own images, and how to illustrate a document with WordArt and charts. ✎✎✎ Alice Wegman is preparing materials for a workshop for new MediaLoft marketing staff. She uses the graphic features of Word to illustrate three handouts on different MediaLoft marketing issues. You will work with Alice as she creates the handouts.

Adding Graphics

Graphic images you can insert in a document include the clip art that comes with Word, photos taken with a digital camera, scanned art, and graphics created in other graphics programs. When you first insert a graphic it is an **inline graphic**—part of the line of text in which it was inserted. You can move an inline graphic just as you would move text. To be able to move a graphic independently of text, you must apply a text wrapping style to it to make it a **floating graphic**, which can be moved anywhere on a page. You can insert clip art or another graphic file into a document using the Picture command on the Insert menu. Alice has written a handout containing tips for writing and designing ads. She wants to illustrate the handout with the MediaLoft logo, a graphic created in another graphics program. She uses the Picture, From File command to insert the logo in the document. She then wraps the text around the logo.

Steps

1. Start **Word**, open the file **WD F-1** from the drive and folder where your Project Files are located, save it as **Ad Tips**, click the **Zoom list arrow** on the Standard toolbar, click **Page Width** if necessary, then read the document to get a feel for its contents
   The document opens in Print Layout view.

2. Click the **Show/Hide ¶ button** ¶ on the Standard toolbar to turn on the display of formatting marks, then click the **Drawing button** on the Standard toolbar to display the Drawing toolbar if it is not already displayed
   The Drawing toolbar, located below the document window, includes buttons for inserting, creating, and modifying graphics.

3. Click before the heading **Create a simple layout**, click **Insert** on the menu bar, point to **Picture**, then click **From File**
   The Insert Picture dialog box opens. You use this dialog box to locate and insert graphic files. Most graphic files are **bitmap graphics**, which are composed of a series of small dots, called **pixels**, that define color and intensity. Bitmap graphics are often saved with a .bmp, .png, .jpg, .wmf, .tif, or .gif file extension. Use the Files of type list arrow in the Insert Picture dialog box to select the type of graphic file you want to insert. To view all the graphic files in a particular location, select All Pictures.

4. Click the **Files of type list arrow**, click **All Pictures** if necessary, use the Look in list arrow to navigate to the drive and folder where your Project Files are located, click the file **Mloft.jpg**, then click **Insert**
   The logo is inserted as an inline graphic at the location of the insertion point. Unless you want a graphic to be part of a line of text, usually the first thing you do after inserting it is to wrap text around it so it becomes a floating graphic. To be able to position a graphic anywhere on a page, you must apply a text wrapping style to it even if there is no text on the page.

5. Click the **logo graphic** to select it
   Squares, called **sizing handles**, appear on the sides and corners of the graphic when it is selected, as shown in Figure F-1. The Picture toolbar also opens. The Picture toolbar includes buttons for modifying graphics.

6. Click the **Text Wrapping button** on the Picture toolbar
   A menu of text wrapping styles opens.

7. Click **Tight**
   The text wraps around the sides of the graphic, as shown in Figure F-2. Notice that the sizing handles change to circles, indicating the graphic is a floating object, and an anchor and a green rotate handle appear. The anchor indicates the floating graphic is **anchored** to the nearest paragraph, so that the graphic will move with the paragraph if the paragraph is moved. The anchor symbol appears only when formatting marks are displayed.

8. Click ¶, deselect the graphic, then click the **Save button** on the Standard toolbar to save your changes

FIGURE F-1: Inline graphic

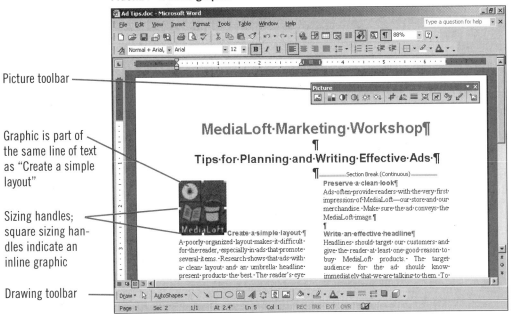

Picture toolbar

Graphic is part of the same line of text as "Create a simple layout"

Sizing handles; square sizing handles indicate an inline graphic

Drawing toolbar

FIGURE F-2: Floating graphic

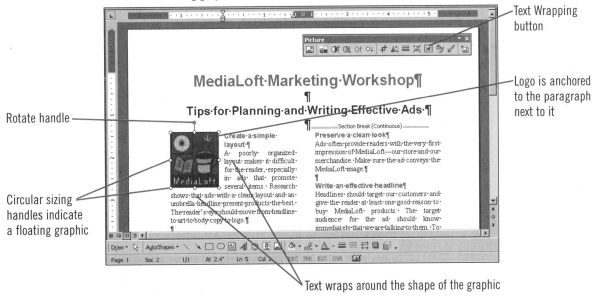

Text Wrapping button

Rotate handle

Logo is anchored to the paragraph next to it

Circular sizing handles indicate a floating graphic

Text wraps around the shape of the graphic

Inserting clips from the Microsoft Design Gallery Live Web site

If you have an Internet connection open when you search for clips using the Insert Clip Art task pane, your search results will automatically include clips from the Microsoft Design Gallery Live Web site, in addition to the clips stored in your Clip Organizer. You can also visit the Microsoft Design Gallery Live Web site to download clips into your Clip Organizer. To visit the Design Gallery Live Web site, click the Clips Online hyperlink in the Insert Clip Art task pane. This opens your browser and connects you to the site, where, after you have read and accepted the License Agreement, you are free to search for and download clips. You can search for clips related to a keyword, in a certain category, or of a particular file type (clip art, photos, sounds, or motion). To download a clip, click the check box under the clip to select it, then click the red arrow to the left of the check box. The clip is automatically downloaded and stored in the appropriate category in your Clip Organizer, making it available for use when you are not connected to the Internet.

Word 2002

Word 2002

Resizing Graphics

Once you insert a graphic into a document, you can change its shape or size by using the mouse to drag a sizing handle, or by using the Picture command on the Format menu to specify an exact height and width for the graphic. Resizing a graphic with the mouse allows you to see how the image looks as you modify it. Using the Picture command to alter a graphic's shape or size allows you to set precise measurements. ✒ Alice enlarges the MediaLoft logo.

QuickTip

Click Ruler on the View menu to display the rulers.

1. Click the **logo graphic** to select it, place the pointer over the **middle-right sizing handle**, when the pointer changes to ↔, drag to the right until the graphic is about 1¾" wide

   As you drag, the dotted outline indicates the size and shape of the graphic. You can refer to the ruler to gauge the measurements as you drag. When you release the mouse button, the image is stretched to be wider. Dragging a side, top, or bottom sizing handle changes only the width or height of a graphic.

QuickTip

If you enlarge a bitmap graphic too much, the dots that make up the picture become visible and the graphic is distorted.

2. Click the **Undo button** 🔙 on the Standard toolbar, place the pointer over the **upper-right sizing handle**, when the pointer changes to ↗ drag up and to the right until the graphic is about **2"** tall and 1¾" wide as shown in Figure F-3

   The image is enlarged. Dragging a corner sizing handle resizes the graphic proportionally so that its width and height are reduced or enlarged by the same percentage. Table F-1 describes other ways to resize objects using the mouse.

3. Double-click the **logo graphic**

   The Format Picture dialog box opens. It includes options for changing the coloring, size, scale, text wrapping, and position of a graphic. You can double-click any graphic object or use the Picture command on the Format menu to open the Format Picture dialog box.

4. Click the **Size tab**

   The Size tab, shown in Figure F-4, allows you to enter precise height and width measurements for a graphic or to scale a graphic by entering the percentage by which you want to reduce or enlarge it. When a graphic is sized to **scale**, its height to width ratio remains the same.

Trouble?

Your height measurement might differ slightly.

5. Change the measurement in the Width text box in the Size and rotate area to **1.5**, then click the **Height text box** in the Size and rotate area

   The height measurement automatically changes to 1.69". When the Lock aspect ratio check box is selected, you need only to enter a height or width measurement. Word calculates the other measurement so that the resized graphic will be proportional.

6. Click **OK**, then save your changes

   The logo is resized to be precisely 1.5" wide and approximately 1.69" tall.

TABLE F-1: Methods for resizing an object using the mouse

do this	to
Drag a corner sizing handle	Resize a clip art or bitmap graphic proportionally from a corner
Press [Shift] and drag a corner sizing handle	Resize a drawing object, such as an AutoShape or WordArt object, proportionally from a corner
Press [Ctrl] and drag a side, top, or bottom sizing handle	Resize any graphic object vertically or horizontally while keeping the center position fixed
Press [Ctrl] and drag a corner sizing handle	Resize any graphic object diagonally while keeping the center position fixed
Press [Shift][Ctrl] and drag a corner sizing handle	Resize any graphic object proportionally while keeping the center position fixed

FIGURE F-3: Dragging to resize an image

Dotted outline shows the size of the graphic as you drag

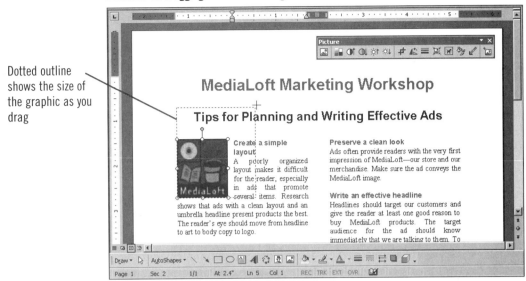

FIGURE F-4: Size tab in the Format Picture dialog box

Set specific height and width measurements (yours might differ)

Change the scale of an object

Select to keep height and width proportional

Select to make scaled measurements relative to the original size

Click to reset image to its original size

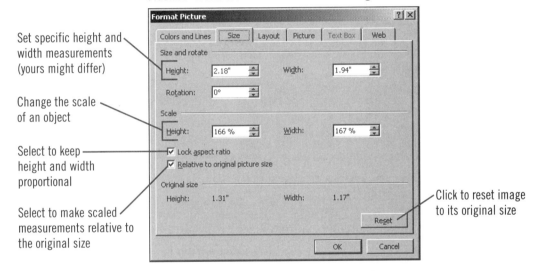

Cropping graphics

If you want to use only part of a picture in a document, you can **crop** the graphic to trim the parts you don't want to use. To crop a graphic, select it, then click the Crop button on the Picture toolbar. The pointer changes to the cropping pointer and cropping handles (solid black lines) appear on all four corners and sides of the graphic. To crop one side of a graphic, drag a side cropping handle inward to where you want to trim the graphic. To crop two sides at once, drag a corner cropping handle inward to the point where you want the corner of the cropped image to be. When you drag a cropping handle, the shape of the cropping pointer changes to correspond to the shape of the cropping handle you are dragging. When you finish adjusting the parameters of the graphic, click the Crop button again to turn off the crop feature. You can also crop a graphic by entering precise crop measurements on the Picture tab in the Format Picture dialog box.

Word 2002

Positioning Graphics

Once you insert a graphic into a document and make it a floating graphic, you can move it by dragging it with the mouse, nudging it with the arrow keys, or setting an exact location for the graphic using the Picture command on the Format menu. Dragging an object with the mouse or using the arrow keys allows you to position a graphic visually. Using the Picture command to position a graphic allows you to place an object precisely on a page. Alice experiments with different positions for the MediaLoft logo to determine which position enhances the document the most.

Steps

QuickTip

To move an object only horizontally or vertically, press [Shift] as you drag.

1. Select the **logo graphic** if necessary, move the pointer over the graphic, when the pointer changes to ⬚, drag the graphic down and to the right as shown in Figure F-5 so its top aligns with the top of the **Create a simple layout** heading

As you drag, the dotted outline indicates the position of the graphic. When you release the mouse button, the graphic is moved and the text wraps around the graphic. Notice that the Create a simple layout heading is now above the graphic.

2. With the graphic selected, press [←] four times, then press [↑] three times

Each time you press an arrow key the graphic is **nudged**—moved a small amount—in that direction. You can also press [Ctrl] and an arrow key to nudge an object in even smaller (one pixel) increments.

QuickTip

You can place a floating graphic anywhere on a page, including outside the margins.

3. Double-click the **graphic**, click the **Layout tab** in the Format Picture dialog box, then click **Advanced**

The Advanced Layout dialog box opens. The Picture Position tab, shown in Figure F-6, allows you to specify an exact position for a graphic relative to some aspect of the document, such as a margin, column, or paragraph.

4. Click the **Picture Position tab** if necessary, click the **Alignment Option button** in the Horizontal section, click the **Alignment list arrow**, click **Centered**, click the **relative to list arrow**, then click **Margin**

The logo will be centered horizontally between the left and right page margins.

5. Change the measurement in the Absolute position text box in the Vertical section to **1.5**, click the **below list arrow**, then click **Margin**

The top of the graphic will be positioned precisely 1.5" below the top margin.

6. Click the **Text Wrapping tab**

You can use the Text Wrapping tab to change the text wrapping style, to wrap text around only one side of a graphic, and to change the distance between the edge of the graphic and the edge of the wrapped text. You want to increase the amount of white space between the sides of the graphic and the wrapped text.

7. Select **Square**, select **0.13** in the Left text box, type **.3**, press **[Tab]**, then type **.3** in the Right text box

The distance between the graphic and the edge of the wrapped text will be .3" on either side.

Trouble?

If the Picture toolbar remains open after you deselect the graphic, close the toolbar.

8. Click **OK** to close the Advanced Layout dialog box, click **OK** to close the Format Picture dialog box, deselect the graphic, then save your changes

The logo is centered between the margins, the top of the graphic is positioned 1.5" below the top margin, and the amount of white space between the left and right sides of the graphic and the wrapped text is increased to .3", as shown in Figure F-7.

FIGURE F-5: Dragging a graphic to move it

Top of graphic aligns with the top of the text

Dotted outline shows the position as you drag

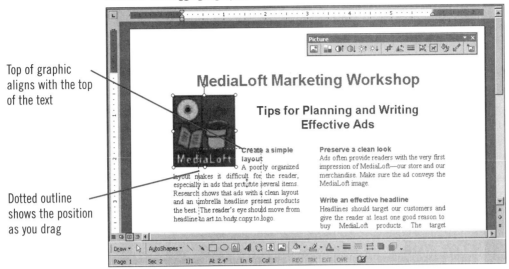

FIGURE F-6: Picture Position tab in the Advanced Layout dialog box

Click to horizontally align a graphic relative to an aspect of the document

Select the aspect of the document you want to position the graphic in relationship to

Click to position a graphic a precise distance from an aspect of the document

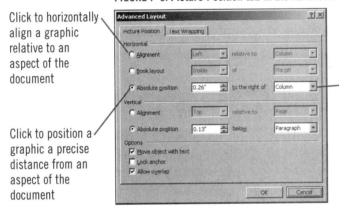

FIGURE F-7: Repositioned logo

Logo is centered and its top is 1.5" from the top margin

1.5" mark on the ruler

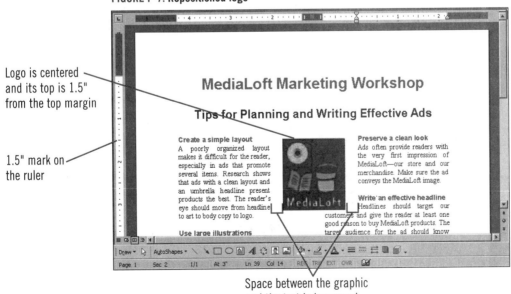

Space between the graphic and the text is increased

Creating Text Boxes

When you want to illustrate your documents with text, you can create a text box. A **text box** is a container that you can fill with text and graphics. Like other drawing objects, text boxes can be resized, formatted with colors, lines, and text wrapping, and positioned anywhere on a page. You can create a text box using the Text Box button on the Drawing toolbar or the Text Box command on the Insert menu. When you insert a text box or another drawing object, a drawing canvas opens in the document. A **drawing canvas** is a workspace for creating your own graphics. You can choose to draw the text box directly in the document, or to draw it in the drawing canvas. Alice wants to add a pull quote to call attention to the main point of the handout. She draws a text box, adds the pull quote text to it, formats the text, and then positions the text box on the page.

Steps

1. Scroll down, click before the **Use large illustrations** heading, then click the **Text Box button** ▣ on the Drawing toolbar
   A drawing canvas opens in the document, as shown in Figure F-8, and the pointer changes to +. You'll draw a text box outside the drawing canvas.

2. Move the + pointer directly under the lower-left corner of the MediaLoft logo, then click and drag down and to the right to draw a text box that is about 1½" wide and 2¾" tall
   When you release the mouse button, the drawing canvas disappears and the insertion point is located in the text box, as shown in Figure F-9. The Text Box toolbar also opens.

3. Type **The reader's eye should move from headline to art to body copy to logo**

4. Select the text, click the **Font list arrow** on the Formatting toolbar, click **Arial**, click the **Font size list arrow**, click **14**, click the **Bold button** ▣, click the **Center button** ▣, click the **Line Spacing list arrow** ▣, click **2.0**, then click outside the text box
   The text is formatted. Notice that the text does not wrap around the text box. By default, text boxes are inserted with the In front of text wrapping style applied.

5. Click the **text box**, double-click the **text box frame**, click the **Size tab** in the Format Text Box dialog box, then change the height to **2.75"** and the width to **1.5"** in the Size and rotate section, if necessary
   When you click a text box with the I pointer, the insertion point moves inside the text box and sizing handles appear. Clicking the frame of a text box with the ▨ pointer selects the text box object itself. Double-clicking the frame opens the Format Text Box dialog box.

6. Click the **Layout tab**, click **Advanced**, click the **Picture Position tab** if necessary, click the **Alignment option button** in the Horizontal section, click the **Alignment list arrow**, click **Centered**, click the **relative to list arrow**, click **Margin**, click the **Absolute position option button** in the Vertical section if necessary, change the measurement in the Absolute position text box to **3.4**, click the **below list arrow**, then click **Margin**
   The text box will be centered between the left and right margins and its top will be precisely 3.4" below the top margin.

7. Click the **Text Wrapping tab**, click **Square**, change the Top, Bottom, Left, and Right measurements to **.3"** in the Distance from text section, click **OK** twice, then deselect the text box
   The text is wrapped in a square around the text box.

8. Click inside the text box, click the **Line Color list arrow** ▣ on the Drawing toolbar, click **No Line**, then deselect the text box
   The thin black border around the text box is removed, as shown in Figure F-10.

9. Press **[Ctrl][End]**, type your name, save your changes, print, then close the file

FIGURE F-8: Drawing canvas

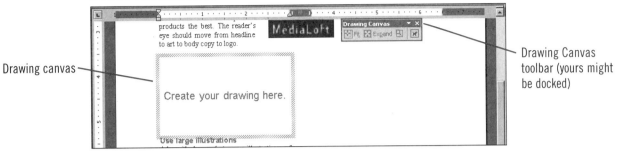

Drawing canvas

Drawing Canvas toolbar (yours might be docked)

FIGURE F-9: Text box

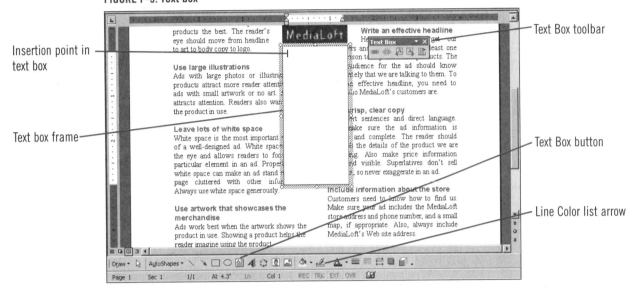

Insertion point in text box

Text box frame

Text Box toolbar

Text Box button

Line Color list arrow

FIGURE F-10: Completed handout with text box

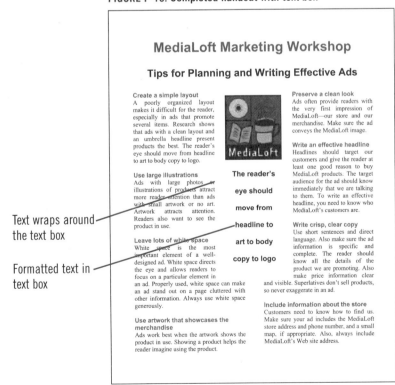

Text wraps around the text box

Formatted text in text box

Creating AutoShapes

You can create your own graphics in Word using AutoShapes. **AutoShapes** are the rectangles, ovals, triangles, lines, block arrows, stars, banners, lightning bolts, hearts, suns, and other drawing objects you can create using the tools on the Drawing toolbar. The Drawing toolbar also includes tools for adding colors, shadows, fills, and three-dimensional effects to your images. Table F-2 describes the buttons on the Drawing toolbar. You can choose to draw a line or shape exactly where you want it in a document, or you can create a graphic in a drawing canvas. It's helpful to use a drawing canvas if your graphic includes multiple items. ✎ Alice creates a handout that illustrates MediaLoft book sales by genre. She uses AutoShapes to create a picture of a stack of books, and then adds the text, to the picture.

Steps

1. Click the **New Blank Document button** ☐ on the Standard toolbar, then save the document as **Genre Sales** to the drive and folder where your Project Files are located

2. Click the **Rectangle button** ▢ on the Drawing toolbar
   When you click an AutoShape button, a drawing canvas opens, the Drawing Canvas toolbar appears, and the pointer changes to +. The Drawing Canvas toolbar contains buttons for sizing the graphics you create in the drawing canvas, and for wrapping text around the drawing canvas. You'll learn more about resizing and positioning the drawing canvas in the next lesson.

> **QuickTip**
>
> To draw a square, click the Rectangle button ▢, then press [Shift] while you drag the + pointer. Similarly, to draw a circle, click the Oval button ○, then press [Shift] while you drag the + pointer.

3. Scroll down until the entire drawing canvas is visible on your screen, place the pointer about ¾" above the lower-left corner of the drawing canvas, then drag down and to the right to create a rectangle that is about **5"** wide and ½" tall
   You do not need to be exact in your measurements as you drag. When you release the mouse button, sizing handles appear around the rectangle to indicate it is selected. Cropping handles also appear around the edges of the drawing canvas.

4. Click **AutoShapes** on the Drawing toolbar, point to **Basic Shapes**, then click the **Sun**
   The AutoShapes menu contains categories of shapes and lines that you can draw.

5. Place the + pointer in the upper-left corner of the drawing canvas, then drag down and to the right to create a sun that is about ½" wide
   The sun shape includes a yellow diamond-shaped adjustment handle. You can drag an **adjustment handle** to change the shape, but not the size, of many AutoShapes.

6. Position the pointer over the adjustment handle until it changes to ⬧, drag the handle to the right about ¼", click the **Fill Color list arrow** 🎨▾ on the Drawing toolbar, click **Gold**, click the **rectangle** to select it, click 🎨▾, then click **Aqua**
   The sun shape becomes narrower and the shapes are filled with color. Notice that when you select a color, the active color changes on the Fill Color button.

> **QuickTip**
>
> You can also double-click the Oval, Line, or Arrow button to draw more than one shape or line. When you are finished drawing, click the button again.

7. Double-click ▢ to activate the rectangle tool, refer to Figure F-11 to draw three more rectangles, click ▢ to turn off the tool, then fill the rectangles with color
   After all four rectangles are drawn, use the sizing handles to resize the rectangles if necessary.

8. Press and hold [**Shift**], click each **rectangle** to select it, click the **3-D Style button** 🔲 on the Drawing toolbar, then click **3-D Style 1** (the first style in the top row)
   The rectangles become three-dimensional, making the group look like a stack of books.

> **QuickTip**
>
> To edit text in an AutoShape, right-click it, then click Edit Text.

9. Deselect the books, right-click the **top book**, click **Add Text**, click the **Font Size list arrow** on the Formatting toolbar, click **20**, then type **Children's - 17%**
   The 3-D rectangle changes to a text box. You can convert any shape to a text box by right-clicking it and clicking Add Text.

10. Add the 20-point text as shown in Figure F-12, then save your changes

FIGURE F-11: AutoShapes in the drawing canvas

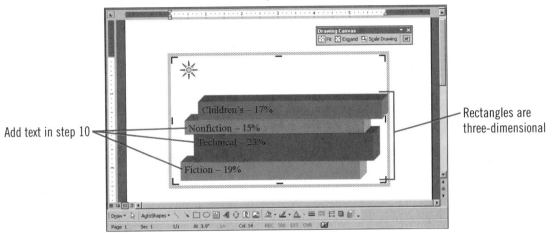

Shape of sun is narrower

Sizing handles indicate rectangle is selected

Cropping handles

Drawing canvas frame

Draw three rectangles in step 7 and fill them with lavender, gold, and pink

Aqua fill

Active color on the Fill Color button is lavender (yours might differ)

FIGURE F-12: Text added to AutoShapes

Children's – 17%
Nonfiction – 15%
Technical – 23%
Fiction – 19%

Add text in step 10

Rectangles are three-dimensional

TABLE F-2: Buttons on the Drawing toolbar

button	use to	button	use to
Draw ▾	Open a menu of commands for grouping, positioning, rotating, and wrapping text around graphics, and for changing an AutoShape to a different shape	(clip art)	Insert a clip art graphic
(select)	Select graphic objects	(picture)	Insert a picture from a file
AutoShapes ▾	Open a menu of drawing options for lines, shapes, and callouts	(fill)	Fill a shape with a color, a texture, a gradient, or a pattern
(line)	Draw a straight line	(line color)	Change the color of a line, arrow, or line around a shape
(arrow)	Draw a straight line with an arrowhead	A ▾	Change the color of text
(rectangle)	Draw a rectangle or square	(line style)	Change the style and weight of a line, arrow, or line around a shape
(oval)	Draw an oval or circle	(dash style)	Change the dash style of a line, arrow, or line around a shape
(text box)	Insert a text box	(arrow style)	Change a line to an arrow; change the style of an arrow
(WordArt)	Insert a WordArt graphic	(shadow)	Add a shadow to a graphic object
(diagram)	Insert a diagram or an organization chart	(3-D)	Make a graphic object three-dimensional

Word 2002

Using the Drawing Canvas

When multiple shapes are contained in a drawing canvas, you can resize and move them as a single graphic object. The Drawing Canvas toolbar includes buttons for sizing a drawing canvas and for wrapping text around it. Once you apply a text wrapping style to a drawing canvas, you can position it anywhere in a document. ✒️ Alice wants to add another three books to the stack. She enlarges the drawing canvas, adds the shapes, sizes the drawing as a single object, and then moves it to the bottom of the page.

Steps

1. Click the **Zoom list arrow** on the Standard toolbar, click **75%**, then click the **stack of books graphic** to make the drawing canvas visible if necessary
   Cropping handles appear around the edges of the drawing canvas.

2. Place the pointer over the **top-middle cropping handle**, when the pointer changes to ⊥, drag the handle to the top of the page, then release the mouse button
   The drawing canvas is enlarged from the top, but the size of the graphic does not change. Dragging a cropping handle resizes the canvas, but not the graphic.

3. Select the **sun**, position the pointer over it until the pointer changes to ⛷, drag the **sun** on top of the right end of the Technical book, then release the mouse button
   The sun shape is moved to the spine of the book, but is hidden beneath the rectangle shape.

4. With the sun shape selected, click the **Draw button** on the Drawing toolbar, point to **Order**, then click **Bring to Front**
   The sun shape is moved on top of the rectangle shape.

5. Double-click the **Rectangle button** 🔲 on the Drawing toolbar, draw three more rectangles on top of the stack of books, click 🔲, then right-click each **rectangle** and add the 20-point text shown in Figure F-13

6. Select each **rectangle**, fill it with any color, then apply the **3D Style 1**

Trouble?

If your Drawing Canvas toolbar is not open, right-click the drawing canvas frame, then click Show Drawing Canvas toolbar on the shortcut menu.

7. Click the **Fit Drawing to Contents button** 🔳 on the Drawing Canvas toolbar
   The drawing canvas is automatically resized to fit the graphic within it.

8. Click the **Zoom list arrow**, click **Whole Page**, then click the **Scale Drawing button** 🔳 on the Drawing Canvas toolbar
   The cropping handles on the drawing canvas change to sizing handles. You can now use the drawing canvas frame to resize the contents of the drawing canvas as a single graphic.

QuickTip

To precisely size or position a drawing canvas, double-click the drawing canvas frame to open the Format Drawing Canvas dialog box.

9. Drag the **bottom-middle sizing handle** down until the graphic is about 6" tall
   Resizing the drawing canvas resizes all the shapes within it. Dragging a top, bottom, or side handle stretches the graphic. Dragging a corner handle resizes the graphic proportionally.

10. Click the **Text Wrapping button** 🔳 on the Drawing Canvas toolbar, click **Square**, place the pointer over the **drawing canvas frame** so it changes to ⛷, drag the **canvas** down and position it so it is centered in the bottom part of the page, deselect the drawing canvas, then save your changes
    Compare your document to Figure F-14. You must wrap text around a drawing canvas to be able to position it anywhere on a page.

FIGURE F-13: New rectangles in drawing canvas

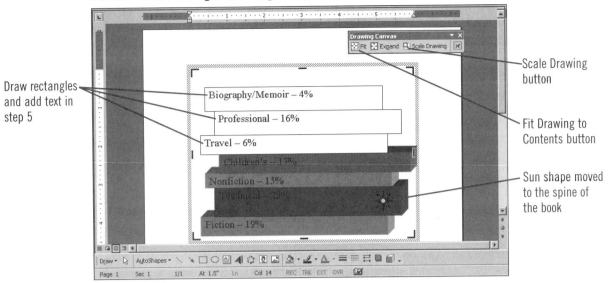

Draw rectangles and add text in step 5

Scale Drawing button

Fit Drawing to Contents button

Sun shape moved to the spine of the book

FIGURE F-14: Resized and repositioned graphic

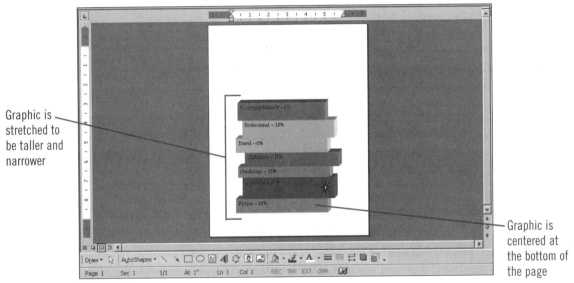

Graphic is stretched to be taller and narrower

Graphic is centered at the bottom of the page

CLUES TO USE

Drawing lines

In addition to drawing straight lines and arrows, you can use the Lines tools on the AutoShapes menu to draw curved, freeform, and scribble lines. Click AutoShapes on the Drawing toolbar, point to Lines, then select the type of line you want to draw. Choose Curve 5 to draw an object with smooth curves, choose Freeform to draw an object with both free-hand and straight-line segments, or choose Scribble to draw a freehand object that looks like it was drawn with a pencil. The lines you draw include vertexes—a **vertex** is either a point where two straight lines meet or the highest point in a curve. To create a curve or freeform line, click the location you want the line to begin, move the mouse, click to insert a vertex, move the mouse, and so on. Double-click to end a curve or freeform line or click near the starting point to close a shape, if that's what you have drawn. Drawing scribble lines is similar to drawing with a pencil: drag the pointer to draw the line, then release the mouse button when you are finished. The best way to learn about drawing curve, freeform, and scribble lines is to experiment. Once you draw a line, you can modify its shape by right-clicking it, clicking Edit Points, and then dragging a vertex to a different location.

Word 2002

Creating WordArt

Another way to give your documents punch and flair is to use WordArt. **WordArt** is a drawing object that contains text formatted with special shapes, patterns, and orientations. You create WordArt using either the WordArt button on the Drawing toolbar or the Picture, WordArt command on the Insert menu. ✐ Alice uses WordArt to create a fun heading for her handout.

Steps

1. **Press [Ctrl][Home], press [Enter], click the Zoom list arrow on the Standard toolbar, click Page Width, then click the Insert WordArt button 🔠 on the Drawing toolbar**
   The WordArt Gallery opens, as shown in Figure F-15. It includes the styles you can choose for your WordArt.

2. **Click the fourth style in the fourth row, then click OK**
   The Edit WordArt Text dialog box opens. You type the text you want to format as WordArt in this dialog box and, if you wish, change the font and font size of the WordArt text.

QuickTip

You can use the Text Wrapping button on the WordArt toolbar to convert the object to a floating graphic.

3. **Type Genre Sales, then click OK**
   The WordArt object appears at the location of the insertion point. Like other graphic objects, the WordArt object is an inline graphic until you wrap text around it.

4. **Click the WordArt object to select it**
   The WordArt toolbar appears when a WordArt object is selected. It includes buttons for editing and modifying WordArt.

Trouble?

If your page goes blank, click the Undo button 🔄 and repeat step 5. Take care not to make the Word Art object taller than 2".

5. **Drag the lower-right corner sizing handle down and to the right to make the object about 2" tall and 6" wide**
   The WordArt is enlarged to span the page between the left and right margins, as shown in Figure F-16.

6. **Click the WordArt Same Letter Heights button 🔠 on the WordArt toolbar, click the WordArt Character Spacing button 🔠 on the WordArt toolbar, then click Loose**
   First, the uppercase and lowercase letters change to become the same height, and then the spacing between the characters is increased.

QuickTip

To change the color of WordArt, click the Format WordArt button 🔳 on the WordArt toolbar, then use the Colors and Lines tab in the Format WordArt dialog box.

7. **Click the WordArt Shape button 🔠 on the WordArt toolbar, then click the Curve Up shape (the first shape in the third row)**
   The shape of the WordArt text changes. You can experiment with different shapes, fonts, colors, and other effects to create WordArt that has the impact you desire.

8. **Click the Zoom list arrow, click Whole Page, click the WordArt Gallery button 🔳 on the WordArt toolbar, click the second style in the third row, click OK, then deselect the WordArt object**
   The WordArt changes to a different style. The completed handout is shown in Figure F-17.

Trouble?

Adjust the colors as necessary.

9. **Press [Ctrl][Home], type your name, save your changes, print the document, then close the file**

FIGURE F-15: **WordArt Gallery**

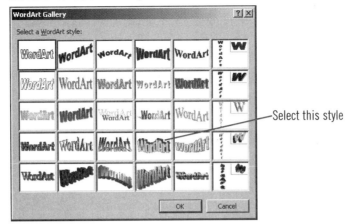

Select this style

FIGURE F-16: **Resized WordArt**

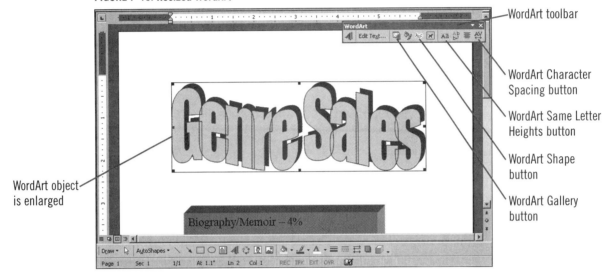

WordArt toolbar

WordArt Character Spacing button

WordArt Same Letter Heights button

WordArt Shape button

WordArt Gallery button

WordArt object is enlarged

FIGURE F-17: **Completed handout with WordArt**

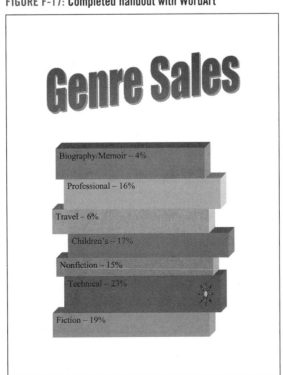

Creating Charts

Word 2002

Adding a chart can be an attractive way to illustrate a document that includes numerical information. A **chart** is a visual representation of numerical data and usually is used to illustrate trends, patterns, or relationships. Word's chart feature allows you to create many types of charts, including bar, column, pie, area, and line charts. You can add a chart to a document using the Picture, Chart command on the Insert menu. ◤▬▬ Alice creates a handout that includes a chart showing the distribution of MediaLoft customers by age and gender.

Steps 1 2 3 4

1. Open the file **WD F-2** from the drive and folder where your Project Files are located, save it as **Age and Gender**, then press **[Ctrl][End]**
   You will insert a chart at the location of the insertion point, which is centered under the title.

2. Click **Insert** on the menu bar, point to **Picture**, then click **Chart**
   A table opens in a datasheet window and a column chart appears in the document. The datasheet and the chart contain placeholder data that you can replace with your own data. The chart is based on the data in the datasheet. Any change you make to the data in the datasheet is made automatically to the chart. Notice that when a chart object is open, the Standard toolbar includes buttons for working with charts.

3. Click the **datasheet title bar** and drag it so that the chart is visible, then move the pointer over the **datasheet**
   The pointer changes to ✛. You use this pointer to select the cells in the datasheet.

   > **QuickTip**
   > Click the Chart Type list arrow 📊 ▾ on the Standard toolbar to change the type of chart.

4. Click the **East cell**, type **Male**, click the **West cell**, type **Female**, click the gray **3 cell** to select the third row, then press **[Delete]**
   When you click a cell and type, the data in the cell is replaced with the text you type. As you edit the datasheet, the changes you make are reflected in the chart.

5. Replace the remaining placeholder text with the data shown in Figure F-18, then click outside the chart to deselect it

6. Click the **chart** to select the object, press **[Ctrl]**, then drag the **lower-right corner sizing handle** down and to the right until the outline of the chart is approximately 7" wide
   The chart is enlarged and still centered.

   > **QuickTip**
   > Point to any part of a chart to see a ScreenTip that identifies the part. You can also use the Chart Objects list arrow on the Standard toolbar to select a part of a chart.

7. Double-click the **chart** to open it, click the **View Datasheet button** 📧 on the Standard toolbar to close the datasheet, click the **legend** to select it, then click the **Format Legend button** 📧 on the Standard toolbar
   The name of the button is Format Legend because the legend is selected. The Format Legend dialog box opens. It includes options for modifying the legend. Select any part of a chart object and use 📧 to open a dialog box with options for formatting that part of the chart.

8. Click the **Placement tab**, click the **Bottom option button**, then click **OK**
   The legend moves below the chart.

9. Click the **value axis** (the Y-axis), click 📧, click the **Number tab** in the Format Axis dialog box, click **Percentage** in the Category list, click the **Decimal places down arrow** twice so **0** appears, click **OK**, then deselect the chart
   Percent signs are added to the Y-axis. The completed handout is shown in Figure F-19.

10. Type **Prepared by** followed by your name centered in the document footer, save your changes, print the handout, close the document, then exit Word

FIGURE F-18: Datasheet and chart object

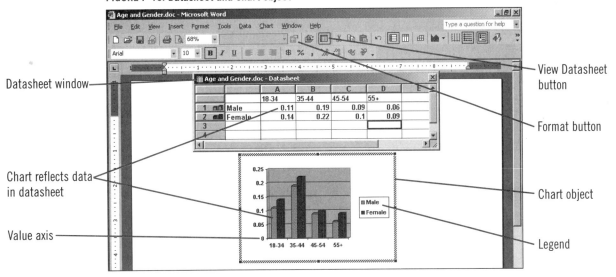

Datasheet window

View Datasheet button

Format button

Chart reflects data in datasheet

Chart object

Value axis

Legend

FIGURE F-19: Completed handout with chart

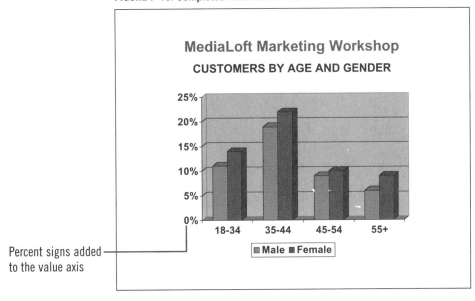

Percent signs added to the value axis

Creating diagrams and organization charts

Diagrams are another way to illustrate concepts in your documents. Word includes a diagram feature that allows you to quickly create and format several types of diagrams, including pyramid, Venn, target, cycle, and radial diagrams, as well as organization charts. To insert a diagram or an organization chart, click the Insert Diagram button [icon] on the Drawing toolbar or use the Diagram command on the Insert menu to open the Diagram Gallery, shown in Figure F-20. Select a diagram type in the Diagram Gallery, then click OK. The diagram appears in a drawing canvas with placeholder text, and the Diagram toolbar opens. The toolbar contains buttons for customizing and formatting the diagram, and for sizing and positioning the drawing canvas. Use the AutoFormat button on the Diagram toolbar to apply colors and shading to your diagram.

FIGURE F-20: Diagram Gallery

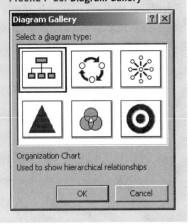

Practice

► Concepts Review

Label the elements shown in Figure F-21.

FIGURE F-21

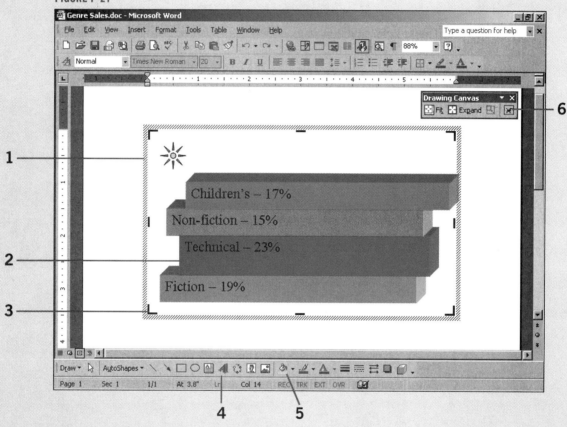

Match each term with the statement that best describes it.

7. Text box
8. Drawing canvas
9. AutoShape
10. Bitmap graphic
11. Chart
12. WordArt
13. Pixels
14. Vertex

a. A graphic object composed of specially formatted text
b. A graphic that is composed of a series of small dots
c. A graphic object that is a container for text and graphics
d. The intersection of two line sections or the highest point on a curve
e. A workspace for creating graphics
f. Dots that define color and intensity in a graphic
g. A graphic object drawn using the tools on the Drawing toolbar
h. A visual representation of numerical data

Select the best answer from the list of choices.

15. Which button can be used to create a text box?
    a. ▣   c. ▲
    b. ◢   d. ▣

16. What must you do to a drawing canvas before moving it to a different location?
    a. Fit the drawing canvas to the contents.
    b. Scale the drawing canvas.
    c. Wrap text around the drawing canvas.
    d. Enter a precise position for the drawing canvas in the Format Drawing Canvas dialog box.

17. What would you drag to change an AutoShape's shape, but not its size or dimensions?
    a. Cropping handle   c. Sizing handle
    b. Adjustment handle   d. Rotate handle

18. Which method would you use to nudge a picture?
    a. Select the picture, then drag it to a new location.
    b. Select the picture, then press an arrow key.
    c. Select the picture, then drag a top, bottom, or side sizing handle.
    d. Select the picture, then drag a corner sizing handle.

19. If you want to create an oval that contains formatted text, what kind of graphic object would you create?
    a. WordArt   c. An AutoShape
    b. A text box   d. A pie chart

20. What style of text wrapping is applied to a text box by default?
    a. In line with text   c. Tight
    b. Square   d. In front of text

▶ Skills Review

1. **Add graphics.**
   a. Start Word, open the file **WD F-3** from the drive and folder where your Project Files are located, then save it as **Farm Flyer**.
   b. Press [Ctrl][End], then insert the file **Farm.jpg** from the drive and folder where your Project Files are located.
   c. Select the photo, apply the Square text wrapping style to it, then save your changes.

2. **Resize graphics.**
   a. Scroll down so that the graphic is at the top of your screen.
   b. Drag the lower-right sizing handle to enlarge the graphic proportionally so that it is about 4" wide and 3" high.
   c. Click the Crop button on the Picture toolbar.
   d. Drag the bottom-middle cropping handle up approximately 1", then click the Crop button again.
   e. Double-click the photo, click the Size tab, then change the width of the photo to 6". (*Hint*: Make sure the Lock aspect ratio check box is selected.)
   f. Save your changes.

Word 2002

3. Position graphics.

  a. Drag the photo up so that its top is aligned with the top margin.

  b. Double-click the photo, click the Layout tab, then click Advanced.

  c. On the Picture Position tab, change the horizontal alignment to centered relative to the margins.

  d. In the Vertical section, change the absolute position to 2" below the margin.

  e. On the Text Wrapping tab, change the wrapping style to Top and bottom, change the Top measurement to 2", then change the Bottom measurement to .3".

  f. Close the Advanced Layout and Format Picture dialog boxes, then save your changes.

4. Create text boxes.

  a. Change the zoom level to Whole Page, then draw a 1.5" x 6" text box at the bottom of the page. (*Note:* Do not draw the text box in the drawing canvas if it opens.)

  b. Change the zoom level to Page Width, type **Mountain Realty** in the text box, format the text in 20-point Arial bold, then center it in the text box.

  c. Press [Enter], type **603-555-3466**, press [Enter], type **www.mountainrealty.com**, then format the text in 11-point Arial bold.

  d. Resize the text box to be 1" high and 4" wide, then move it to the lower-left corner of the page, aligned with the left and bottom margin.

  e. Fill the text box with Blue-Gray, change the font color of the text to White, then remove the line from around the text box.

  f. With the text box selected, click Draw on the Drawing toolbar, point to Change AutoShape, point to Basic Shapes, then click the Oval. (*Note:* Adjust the text size or oval size if necessary)

  g. Deselect the text box, then save your changes.

5. Create AutoShapes.

  a. Click AutoShapes on the Drawing toolbar, point to Basic Shapes, then click the Isosceles Triangle shape.

  b. Draw an isosceles triangle in the drawing canvas, then fill it with Violet. (*Note:* The drawing canvas appears on a new page 2. You will resize and position the drawing canvas after you finish drawing in it.)

  c. Draw three more isosceles triangles in the drawing canvas, then fill them with Lavender, Blue-Gray, and Indigo.

  d. Drag the triangles to position them so they overlap each other to look like mountains.

  e. Draw a sun shape in the drawing canvas, fill it with Gold, then position it so it overlaps the tops of the mountains. Resize the sun if necessary.

  f. Select the sun, click Draw on the Drawing toolbar, point to Order, then click Send to Back.

  g. Use the Order commands to change the order of the triangles and the sun so that the shapes look like a mountain range with the sun setting behind it. Resize and reposition the shapes as necessary to create a mountain effect, then save your changes.

6. Use the drawing canvas.

  a. Fit the drawing canvas to the mountain range graphic.

  b. Apply the Square text wrapping style to the drawing canvas. (*Hint:* You might need to scroll the document to locate the drawing canvas after you apply text wrapping to it.)

  c. Click the Scale Drawing button, then resize the drawing canvas so the graphic is approximately 1.5" wide and 1" tall. Adjust the shapes in the drawing canvas if the graphic looks awkward after resizing it.

  d. Change the zoom level to Whole Page, move the drawing canvas to the lower-right corner of the page, aligned with the right and bottom margins, then deselect the drawing canvas.

  e. Save your changes, then press [Ctrl][Home] to move the insertion point to the top of the document (the beginning of the text).

7. Create WordArt.

a. Insert a WordArt object, select any horizontal WordArt style, type **Farmhouse**, then click OK.

b. Apply Square text wrapping to the WordArt object, then move it above the photograph if necessary.

c. Resize the WordArt object to be 6" wide and 1.25" tall, then position it so it is 1" below the top of the page and centered between the margins.

d. Open the WordArt Gallery, then change the style to the fifth style in the second row.

e. Type **Contact** followed by your name in the document footer, center the text, then format it in 12-point Arial.

f. Save your changes to the flyer, print a copy, then close the file.

8. Create charts.

a. Open a new, blank document, then save it as **Realty Sales** to the drive and folder where your Project Files are located.

b. Click the Center button, type **Mountain Realty 2003 Sales**, then format the text in 26-point Arial bold.

c. Press [Enter] twice, then insert a chart.

d. Click the Chart Type list arrow on the Standard toolbar, then click Pie Chart.

e. Select the second and third rows in the datasheet, then press [Delete].

f. Replace the data in the datasheet with the data shown in Figure F-22, then close the datasheet.

g. Select the legend, click the Format Legend button, then change the placement of the legend to Bottom.

h. Use the Chart Objects list arrow to select the Plot Area, open the Format Plot Area dialog box, then change the Border and Area patterns to None.

i. Use the Chart Objects list arrow to select Series "Pie 1," open the Format Data Series dialog box, click the Data Labels tab, then make the data labels show the percentage.

j. Resize the chart object proportionally so it is about 5" wide.

k. Type **Prepared by** followed by your name centered in the document footer, save your changes, print the document, close the file, then exit Word.

FIGURE F-22

	A	B	C	D	E
	Houses	Land	Farms	Businesses	
1 — Pie 1	11.3	4.1	4.4	6.2	
2					
3					

Realty Sales.doc - Datasheet

► Independent Challenge 1

You are starting a business and need to design a letterhead. Your letterhead will include a logo, which you'll design using AutoShapes, as well as your name and contact information. Figure F-23 shows a sample letterhead.

FIGURE F-23

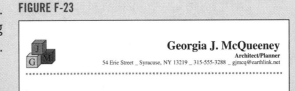

Georgia J. McQueeney
Architect/Planner
54 Erie Street _ Syracuse, NY 13219 _ 315-555-3288 _ gjmcq@earthlink.net

a. Start Word, open a new blank document, then save it as **Letterhead** to the drive and folder where your Project Files are located.

b. Identify the nature of your business, then examine the shapes available on the AutoShapes menus and decide what kind of logo to create.

c. Using pencil and paper, sketch a design for your letterhead. Determine the positions for your logo, name, address, and any other design elements you want to include. You will create and organize all the elements of your letterhead in a drawing canvas.

d. Using AutoShapes, create your logo in a drawing canvas. Use the buttons on the Drawing toolbar to enhance the logo with color, text, lines, shadows, and other effects.

e. Resize the logo and position it in the drawing canvas.

f. In the drawing canvas, create a text box that includes your name, address, and other important contact information. Format the text and the text box using the buttons on the Formatting and Drawing toolbars.

g. Resize the text box as necessary and position it in the drawing canvas.

h. Add to the drawing canvas any other design elements you want to include.

i. When you are satisfied with the layout of your letterhead in the drawing canvas, fit the drawing canvas to its contents, then resize the drawing canvas as necessary.

j. Wrap text around the drawing canvas, then position it on the page.

k. Save your changes, preview the letterhead, print a copy, close the file, then exit Word.

► Independent Challenge 2

You design ads for GoTroppo.com, a company that specializes in discounted travel to tropical destinations. Your next assignment is to design a full-page ad for a travel magazine. Your ad will contain a photograph of a vacation scene, shown in Figure F-24, the text "Your vacation begins here and now," and the Web address "www.gotroppo.com."

a. Start Word, open a new, blank document, then save it as **GoTroppo Ad** to the drive and folder where your Project Files are located.

b. Change all four page margins to .7".

FIGURE F-24

c. Insert the file **Vacation.jpg** from the drive and folder where your Project Files are located, then examine the photo. Think about how you can use this photo effectively in your ad.

d. Using pencil and paper, sketch the layout for your ad. You can use AutoShapes, lines, text boxes, WordArt, and any other design elements in your ad to make it powerful and eye-catching.

e. Apply a text wrapping style to the photograph to make it a floating graphic, then format the photograph as you planned. You can crop it, resize it, move it, and combine it with other design elements.

f. Using text boxes or WordArt, add the text **Your vacation begins here and now** and the Web address **www.gotroppo.com** to the ad.

g. Use the buttons on the Drawing and Formatting toolbars to format the graphic objects.

h. Adjust the layout and design of the ad: adjust the colors, add or remove design elements, and resize and reposition the objects if necessary.

i. When you are satisfied with your ad, type your name in the document header, save your changes, print a copy, close the document, then exit Word.

Independent Challenge 3

You are a graphic designer. The public library has hired you to design a bookmark for Literacy Week. Their only request is that the bookmark includes the words Literacy Week. You'll create three different bookmarks for the library.

a. Start Word, open a new, blank document, then save it as **Bookmarks** to the drive and folder where your Project Files are located.

b. Change the page orientation to landscape, change all four page margins to .7", and change the zoom level to Whole Page.

c. Draw three rectangles in a drawing canvas. Resize the rectangles to be 2.5" x 6.5" and move them so they do not overlap. Each rectangle will become a bookmark.

d. In the first rectangle, design a bookmark using AutoShapes.

e. In the second rectangle, design a bookmark using WordArt.

f. In the third rectangle, design a bookmark using clip art.

g. Use the buttons on the Drawing toolbar to format the bookmarks with fills, colors, lines, and other effects. Be sure to add the words Literacy Week to each bookmark.

h. Type your name in the document header, save your changes, print, close the document, then exit Word.

 ## Independent Challenge 4

One way to find graphic images to use in your documents is to download them from the Web. Many Web sites feature images that are in the public domain, which means they have no copyright restrictions. You are free to download these images and use them in your documents, although often you must acknowledge the artist or identify the source. Other Web sites include images that are copyrighted and require written permission, and often payment, to use. Before downloading and using graphics from the Web, it's important to research and establish their copyright status and permission requirements. In this exercise you will download photographs from the Web and research their copyright restrictions.

a. Start Word, open the file WD F-4 from the drive and folder where your Project Files are located, then save it as **Copyright Info**. This document contains a table that you will fill with the photos you find on the Web and the copyright restrictions for those photos.

b. Use your favorite search engine to search the Web for photographs. Use the keywords **photo archives** to conduct your search. If your search does not result in appropriate links, try looking at the following Web sites: http://pictures.fws.gov, http://gimp-savvy.com, http://www-pao.ksc.nasa.gov, or http://vulcan.wr.usgs.gov.

c. Find at least three Web sites that contain photos you could use in a document. Save a photo from each Web site to your computer, and note the URL and copyright restrictions. To save an image from a Web page, right-click the image, then click the appropriate command on the shortcut menu.

d. Insert the photos you saved from the Web in the Photo column of the table. Resize the photos proportionally so that they are no more than 1.5" tall or 1.5" wide. Wrap text around the photos and center them in the table cells.

e. For each photo, enter the URL and the copyright restrictions for the photo in the table. In the Copyright Restrictions column, indicate if the photo is copyright or in the public domain, and note the requirements for using that photo in a document.

f. Type your name in the document header, save your changes, print a copy, close the file, then exit Word.

▶ Visual Workshop

Using WD F-5.doc and Surfing.jpg (found in the drive and folder where your Project Files are located), create the flyer shown in Figure F-25. Type your name in the header, save the flyer as **Surf Safe**, then print a copy.

FIGURE F-25

NEVER SURF ALONE

Follow the rules

All beginning surfers need to follow basic safety rules before heading into the waves. The key to safe surfing is caution and awareness.

Wear sunscreen

Sunscreen helps prevent skin cancer and aging of the skin. 30+ SPF broad spectrum sunscreen screens out both UVA and UVB rays and provides more than 30 times your natural sunburn protection. Apply sunscreen at least 15 minutes before exposing yourself to the sun, and reapply it every two hours or after swimming, drying with a towel, or excessive perspiration. Zinc cream also helps prevent sunburn and guards against harmful UV rays.

Dress appropriately

Wear a wet suit or a rash vest. Choose a wet suit that is appropriate for the water temperature. Rash vests help protect against UV rays.

Use a safe surfboard

A safe surfboard is a surfboard that suits your ability. Beginners need a big, thick surfboard for stability.

Learn how to escape rips

A rip current is a volume of water moving out to sea: the bigger the surf, the stronger the rips associated with it. Indicators of rips include:

- Brown water caused by stirred up sand
- Foam on the surface of the water that trails past the break
- Waves breaking on both sides of a rip current
- A rippled appearance between calm water
- Debris floating out to sea

If you are dragged out by a rip, don't panic! Stay calm and examine the rip conditions before trying to escape the current. Poor swimmers should ride the rip out from the beach and then swim parallel to the shore for 30 or 40 meters. Once you have escaped the rip, swim toward the shore where the waves are breaking. You can also probe with your feet to see if a sand bar has formed near the edge of the rip. Strong swimmers should swim at a 45 degree angle across the rip.

Study the surf

Always study the surf before going in. Select a safe beach with waves under 1 meter, and pick waves that are suitable for your ability.

Unit
G

Creating
a Web Site

Objectives

- ▶ **Plan a Web site**
- ▶ **Create a Web page**
- ▶ **Format a Web page with themes**
- ▶ **Illustrate a Web page with graphics**
- ▶ **Save a document as a Web page**
- ▶ **Add hyperlinks**
- ▶ **Modify hyperlinks**
- ▶ **Preview a Web page in a browser**

Creating a Web site and posting it on the Internet or an intranet is a powerful way to share information with other people. The Web page formatting features of Word allow you to easily create professional-looking Web pages from scratch or to save an existing document in HTML format so it can be viewed using a browser. In this unit, you learn how to create a new Web page and how to save an existing document as a Web page. You also learn how to edit and format Web pages, create and modify hyperlinks, and preview a Web page in a browser. ⟅══ MediaLoft is sponsoring the Seattle Writers Festival, a major public event featuring prominent writers from around the world. Alice Wegman needs to create a Web site that she will post on the World Wide Web to promote the event and provide information to the public. You will work with Alice as she creates the Seattle Writers Festival Web site.

Planning a Web Site

A **Web page** is a document that can be stored on a computer called a Web server and viewed on the World Wide Web or on an intranet using a **browser,** a software program used to access and display Web pages. A **Web site** is a group of associated Web pages that are linked together with hyperlinks. Before creating a Web page or a Web site, it's important to plan its content and organization. The **home page** is the main page of a Web site, and is the first Web page viewers see when they open a site. Usually, it is the first page you plan and create. ▰▰▰ The Seattle Writers Festival Web site will include a home page that serves both as an introduction to the festival and as a table of contents for the other Web pages in the site. Before creating the home page, Alice identifies the content she wants to include, plans the organization of the Web site, and sketches the design for each Web page.

▶ Identify the goal of the Web site

A successful Web site has a clear purpose. For example, it might promote a product, communicate information, or facilitate a transaction. Alice's Web site will communicate information about the Seattle Writers Festival to the public.

▶ Sketch the Web site

Identify the information you want to include on each Web page, sketch the layout and design of each Web page, and map the links between the pages in the Web site. A well-designed Web site is visually interesting and easy for viewers to use. Figure G-1 shows the sketch of Alice's Web site.

▶ Create each Web page and save it in HTML format

You can create a Web page from scratch in Word, use a Word template to create a standard type of Web page, or convert an existing document to a Web page. When you create a Web page in Word, you save it in HTML format. **HTML** (Hypertext Markup Language) is the programming language used to describe how each element of a Web page should appear when viewed with a browser. Alice will use a blank Web page template to create her home page. She will create the Program of Events Web page by saving an existing document in HTML format. Files saved in HTML format can be recognized by their .htm or .html file extension.

▶ Determine the filenaming convention to use

Different operating systems place various restrictions on Web site filenames. It's safest to name Web pages using the standard eight-dot-three filenaming convention, which specifies that a filename have a maximum of eight letters followed by a period and a three-letter file extension—mypage.htm or chap_1.htm, for example. Alice will use the eight-dot-three naming convention for her Web pages.

▶ Format each Web page

You can use the standard Word formatting features to enhance Web pages with fonts, backgrounds, graphics, lines, tables, and other format effects. Word also includes visual themes that you can apply to Web pages to format them quickly. The look of a Web page impacts the viewer as much as its content, so it's important to select fonts, colors, and graphics that complement the goal of your Web site. Alice will apply a theme that expresses the spirit of the writers festival to each Web page. A consistent look between Web pages is an important factor in Web site design.

▶ Create the hyperlinks between Web pages

Hyperlinks are text or graphics that viewers can click to open a file, another Web page, or an e-mail message, or click to jump to a specific location in the same file. Hyperlinks are commonly used to link the pages of a Web site to each other. Alice will add hyperlinks that link the home page to other Web pages in her Web site. She will also add links from the home page to other Web sites on the Internet and to an e-mail message to MediaLoft.

▶ View the Web site using a browser

Before publishing your Web site to the Web or an intranet, it's important to view your Web pages in a browser to make sure they look and work as you intended. Alice will use the Web Page Preview feature to check the formatting of each Web page in her browser and to test the hyperlinks.

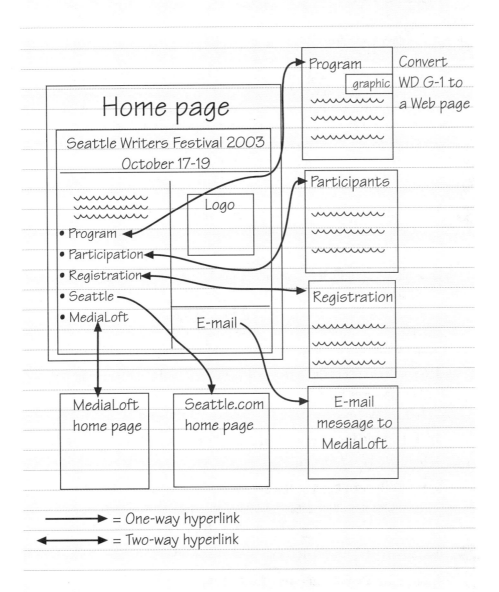

Creating a Web site with the Web Page Wizard

Once you have determined the content and organization of a Web site, one quick way to create it is to use the Web Page Wizard. Through a series of dialog boxes, the Wizard prompts you to: enter a title and save as location for your Web site; choose between using a frame or a separate Web page for the hyperlinks between pages; select the files or templates to include as Web pages; organize and name the Web pages and hyperlinks; and select a common visual theme to apply to each page. When you are finished tailoring your selection, Word creates the Web site for you and the first Web page appears in the document window. You can then use Word's formatting features to customize each page in the Web site. To start the Web Page Wizard, click the General Templates hyperlink in the New Document task pane, click the Web Pages tab in the Templates dialog box, click the Web Page Wizard icon, then click OK to open the Web Page Wizard. Click Next to begin, then answer the questions and choose from the options in each Wizard dialog box, clicking Next to move to the next dialog box. When you are satisfied with your selections, click Finish.

Word 2002

Creating a Web Page

Creating a Web page involves creating a document that uses HTML formatting. HTML places codes, called **tags**, around the elements of a Web page to describe how each element should appear when viewed with a browser. When you create a Web page in Word, you use the usual Word buttons and commands to edit and format it and Word automatically inserts the HTML tags for you. A quick way to create a new Web page is to start with a template. Word includes a template for a new blank Web page, as well as templates for many standard types of Web pages. Because text and graphics align and position differently on Web pages than in Word documents, it's helpful to use a table to structure the layout of a Web page. Alice begins by creating the home page. She starts with a new blank Web page, inserts a table to structure the layout of the home page, adds text, and then saves the Web page in HTML format.

QuickTip

To create a Web page that is based on a different template, click General Templates in the New Document task pane, click the Web Pages tab in the Templates dialog box, select a template, then click OK.

1. Start **Word**, then click **Blank Web Page** in the New Document task pane
A blank Web page opens in the document window in Web Layout view, which shows a Web page as it will appear when viewed in a Web browser.

2. Click the **Zoom list arrow** on the Standard toolbar, click **100%** if necessary, click the **Insert Table button** on the Standard toolbar, point to the second box in the third row of the grid to create a 3 x 2 Table, then click
A table with two columns and three rows is inserted. After you finish using the table to help lay out the design of the Web page, you will remove the table borders.

3. Select the **two cells** in the first row, click **Table** on the menu bar, click **Merge Cells**, then deselect the row
Two cells in the first row merge to become a single cell.

4. Click in the first row, type **Seattle Writers Festival 2003**, press **[Enter]** twice, type **October 17-19**, then press **[Enter]**

5. Select the **two cells** in the second and third rows of the first column, click **Table** on the menu bar, click **Merge Cells**, then deselect the cell
The two cells in the first column merge to become a single cell.

QuickTip

There are no margins in Web Layout view and text wraps to fit the window.

6. Type the text shown in Figure G-2 in the table cells

7. Click the **Save button** on the Standard toolbar
The Save As dialog box opens. Word assigns a default page title and filename for the Web page and indicates Web Page (*.htm; *html) as the Save as type. Web pages are automatically saved in HTML format.

QuickTip

To edit a page title, click Properties on the File menu, click the Summary tab, then type a new title in the Title text box.

8. Click **Change Title**, type **Seattle Writers Festival - Home (Your Name)** in the Set Page Title dialog box, then click **OK**
The page title appears in the title bar when the Web page is viewed with a browser. It's important to assign a page title that describes the Web page for visitors.

9. Drag to select **Seattle Writers Festival 2003.htm** in the File name text box, type **swfhome**, then use the Save in list arrow to navigate to the drive and folder where your Project Files are located
The filename appears in the title bar when the Web page is viewed in Word. Compare your Save As dialog box with Figure G-3. Word automatically assigns the .htm file extension when Web Page (*.htm; *.html) is selected as the Save as type, so you do not need to type it.

10. Click **Save**
The filename swfhome appears in the title bar. Depending on your Windows settings, the filename extension may or may not appear after the filename.

FIGURE G-2: Web page in Web Layout view

New Web Page
button

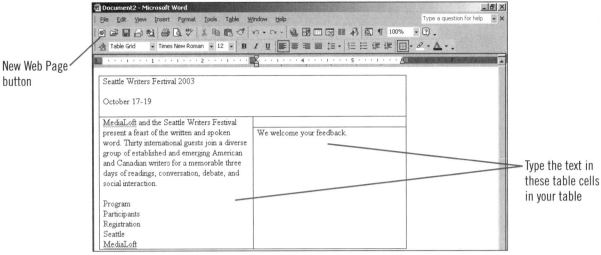

Type the text in
these table cells
in your table

FIGURE G-3: Save As dialog box

Page title of Web
page (yours will
include your name)

Filename of
Web page

File will be saved
in HTML format

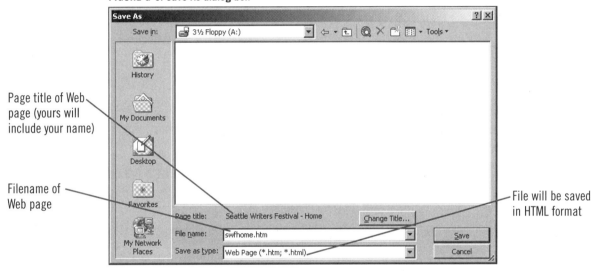

Adding frames to a Web page

Many Web pages you visit on the Internet include frames for displaying fixed information. A frame is a section of a Web page window in which a separate Web page can be displayed. Frames commonly contain hyperlinks and other navigation elements that help visitors browse a Web site. A header that remains at the top of the screen while visitors browse a Web site is one example of a frame; a left column that contains hyperlinks to each page in the Web site and stays on the screen while readers visit different pages is another example. You can add a frame to a Web page by pointing to Frames on the Format menu, and then clicking the type of frame you want to add. Click New Frames Page to open the Frames toolbar, which you can use to select a location (left, right, above, or below) for a new, empty frame. Alternately, if you have applied heading styles to text in the current Web page, you can click Table of Contents in Frame to create a frame that includes hyperlinks to each heading in the Web page.

Formatting a Web Page with Themes

Word includes a multitude of themes that you can apply to Web pages to quickly give them an attractive and consistent look. A **theme** is a set of complementary design elements that you can apply to Web pages, e-mail messages, and other documents that are viewed on-screen. Themes include Web page backgrounds, styles for headings and hyperlinks, picture bullets, horizontal lines, table borders, and other specially designed formats that work well together. You can apply a theme to a Web page using the Theme command on the Format menu. Alice applies a theme to the Web page, formats the text using the theme styles, and adds a horizontal line and bullets. She then experiments with alternate themes to find a design that more closely matches the character of the Writers Festival.

Steps 1 2 3 4

1. Click **Format** on the menu bar, click **Theme**, scroll down the Choose a Theme list box, then click **Refined**

   A preview of the Refined theme appears in the Theme dialog box, as shown in Figure G-4. The theme includes a background and styles for text, hyperlinks, bullet characters, and horizontal lines.

2. Click **OK**

   The theme background is added to the Web page and the Normal style that comes with the theme is applied to the text.

3. Select **Seattle Writers Festival 2003**, click the **Style list arrow** on the Formatting toolbar, click **Heading 1** in the Style list, then deselect the text

   The Heading 1 style—24-point Times New Roman white—is applied to the heading text.

4. Select **October 17-19**, click the Style list arrow, click **Heading 2**, then deselect the text

   The Heading 2 style—18-point Times New Roman white—is applied to the date text.

5. Select the **heading** and the **date**, click the **Center button** 🔲 on the Formatting toolbar, move the pointer over the table, click the **table move handle** ⊞ to select the table, then click 🔲

   The heading, date, and table are centered on the Web page.

6. Place the insertion point in the blank line between the heading and the date, click the **Outside Border list arrow** 🔲 on the Formatting toolbar, then click the **Horizontal Line button** 🔲

   A horizontal line formatted in the theme design is added below the heading.

7. Select the five-line list at the bottom of the first column, then click the **Bullets button** 🔲 on the Formatting toolbar

   The list is formatted using bullets from the theme design.

8. Click **Format** on the menu bar, click **Theme**, scroll down the Choose a Theme list box, select **Sumi Painting**, then click **OK**

   The background and the text, line, and bullet styles applied to the Web page change to the designs used in the Sumi Painting theme. You do not need to reapply the styles to a Web page when you change its theme.

9. Select **Seattle Writers Festival 2003**, click the **Bold button** 🅱 on the Formatting toolbar, deselect the text, then save your changes

   The heading is formatted in bold. Once you have applied styles to text you can customize the format to suit your purpose. Compare your Web page with Figure G-5.

FIGURE G-4: Refined theme in the Theme dialog box

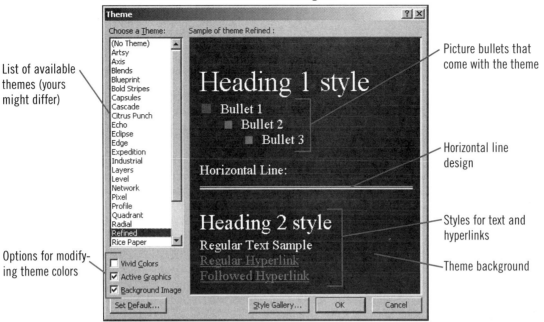

List of available themes (yours might differ)

Options for modifying theme colors

Picture bullets that come with the theme

Horizontal line design

Styles for text and hyperlinks

Theme background

FIGURE G-5: Sumi Painting theme applied to the Web page

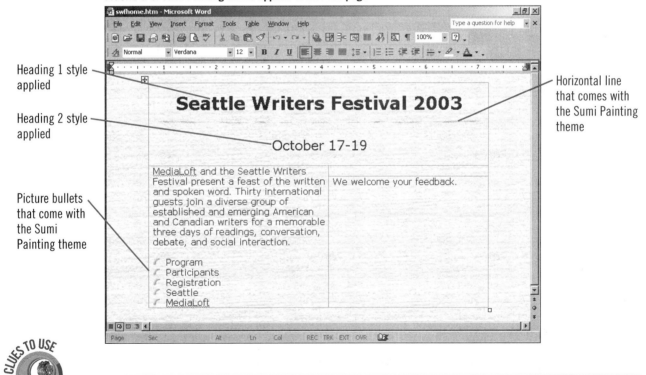

Heading 1 style applied

Heading 2 style applied

Picture bullets that come with the Sumi Painting theme

Horizontal line that comes with the Sumi Painting theme

CLUES TO USE

Managing Web page files

When you save a document as a Web page, Word automatically creates a supporting folder in the same location as the .htm file. This folder has the same name as the .htm file plus the suffix _files. It houses the supporting files associated with the Web page. For example, when you create a new Web page or save an existing document as an .htm file, each graphic—including the bullets, background textures, horizontal lines, and other graphics included on the Web page—is automatically converted to a GIF or JPEG format file and saved in the supporting folder. Be aware that if you copy or move a Web page to a different location, it's important that you copy or move the supporting folder (and all the files in it) along with the .htm file, otherwise the links between the .htm file and the supporting files may be broken. If a browser cannot locate the graphic files associated with a Web page, the browser will display a placeholder (often a red X) instead of a graphic.

Illustrating a Web Page with Graphics

You can illustrate your Web pages with pictures, clip art, WordArt, text boxes, AutoShapes, and other graphic objects. When you insert a graphic on a Web page, it is inserted as an inline graphic and you must apply text wrapping to be able to move it independently of the line of text. Floating graphics align and position differently on Web pages than in Word documents, however, because browsers do not support the same graphic formatting options as Word. For example, a floating graphic with square text wrapping can only be left- or right-aligned on a Web page, whereas you can position a floating graphic anywhere in a Word document. For this reason, it's important to use Web Layout view to position graphics on a Web page. If you want to position floating graphics or text precisely on a Web page, you can create a table and then insert the text or graphics in the table cells. Alice wants the MediaLoft logo to appear to the right of center on the Web page. She inserts the logo in the blank cell in the table, and then adjusts the table formatting to make the Web page attractive.

Steps 1 2 3 4

QuickTip

To insert a text file in a table cell, click Insert on the menu bar, click File, select the file, then click Insert.

1. Place the insertion point in the blank cell in the second column of the table, click **Insert** on the menu bar, point to **Picture**, then click **From File**

The Insert Picture dialog box opens.

2. Use the Look in list arrow to navigate to the drive and folder where your Project Files are located, click the file **mloft.jpg**, then click **Insert**

The logo is inserted in the cell as an inline graphic.

QuickTip

To resize a graphic, crop it, or change the text wrapping style, double-click the graphic to open the Format Picture dialog box.

3. Click the **logo** to select it, click the **Center button** 🗐 on the Formatting toolbar, press [→], then press [**Enter**]

The graphic is centered in the table cell and a blank line is inserted under the logo.

4. Position the pointer over the border between the first and second columns until the pointer changes to ◄‖►, then drag the border to approximately the 4¼" **mark** on the horizontal ruler

The first column widens and the second column narrows. The logo remains centered in the table cell.

5. Select **We welcome your feedback.**, click 🗐, then click in the table to deselect the text

The text is centered in the table cell, as shown in Figure G-6. In Web Layout view, text and graphics are positioned as they are in a Web browser.

Trouble?

If gridlines appear on your Web page after you remove the borders, click Table on the menu bar, then click Hide Gridlines.

6. Click the **table move handle** ⊞ to select the table, click the **Horizontal Line list arrow** 🔳▾ on the Formatting toolbar, click the **No Border button** 🔲, deselect the table, then save your changes

Removing the table borders masks that the underlying structure of the Web page is a table, as shown in Figure G-7. The text on the left is now a wide column and the logo and text under the logo are positioned to the right of center. By inserting text and graphics in a table, you can position them exactly where you want.

FIGURE G-6: Logo and text centered in the second column

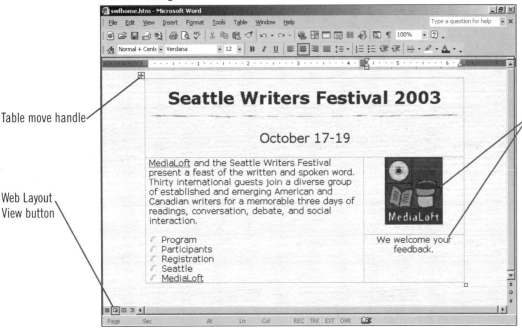

Table move handle

Web Layout View button

Logo and text are centered in the table cells

FIGURE G-7: Web page with table borders removed

Adding alternate text for graphics

Graphics can take a long time to appear on a Web page, so some people turn off the display of graphics in their browsers so that they can download and view Web pages more quickly. If you don't want visitors to your Web page to see empty space where you intended that they see a graphic, you can add alternate text to appear on the Web page instead of the graphic.

Alternate text will also appear in some browsers while the graphic is loading. To add alternate text to a Web page, select the graphic, then click the Picture command on the Format menu. On the Web tab in the Format Picture dialog box, type the text you want to appear in lieu of the graphic, then click OK.

Saving a Document as a Web Page

When you save an existing document as a Web page, Word converts the content and formatting of the Word file to HTML and displays the Web page as it will appear in a browser. Any formatting that is not supported by Web browsers is either converted to similar supported formatting or removed from the Web page. For example, if you save a document that contains a floating graphic in HTML format, the graphic will be left- or right-aligned on the Web page. Table G-1 describes several common formatting elements that are not supported by Web browsers. You can save a document as a Web page using the Save as Web Page command on the File menu. ➤ Alice wants to add a Web page that includes the festival program of events to her Web site. Rather than create the Web page from scratch, she converts an existing document to HTML format. She then adjusts the formatting of the new Web page and applies the Sumi Painting theme.

Steps 1234

1. Open the file **WD G-1** from the drive and folder where your Project Files are located, click the **Zoom list arrow** on the Standard toolbar, then click **Two Pages**

   The document opens in Print Layout view, as shown in Figure G-8. Notice that the document is two pages long, the text is formatted in three columns, and the graphic on the first page is centered.

QuickTip

To create a Web page that is compatible with a specific browser, click Tools on the menu bar, click Options, click the General tab, click Web Options, then select from the options on the Browsers tab in the Web Options dialog box.

2. Click **File** on the menu bar, click **Save as Web Page**, click **Change Title**, type **Seattle Writers Festival – Program of Events (Your Name)** in the Set Page Title dialog box, click **OK**, select **WD G-1.htm** in the Filename text box, type **swfevent**, then click **Save**

   A dialog box opens and informs you that browsers do not support some of the formatting features of the document. It says the floating graphic will be left- or right-aligned in the Web page. You can click Tell Me More in the dialog box to learn more about features not supported by Web browsers.

3. Click **Continue**

   A copy of the document is saved in HTML format with the filename "swfevent" and the page title "Seattle Writers Festival – Events (Your Name)." The Web page appears in Web Layout view. Notice that the graphic is now left-aligned on the Web page.

4. Click the **Zoom list arrow** on the Standard toolbar, click **100%** if necessary, then scroll to the bottom of the Web page

   The text is now formatted in a single column, there are no margins on the Web page, and the document is one long page.

5. Press **[Ctrl][Home]**, double-click the **graphic** to open the Format Picture dialog box, click the **Size tab**, select **3.76** in the Height text box, type **2**, then click **OK**

   The size of the graphic is reduced.

QuickTip

To be able to position a graphic precisely on a Web page, you must insert the graphic in a table or make it an inline graphic.

6. Drag the **graphic** to the upper-right corner of the Web page, then deselect the graphic

   The graphic jumps into place in the upper-right corner when you release the mouse button.

7. Click **Format** on the menu bar, click **Theme**, click **Sumi Painting** in the Choose a Theme list box, click **OK**, then save your changes

   The Sumi Painting theme is applied to the Web page, giving it a look that is consistent with the home page. Notice that the bullet characters change to the picture bullets included with the theme. The font of the body text also changes to the Normal style font used in the theme (12-point Verdana). Compare your Web page with Figure G-9.

FIGURE G-8: Word document in Print Layout view

Floating graphic is centered

Document is two pages long

Text is formatted in columns

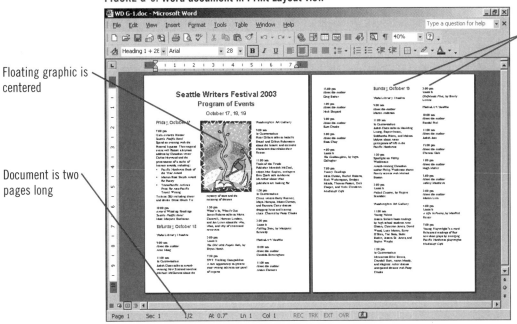

FIGURE G-9: Web page in Web Layout view

Body text changes to Sumi Painting theme Normal style

Bullets change to Sumi Painting theme picture bullets

Graphic is moved to the upper-right corner

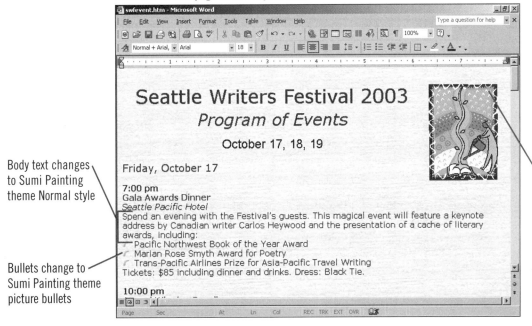

TABLE G-1: Word features that are not supported by Web browsers

feature	result when viewed with a browser
Character formatting	Shadow text becomes bold, small caps become all caps, and embossed, engraved, and outline text becomes solid; character scale changes to 100%; drop caps are removed
Paragraph formatting	Indents are removed, tabs might not align correctly, and border and shading styles might change
Page layout	Margins, columns, page numbers, page borders, and headers and footers are removed; all footnotes are moved to the end of the document
Graphics	Floating graphics, including pictures, AutoShapes, text boxes, and WordArt, are left- or right-aligned
Tables	Decorative cell borders become box borders, diagonal borders are removed, vertical text is changed to horizontal

Adding Hyperlinks

Hyperlinks allow readers to link to (or "jump") to a Web page, e-mail address, file, or a specific location in a document. When you create a hyperlink in a document, you select the text or graphic you want to use as a hyperlink and then specify the location you want to jump to when the hyperlink is clicked. You create hyperlinks using the Insert Hyperlink button on the Standard toolbar. Text that is formatted as a hyperlink appears as colored, underlined text. ✏️ To make navigating the Events Web page easier, Alice creates hyperlinks that jump from the dates in the third line of the Web page to the schedule for those dates farther down the Web page. She then inserts several hyperlinks on her home page: one to link to the Events Web page, one to link to the Seattle.com Web site on the Internet, and one to link to an e-mail message to MediaLoft.

Steps 1 2 3 4

1. Select **19** in the third line of the Events Web page, then click the **Insert Hyperlink button** 🖳 on the Standard toolbar

   The Insert Hyperlink dialog box opens. You use this dialog box to specify the location of the Web page, file, e-mail address, or position in the current document you want to jump to when the hyperlink—in this case, the text "19"—is clicked.

2. Click **Place in This Document** in the Link to section

   All the headings in the Web page are displayed in the dialog box, as shown in Figure G-10. In this context, "heading" is any text to which a heading style has been applied.

QuickTip
Press [Ctrl] and click any hyperlink in Word to follow the hyperlink.

3. Click **Sunday, October 19** in the Select a place in this document section, then click **OK**

   The selected text, "19", is formatted in bright blue and underlined, the hyperlink style when the Sumi Painting theme is applied. When the Web page is viewed in a browser, clicking the 19 hyperlink will jump the viewer to the heading "Sunday, October 19" farther down the Web page.

4. Select **18**, click 🖳, click **Saturday, October 18** in the Insert Hyperlink dialog box, click **OK**, select **17**, click 🖳, click **Friday, October 17**, click **OK**, save your changes, then close the file

   The numbers 18 and 17 are formatted as hyperlinks to the headings for those dates in the Web page. After you save and close the file, the home page appears in the document window.

5. Select **Program** in the bulleted list, click 🖳, click **Existing File or Web Page** in the Link to section, use the Look in list arrow to navigate to the drive and folder where your Project Files are located, then click **swfevent.htm**

   The filename swfevent.htm appears in the Address text box, as shown in Figure G-11.

QuickTip
To create a ScreenTip that appears in a browser, click ScreenTip in the Insert Hyperlink dialog box, then in the Set Hyperlink ScreenTip dialog box, type the text you want to appear.

6. Click **OK**

   "Program" is formatted as a hyperlink to the Program of Events Web page. If you point to a hyperlink in Word, the address of the file or Web page it links to appears in a ScreenTip.

7. Select **Seattle** in the list, click 🖳, type **www.seattle.com** in the Address text box in the Insert Hyperlink dialog box, then click **OK**

   As you type the Web address, Word automatically adds "http://" in front of "www". A Web address is also called a **URL**, which stands for Uniform Resource Locator. "Seattle" is formatted as a hyperlink to the Seattle.com Web site on the Internet.

QuickTip
By default, Word automatically creates a hyperlink to an e-mail address or URL when you type the address or URL in a document or Web page.

8. Select **feedback** under the logo, click 🖳, then click **E-mail Address** in the Link to section of the Insert Hyperlink dialog box

   The Insert Hyperlink dialog box changes so you can create a link to an e-mail message.

9. Type **swf@medialoft.com** in the E-mail address text box, type **Seattle Writers Festival** in the Subject text box, click **OK**, then save your changes

   "Feedback" is formatted as a hyperlink, as shown in Figure G-12.

FIGURE G-10: Creating a hyperlink to a heading

Creates a hyperlink to a Web page or file

Creates a hyperlink to a location in the current file

Creates a hyperlink to a new blank document

Creates a hyperlink to an e-mail address

Text selected to be formatted as a hyperlink

These headings in the document are formatted with heading styles

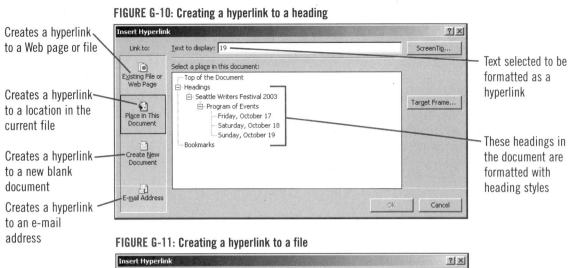

FIGURE G-11: Creating a hyperlink to a file

File to jump to when the hyperlink is clicked

Click to change the default ScreenTip for the hyperlink

Click to browse the Internet for a specific URL to link to

Files and folders in the active drive or folder (yours might differ)

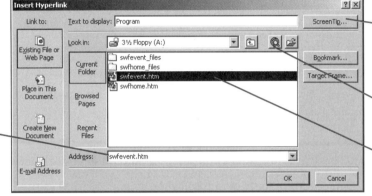

FIGURE G-12: Hyperlinks in the Web page

Hyperlinks are colored and underlined

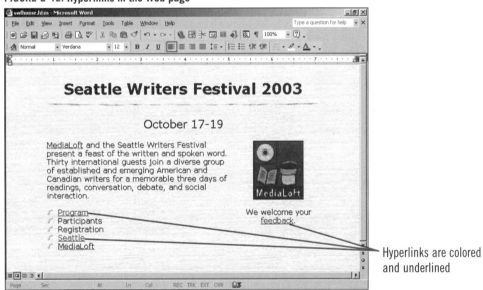

CLUES TO USE

Pasting text as a hyperlink

You can quickly create a hyperlink to a specific location in any document by copying text from the destination location and pasting it as a hyperlink. To copy and paste text as a hyperlink, select the text you want to jump to, copy it to the Clipboard, place the insertion point in the location you want to insert the hyperlink, click Edit on the menu bar, then click Paste as Hyperlink. The text you copied is pasted and formatted as a hyperlink.

Modifying Hyperlinks

Over time, you might need to edit the hyperlinks on your Web pages with new information or remove them altogether. When you edit a hyperlink, you can change the hyperlink destination, the hyperlink text, or the ScreenTip that displays when a viewer points to the hyperlink. You can easily update or remove a hyperlink by right-clicking it and selecting the Edit Hyperlink or Remove Hyperlink command on the shortcut menu. Alice changes the hyperlink text for the Program and Seattle hyperlinks to make them more descriptive. She also adds a ScreenTip to the Seattle hyperlink so that visitors to the home page will better understand what the link offers.

Steps

1. **Right-click Program, then click Edit Hyperlink on the shortcut menu**
   The Edit Hyperlink dialog box opens.

2. **Click after Program in the Text to display text box, press [Spacebar], type of Festival Events, then click OK**
   The hyperlink text changes to "Program of Festival Events" on the Web page.

3. **Right-click Seattle, click Edit Hyperlink, then click ScreenTip in the Edit Hyperlink dialog box**
   The Set Hyperlink ScreenTip dialog box opens, as shown in Figure G-14. Any text you type in this dialog box will appear as a ScreenTip when a viewer points to the hyperlink.

4. **Type Hotels, dining, and entertainment in Seattle in the ScreenTip text box, then click OK**

5. **Click in front of Seattle in the Text to display text box in the Edit Hyperlink dialog box, type Visiting, press [Spacebar], click OK, then save your changes**
   The hyperlink text changes to "Visiting Seattle."

6. **Point to Visiting Seattle**
   The ScreenTip you added appears, as shown in Figure G-15.

CLUES TO USE

Adding comments to Web pages and documents

A comment is an embedded note that you add to a document or a Web page. Comments appear in a balloon in the right margin of a document in Print Layout or Web Layout view, as shown in Figure G-13, and are generally used to facilitate collaboration when two or more people are working on the same document or Web page.

To insert a comment in a document, select the text you want to comment upon, click Insert on the menu bar, click Comment, type your comment in the comment balloon that appears, then click outside the balloon. To respond to a comment, click in the comment balloon, click Comment on the Insert menu, then type a response in the new comment balloon that opens. To delete a comment, right-click it, then click Delete Comment on the shortcut menu. Note that comments also appear on a Web page when it is viewed in a browser. Comments appear as ScreenTips in a browser when a reader points to a comment mark (usually the author's initials in brackets).

Before you publish Web pages be sure to remove any comments you don't want others to see.

FIGURE G-13: Comment in a document

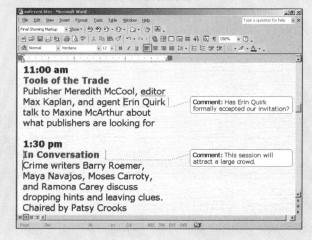

FIGURE G-14: Set Hyperlink ScreenTip dialog box

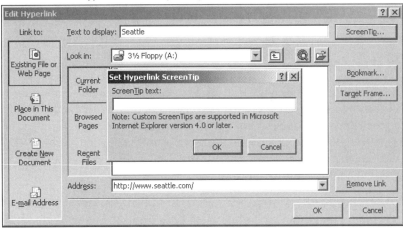

FIGURE G-15: ScreenTip and edited hyperlinks

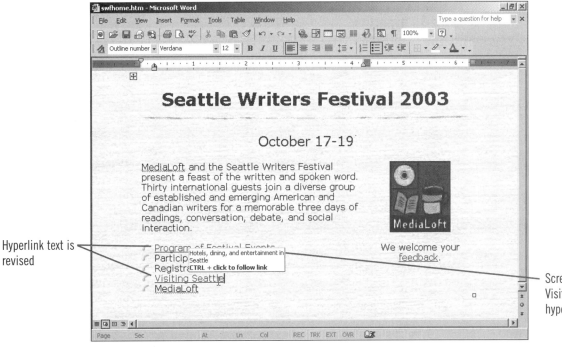

Hyperlink text is revised

ScreenTip for the Visiting Seattle hyperlink

E-mailing a document from Word

Another way to share information online is to e-mail a Word document to others. To e-mail a document directly from Word, open the document, then click the E-mail button 🖃 on the Standard toolbar. An e-mail message header opens in the program window. Type the e-mail address(es) of the recipient(s) in the To and Cc text boxes in the message header, separating multiple addresses with a comma or a semicolon. When you are ready to send the file, click Send a Copy on the e-mail header toolbar. Your default e-mail program sends a copy of the document to each recipient.

Preview a Web Page in a Browser

Before you publish Web pages to the Web or an intranet, it's important to preview the pages in a browser to make sure they look as you intended. You can use the Web Page Preview command on the Edit menu to open a copy of a Web page in your default browser. When previewing a Web page, you should check for formatting errors and test each hyperlink. ✒ Alice previews the Web site in her browser and tests the hyperlinks. After viewing the Program Web page, she uses Word to adjust its formatting.

Steps

Trouble?

You must have a Web browser installed on your computer to complete this lesson. If your default browser is not Internet Explorer 5, your screens might not match the figures in the lesson and some features might not be available.

1. **Click File on the menu bar, click Web Page Preview, then click the Maximize button on the browser title bar if necessary**
   The browser opens and the home page is displayed in the browser window, as shown in Figure G-16. Notice that the page title—Seattle Writers Festival - Home—appears in the browser title bar. Your page title will also include your name.

2. **Click the Program of Festival Events hyperlink**
   The Seattle Writers Festival – Program of Events Web page opens in the browser window.

3. **Click the 19 hyperlink**
   The browser jumps down the page and displays the program for Sunday, October 19 in the browser window.

4. **Click the Back button ⇐ Back on the browser toolbar**
   The top of the Program of Events Web page is displayed in the browser window. The browser toolbar includes buttons for navigating between Web pages, searching the Internet, and printing and editing the current Web page.

Trouble?

If the Edit with Microsoft Word button is not available in your browser, click the Word Program button on the taskbar to switch to Word, then open swfevent.htm.

5. **Click the Edit with Microsoft Word button 📖 on the browser toolbar**
   The Program of Events Web page appears in a Word document window.

6. **Click the Zoom list arrow on the Standard toolbar, click 100% if necessary, select Tickets under the bulleted list, press and hold [Ctrl], select Dress, release [Ctrl], click the Bold button 🅱 on the Formatting toolbar, save your changes, then close the file**
   The home page appears in the Word document window. You want to check that your changes to the Program of Events Web page will preview correctly in the browser.

QuickTip

To view or edit the HTML tags for a Web page, click View on the browser title bar, then click Source.

7. **Click File on the menu bar, click Web Page Preview, then click the Program of Festival Events hyperlink**
   The revised Program of Events Web page appears in the browser, as shown in Figure G-17.

8. **Click the Print button 🖨 on the browser toolbar to print a copy of the swfevent Web page, click ⇐ Back, then point to the Visiting Seattle hyperlink**
   The ScreenTip you created for the hyperlink appears. The URL of the Seattle.com Web site also appears in the status bar. If you are connected to the Internet you can click the Visiting Seattle hyperlink to open the Seattle.com Web site in your browser window. Click the Back button on the browser toolbar to return to the Seattle Writers Festival home page when you are finished.

Trouble?

If an e-mail message does not open, continue with step 10.

9. **Click the feedback hyperlink**
   An e-mail message that is automatically addressed to swf@medialoft.com with the subject "Seattle Writers Festival" opens in your default e-mail program.

10. **Close the e-mail message, click 🖨 to print the swfhome Web page, exit your browser, then exit Word**

FIGURE G-16: **Home page in Internet Explorer**

Page title (yours will include your name)

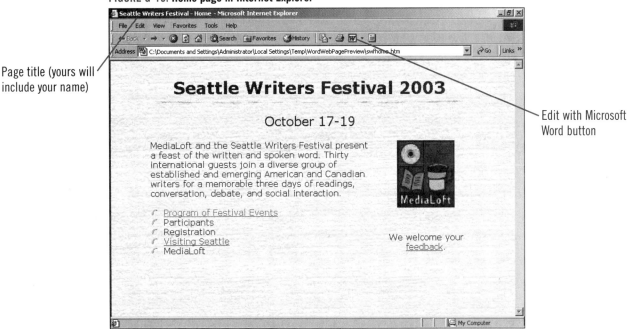

Edit with Microsoft Word button

FIGURE G-17: **Program of Events page in Internet Explorer**

Print button

Text is bold

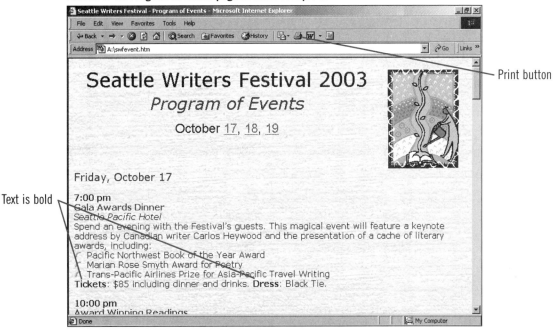

Posting a Web site to the Web or an intranet

To make your Web site available to others, you must post (or publish) it to the Web or to a local intranet. Publishing a Web site involves copying the HTML files and the supporting folders and files to a Web server—either your Internet Service Provider's (ISP) server, if you want to publish it to the Internet, or the server for your local intranet. Check with your ISP or your network administrator for instructions on how to post your Web pages to the correct server.

Practice

► Concepts Review

Label each element shown in Figure G-18.

FIGURE G-18

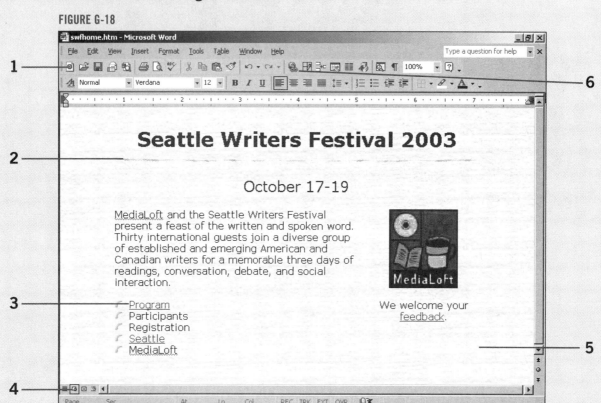

Match each term with the statement that best describes it.

7. Hyperlink
8. Web page
9. Home page
10. HTML
11. Theme
12. Web site
13. Browser
14. URL

a. The main page of a Web site
b. A software program used to access and display Web pages
c. A document that can be viewed using a browser
d. A group of associated Web pages
e. The address of a Web page on the World Wide Web
f. A programming language used to create Web pages
g. Text or graphic that jumps the viewer to a different location when clicked
h. A set of common design elements that can be applied to a Web page

Select the best answer from the list of choices.

15. Which of the following is *not* a design element included in a theme?
a. Web page background
b. Horizontal line style
c. Font effects
d. Picture bullets

16. Which of the following *cannot* be opened using a hyperlink?
    a. Support folders
    b. Web pages
    c. E-mail messages
    d. Files

17. Which of the following formats is supported by Web browsers?
    a. Headers and footers
    b. Page numbers
    c. Columns of text
    d. Inline graphics

18. What does using the Save as Web Page command accomplish?
    a. Opens the active file in a browser
    b. Converts the active file to HTML format
    c. Applies a Web theme to the active file
    d. Converts floating graphics to inline graphics

19. Where does the page title of a Web page appear?
    a. On the home page
    b. In the Word title bar
    c. In the name of the supporting folder
    d. In the browser title bar

20. Which of the following statements is false?
    a. The supporting folder for a Web page holds GIF and JPEG files.
    b. When you save a document as a Web page, Word adds HTML tags to the file.
    c. You can use the Center button to center a floating graphic in Web Layout view.
    d. Hyperlink text is underlined.

▶ Skills Review

1. **Create a Web page.**
   a. Study the sketch for the Web site devoted to literacy issues shown in Figure G-19.
   b. Start Word and create a blank Web page.
   c. Create a table with two columns and three rows, select the table, then AutoFit the table to fit the window. (*Hint:* Click Table on the menu bar, point to AutoFit, click AutoFit to window.)
   d. Merge the two cells in the first row of the table, then type Literacy Facts in the first row.
   e. Merge the cells in rows 2 and 3 in the second column, click Insert on the menu bar, click File, navigate to the drive and folder where your Project Files are located, select WD G-2, then click Insert.
   f. In the last cell of the first column, type the following three-item list: What you can do, Literacy Volunteers of America, Contact us.
   g. Save the file as a Web page to the drive and folder where your Project Files are located with the page title Literacy Facts – Home and the filename literacy.

2. **Format a Web page with themes.**
   a. Apply the Poetic or Network theme to the Web page. (*Note:* Select a different theme if neither of these themes is available to you.)
   b. Format Literacy Facts in the Heading 1 style, center the text, then press [Enter].
   c. Insert a horizontal line below the heading.
   d. Apply bullets to the list in the last cell of the first column, then save your changes.

3. **Illustrate a Web page with graphics.**
   a. In the blank cell in the first column, insert the graphic file reader.gif from the drive and folder where your Project Files are located.
   b. Center the graphic in the cell, press [Enter], type Literacy is not just reading and writing; the ability to perform basic math and solve problems is also important., press [Enter], then change the font size of the text to 10.
   c. Drag the border between the first and second columns to approximately the 2¼" mark on the horizontal ruler.
   d. Click Format on the menu bar, point to Background, click Fill Effects, click the Gradient tab, select the Two Colors Option button in the Colors section, click the Color 1 list arrow, click Lavender, click the Color 2 list arrow, click Light Yellow, then click OK.

e. Select the table, remove the table borders, then save your changes.

4. **Save a document as a Web page.**

   a. Open the file WD G-3 from the drive and folder where your Project Files are located.

   b. Examine the document, then save it as a Web page with the page title **Literacy – what you can do** and the filename **whattodo**.

   c. Read the message about formatting changes, then click Continue.

   d. Apply the theme you used with the Literacy page to the Web page, then apply the Heading 1 style to the heading.

   e. Double-click the graphic, click the Layout tab, change its text wrapping style to In line with text, then move it before Literacy in the heading.

   f. Change the background to a lavender and light yellow gradient. (*Hint*: See Step 3d).

   g. Save your changes, then close the file.

5. **Add hyperlinks.**

   a. In the Literacy Facts file, select What you can do, then format it as a hyperlink to the whattodo.htm file.

   b. Format Literacy Volunteers of America as a hyperlink to the Web address **www.literacyvolunteers.com**.

   c. Format Contact us as a hyperlink to your e-mail address with the message subject **Literacy information**. (*Note:* If you do not have an e-mail address, skip this step.)

   d. Save your changes.

6. **Modify hyperlinks.**

   a. Right-click the Contact us hyperlink, click Edit Hyperlink, then change the Text to display to **For more information on literacy, contact** followed by your name.

   b. Edit the Literacy Volunteers of America hyperlink so that the ScreenTip says **Information on LVA and links to literacy Web sites**.

   c. Edit the What you can do hyperlink so that the ScreenTip says **Simple actions you can take to help eliminate illiteracy**.

   d. Save your changes.

7. **Preview a Web page in a browser.**

   a. Preview the Literacy Facts Web page in your browser, test all the hyperlinks, then print a copy of the Literacy Facts Web page.

   b. Open the whattodo.htm file in Word.

   c. Press [Ctrl][End], press [Enter], type **For more information, contact** followed by your name, format your name as a hyperlink to your e-mail address, then save your changes.

   d. Preview the Literacy - what you can do Web page in your browser, test the hyperlink, then print the page.

   e. Close the browser, close all open Word files, then exit Word.

FIGURE G-19

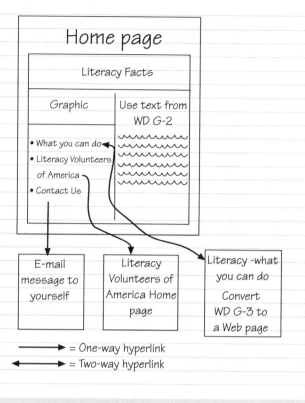

Independent Challenge 1

You have written a story about a recent hiking expedition you took and want to share it and some photos with your family and friends. You decide to create a Web page. Figure G-20 shows how you will arrange the photos.

FIGURE G-20

Rising Wolf Mountain (elev. 9513 feet)

Jackson enjoying the view

a. Start Word, open a blank Web page, save the Web page with the page title **A long walk with Jackson** and the filename **longwalk** to the drive and folder where your Project Files are located, then change the zoom level to 100% if necessary.

b. Insert a table with two columns and four rows, merge the two cells in the first row, merge the three cells in the second column, select the table, then AutoFit the table to fit the window.

c. Type **A long walk with Jackson** in the first row of the table, then press [Enter].

d. Click in the second column, then insert the file WD G-4 from the drive and folder where your Project Files are located. (*Hint*: Use the File command on the Insert menu.)

e. Click in the first blank cell in the first column, then insert the graphic file rwolf.jpg from the drive and folder where your Project Files are located.

f. Press [Enter], then type **Rising Wolf Mountain (elev. 9513 feet)**.

g. In the last blank cell in the first column, insert the graphic file jackson.jpg from the drive and folder where your Project Files are located, then resize the photo proportionally to be the same width as the Rising Wolf Mountain photo.

h. Press [Enter], then type **Jackson enjoying the view**.

i. Drag the border between the first and second columns left to approximately the 3¼" mark.

j. Apply a theme, then format the Web page using theme elements and other formatting features.

k. Select Glacier National Park in the first paragraph in the second column, format it as a hyperlink to the URL **www.nps.gov/glac/home.htm** with the ScreenTip **Glacier National Park Website Visitor Center**.

l. Press [Ctrl][End], press [Enter], type **E-mail** followed by your name, center the text, then format your name as a hyperlink to your e-mail address, if you have one.

m. Resize the table rows and columns as necessary to make the Web page attractive, remove the borders from the table, save your changes, preview the Web page in your browser, then test the hyperlinks.

n. Switch to Word, make any necessary adjustments, save your changes, preview the Web page in your browser, print a copy, close the browser, close the file in Word, then exit Word.

 # Independent Challenge 2

You and your partner have just started a mail-order business called Monet's Garden. You create a small Web site that includes a home page and a list of your products and prices.

a. Start Word, open the Templates dialog box, double-click Web Page Wizard on the Web pages tab, then click Next.

b. Name the Web site **Monet's Garden**, click Browse, navigate to the drive and folder where your Project Files are located, click Open, then click Next.

c. Click Separate Page, then click Next.

d. Click Remove Page three times to remove each Web page, click Add Template Page, select Right-aligned Column, click OK, click Add Existing File, navigate to the drive and folder where your Project Files are located, click WD G-5, click Open, then click Next.

e. Select Right-aligned Column in the list, click Rename, type **Monet's Garden Home**, click OK, click WD G-5, click Rename, type **Products and Prices**, click OK, then click Next.

f. Click Browse Themes, select the Nature theme (or another theme), click OK, click Next, then click Finish.

g. After the wizard creates the Web site, the default contents page of the Web site opens in Word. It has the file-name default.htm. This page provides links to the other pages in the Web site.

h. Select the table on the default.htm page, remove the borders, then save your changes.

i. Press [Ctrl], click the Monet's Garden Home hyperlink on the default.htm page to open the home page in your browser, then open the Monet's Garden Home page in Word.

j. At the top of the home page, type **Order** in the blank table cell, format Order as a hyperlink to the e-mail address **monetsgarden@monad.net**, then remove the table borders.

k. Replace the main heading placeholder with **Monet's Garden,** replace the first section heading placeholder with **Professionally Designed Perennial Gardens!,** then replace the first body paragraph with the following: **If you've admired perennial gardens but thought it would be too complicated or expensive to create your own, here's great news. Our fail-proof garden packages will get you off to a sure-fire start and guarantee you glorious blooms for years to come.**

l. Delete the remaining placeholder text in the first column, delete the caption placeholder in the second column, then replace the graphic with an appropriate clip art image.

m. Adjust the formatting of the Web page to make it attractive, press [Ctrl][End], type **For more information, contact** followed by your name, make your name a hyperlink to your e-mail address, then save your changes.

n. Open the Products and Prices page in Word.

o. At the top of the Products and Prices page, type **Order** in the blank table cell, right-align Order, format it as a hyperlink to the e-mail address **monetsgarden@monad.net**, then remove the table borders.

p. Scroll down the Web page, read the comment, change 60 to 30 in the Web page text, then delete the comment. (*Hint*: Right-click the comment, then click Delete comment.)

q. Apply styles and other formatting to the Web page to make it attractive and give it a look consistent with the Monet's Garden Home page, press [Ctrl][End], type **For more information, contact** followed by your name, make your name a hyperlink to your e-mail address, then save your changes.

r. Preview the Web site in your browser, test the hyperlinks, print a copy of the home page and the Products and Prices page, exit your browser, close all open files, then exit Word.

▶ Independent Challenge 3

You are in charge of publicity for the Sydney Triathlon 2003 World Cup. One of your responsibilities is to create a Web site to provide details of the event. You have created the content for the Web pages as Word documents, and now need to save and format them as Web pages. Your Web site will include a home page and three other Web pages. One of the Web pages is shown in Figure G-21.

FIGURE G-21

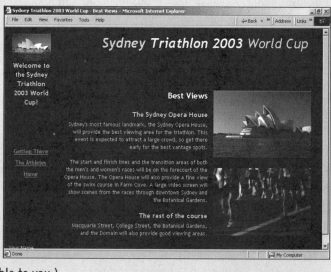

a. Start Word, open the file WD G-6 from the drive and folder where your Project Files are located, then save it as a Web page with the page title **Sydney Triathlon 2003 World Cup - Home** and the filename **tri_home**.

b. Apply the Geared Up Factory or Cascade theme, but first remove the check from the Background Image check box in the Theme dialog box. (*Note*: Use a different theme if neither of these themes is available to you.)

c. Press [Ctrl][A], then change the font size to 10.

d. Apply the Heading 1 style to the heading Sydney Triathlon 2003 World Cup in the first row of the table, right-align the text, apply italic, select Sydney Triathlon 2003 in the heading, apply bold, select Triathlon 2003, then change the font color to a different color.

e. Apply the Heading 4 style to Welcome to the Sydney Triathlon 2003 World Cup! in the upper-left cell of the table, apply bold, then center the text.

f. Read the remaining text on the Web page, then format it with heading styles, fonts, font colors, and other formatting effects to make it look attractive. Preview the Web page in your browser.

g. Remove the table borders from the Web page, press [Ctrl][End], type your name, save your changes, then close the file.

h. Open the files listed in the table from the drive and folder where your Project Files are located, then save them as Web pages with the page titles and filenames listed in the table.

Project File	Page Title	Filename
WD G-7	Sydney Triathlon 2003 World Cup – Best Views	tri_view
WD G-8	Sydney Triathlon 2003 World Cup – Getting There	tri_get
WD G-9	Sydney Triathlon 2003 World Cup – The Athletes	tri_athl

i. In Word, open the tri_home.htm file, then change the zoom level to 100% if necessary.

j. Select Best Views, then format it as a hyperlink to the tri_view.htm file. Format Getting There and The Athletes as hyperlinks to the tri_get.htm and tri_athl.htm files, then save your changes.

k. Open each of the remaining three files—tri_view.htm, tri_get.htm, and tri_athl.htm—and format the text in the left column of each Web page as a hyperlink to the appropriate file. Save your changes, then close each Web page.

l. Preview the home page in your browser. Test each hyperlink on the home page and on the other Web pages.

m. Examine each Web page in your browser, make any necessary formatting adjustments in Word, print a copy of each Web page from your browser, then close your browser, close all open files, and exit Word.

Independent Challenge 4

In this independent challenge you will use the Personal Web page template to create a Web page that provides information about you and your interests. Your Web page will include hyperlinks to Web sites that you think will be useful to people who share your passions.

a. Start Word, open the Templates dialog box, then create a new Web page based on the Personal Web page template.

b. Save the Web page with the filename **my_page** to the drive and folder where your Project Files are located. Use your name for the page title.

c. Under Contents, delete the Work Information and Current Projects items, then scroll down and delete the placeholders in the Work Information and Current projects sections of the Web page. (*Note:* Delete from the heading for each section to the "Back to top" hyperlink.)

d. Use your favorite search engine to search for Web sites related to your interests. Write down the page titles and URLs of at least three Web sites that you think are worth visiting.

e. Replace the placeholder text in the Favorite Links section with the names of the three Web sites you liked. Format each name as a hyperlink to the Web site, and create a ScreenTip that explains why you think it's a good Web site.

f. Replace the remaining placeholder text in the Web page with information about yourself.

g. Format your e-mail and Web addresses as hyperlinks to those addresses. Edit each Back to top hyperlink so that it jumps to the main heading at the top of the page rather than to the top of the document.

h. Illustrate the Web page with a clip art graphic. Create a table to position the graphic if necessary.

i. Format the Web page with a background, heading styles, lines, bullets, fonts, colors, and any other formatting features.

j. Save your changes, preview the Web page in your browser, test each hyperlink, then make any necessary adjustments.

k. Save your changes, preview the Web page in your browser again, print a copy, close the browser, close the file, then exit Word.

▶ Visual Workshop

Create the Web pages shown in Figure G-22 using the graphic files rest.jpg, bridge.jpg, and studlamp.jpg, found on the drive and folder where your Project Files are located. Save the home page with the page title **Gallery Azul Home (Your Name)** and the filename **azulhome**. Save the exhibit page with the page title **Gallery Azul Exhibit (Your Name)** and the filename **azulexhb**. On the home page, create a hyperlink to the exhibit page and a hyperlink to the e-mail address **GalleryAzul@ptown.net**. On the Exhibit page, create a hyperlink to the home page. View the Web pages in your browser, then print a copy of each Web page.

FIGURE G-22

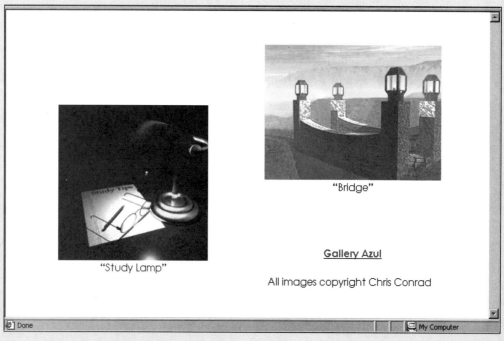

Merging

Word Documents

Objectives

- ▶ **Understand mail merge**
- ▶ **Create a main document**
- ▶ **Design a data source**
- ▶ **Enter and edit records**
- ▶ **Add merge fields**
- ▶ **Merge data**
- ▶ **Create labels**
- ▶ **Sort and filter records**

A mail merge operation combines a standard document, such as a form letter, with customized data, such as a set of names and addresses, to create a set of personalized documents. You can perform a mail merge to create documents used in mass mailings, such as letters and labels. You also can use mail merge to create documents that include customized information, such as business cards. In this unit you learn how to use the Mail Merge Wizard to set up and perform a mail merge. Alice Wegman needs to send a welcome letter to the new members of the MediaLoft Coffee Club, a program designed to attract customers to the MediaLoft Café. She also needs to send a brochure to all the members of the club. She uses mail merge to create a personalized form letter and mailing labels for the brochures.

Word 2002

Understanding Mail Merge

When you perform a mail merge, you merge a standard document with a file that contains customized information for many individuals or items. The document with the standard text is called the **main document**. The file with the unique data for individual people or items is called the **data source**. Merging the main document with a data source results in a merged document that contains customized versions of the main document, as shown in Figure H-1. The Mail Merge Wizard steps you through the process of setting up and performing a mail merge. Alice uses the Mail Merge Wizard to create her form letters and mailing labels. Before beginning, she explores the steps involved in performing a mail merge.

▶ **Create the main document**

The main document contains the text—often called **boilerplate text**—that appears in every version of the merged document. The main document also includes the merge fields, which indicate where the customized information will be inserted when you perform the merge. You insert the merge fields in the main document after you have created or selected the data source.

▶ **Create a data source or select an existing data source**

The data source is a file that contains the unique information for each individual or item. It provides the information that varies in every version of the merged document. A data source is composed of data fields and data records. A **data field** is a category of information, such as last name, first name, street address, city, or postal code. A **data record** is a complete set of related information for an individual or an item, such as one person's name and address. It is easiest to think of a data source file as a table: the header row contains the names of the data fields (the **field names**), and each row in the table is an individual data record. You can use the Mail Merge Wizard to create a new data source, or you can merge a main document with an existing data source, such as a data source created in Word, an Outlook Contact List, or an Access database.

▶ **Identify the fields to include in the data source and enter the records**

When you create a new data source, you must first identify the fields to include. It's important to think of and include all the fields before you begin to enter data. For example, if you are creating a data source that will include addresses, you might need to include fields for a person's middle name, title, department name, or country, even though every address in the data source will not include that information. Once you have identified the fields and set up your data source, you are ready to enter the data for each record.

▶ **Add merge fields to the main document**

A **merge field** is a placeholder that you insert in the main document to indicate where the data from each record should be inserted when you perform the merge. For example, in the location you want to insert a zip code, you insert a zip code merge field. The merge fields in a main document must correspond with the field names in the associated data source. Merge fields must be inserted, not typed, in the main document. The Mail Merge Wizard provides access to the dialog boxes you use to insert merge fields.

▶ **Merge the data from the data source into the main document**

Once you have established your data source and inserted the merge fields in the main document, you are ready to perform the merge. You can merge to a new file, which will contain a customized version of the main document for each record in the data source, or you can merge directly to a printer, fax, or e-mail message.

FIGURE H-1: Mail merge process

Data source document

Field name

Store	Title	First Name	Last Name	Address Line 1	City	State	Zip Code	Country
Seattle	Ms.	Linda	Barker	62 Cloud St.	Bellevue	WA	83459	US
Boston	Mr.	Bob	Cruz	23 Plum St.	Boston	MA	02483	US
Chicago	Ms.	Joan	Yatco	456 Elm St.	Chicago	IL	60603	US
Seattle	Ms.	Anne	Butler	48 East Ave.	Vancouver	BC	V6F 1AH	CANADA
Boston	Mr.	Fred	Silver	56 Pearl St.	Cambridge	MA	02139	US

Data record

Main document

MediaLoft
Corporate Headquarters • 821 Post Street • San Francisco, CA 94108
Tel: (415) 555-2398 • Fax: (415) 555-2393 • www.medialoft.com

May 12, 2003

««AddressBlock»»

««GreetingLine»»

Welcome to the MediaLoft «Store» Coffee Club! This month's featured coffee is Kealakekua Sunrise, a rich blend of organic Kona beans with a hint of macadamia – the twin flavors of Hawaii.

Your membership entitles you to a free cup of the featured coffee any Saturday morning at the MediaLoft Café. In addition you will receive a 10% discount on all coffees and coffee-related products. We'll hope you'll join us each Saturday at MediaLoft.

Sincerely,

Alice Wegman
Marketing Manager

Merge fields

Boilerplate text

Merged document

MediaLoft
Corporate Headquarters • 821 Post Street • San Francisco, CA 94108
Tel: (415) 555-2398 • Fax: (415) 555-2393 • www.medialoft.com

May 12, 2003

Ms. Linda Barker
62 Cloud St.
Bellevue, WA 83459

Dear Ms. Barker:

Welcome to the MediaLoft Seattle Coffee Club! This month's featured coffee is Kealakekua Sunrise, a rich blend of organic Kona beans with a hint of macadamia – the twin flavors of Hawaii.

Your membership entitles you to a free cup of the featured coffee any Saturday morning at the MediaLoft Café. In addition you will receive a 10% discount on all coffees and coffee-related products. We'll hope you'll join us each Saturday at MediaLoft.

Sincerely,

Alice Wegman
Marketing Manager

Customized information

CLUES TO USE

Understanding compare and merge

The Word compare and merge feature is different from mail merge. Mail merge combines a main document with a file containing customized information to create a set of unique documents. Compare and merge is used to compare any two documents—usually an original document and an edited copy of the original—to create a third document that shows the differences between the two. To compare and merge two documents, open the edited copy of the document, click Tools on the menu bar, then click Compare and Merge Documents. In the Compare and Merge dialog box, select the original document, click the Merge button list arrow, then click Merge into new document. A new merge document showing the differences between the edited document and the original document opens. The differences between the two documents are shown as tracked changes (colored and underlined text). You can then examine the merged document, edit it, and save it with a new filename.

Creating a Main Document

Word 2002

The first step in performing a mail merge is to create the main document—the file that contains the boilerplate text. You can create a main document from scratch, save an existing document as a main document, or use a mail merge template to create a main document. The Mail Merge Wizard walks you through the process of selecting the type of main document to create. Alice uses an existing form letter for her main document. She begins by starting the Mail Merge Wizard.

QuickTip

You can click an option button in the task pane to read a description of each type of merge document.

1. Start **Word**, click **Tools** on the menu bar, point to **Letters and Mailings**, then click **Mail Merge Wizard**

The Mail Merge task pane opens, as shown in Figure H-2, and displays information for the first step in the mail merge process: selecting the type of merge document to create.

2. Make sure the **Letters option button** is selected, then click **Next: Starting document** to continue with the next wizard step

The task pane displays the options for the second step: selecting the main document. You can use the current document, start with a mail merge template, or use an existing file.

QuickTip

If you choose "Use the current document" and the current document is blank, you can create a main document from scratch. Either type the boilerplate text at this wizard step, or wait until the wizard prompts you to do so.

3. Select the **Start from existing document option button**, select **More files** in the Start from existing list box if necessary, then click **Open**

The Open dialog box opens.

4. Use the Look in list arrow to navigate to the drive and folder where your Project Files are located, select the file **WD H-1**, then click **Open**

The letter that opens contains the boilerplate text for the main document. Notice the filename in the title bar is Document1. When you create a main document that is based on an existing document, Word gives the main document a default temporary filename.

5. Click the **Save button** 🖫 on the Standard toolbar, then save the main document with the filename **Coffee Letter Main** to the drive and folder where your Project Files are located

It's a good idea to include "main" in the filename so that you can easily recognize the file as a main document.

6. Click the **Zoom list arrow** on the Standard toolbar, click **Text Width**, select **April 9, 2003** in the letter, type today's date, scroll down, select **Alice Wegman**, type your name, press **[Ctrl][Home]**, then save your changes

The edited main document is shown in Figure H-3.

7. Click **Next: Select recipients** to continue with the next wizard step

You will continue with Step 3 of 6 in the next lesson.

Working with smart tags

Smart tags are labels applied to data (text) that Word recognizes as a date, address, place, name, or other type of data. Text that is labeled with a smart tag is marked with a dotted purple underline. Smart tags allow you to use Word to perform tasks that you would normally need to do in another Office program. For example, in Word you can click a smart tag labeling a person's name to add the person's name and address to one of your contact lists in Outlook, without having to open Outlook first. To find out the kinds of actions you can take with a smart tag, point to the smart tag, click the Smart Tag Actions button that appears, then select from the menu of options.

FIGURE H-2: **Step 1 of 6 Mail Merge task pane**

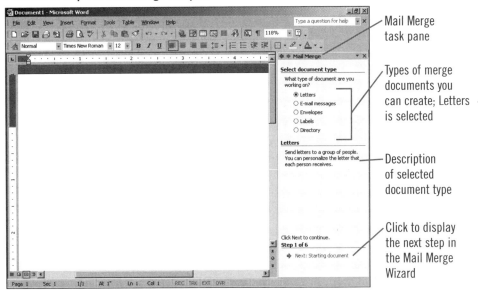

Mail Merge task pane

Types of merge documents you can create; Letters is selected

Description of selected document type

Click to display the next step in the Mail Merge Wizard

FIGURE H-3: **Main document with the Step 2 of 6 Mail Merge task pane**

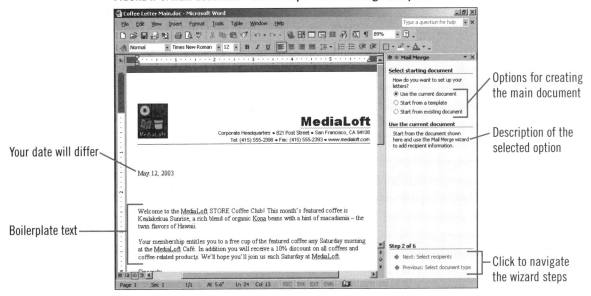

Your date will differ

Boilerplate text

Options for creating the main document

Description of the selected option

Click to navigate the wizard steps

CLUES TO USE

Using a mail merge template

If you are creating a letter, fax, or directory, you can use a mail merge template to start your main document. Each template includes boilerplate text, which you can customize, and merge fields, which you can match to the field names in your data source. To create a main document that is based on a mail merge template, click the Start from a template option button in the Step 2 of 6 Mail Merge task pane, then click Select template. In the Templates dialog box that opens, select a template on the Mail Merge tab, then click OK to create the document. Once you have created the main document, you can customize it with your own information: edit the boilerplate text, change the document format, or add, remove, or modify the merge fields. Before performing the merge, make sure to match the names of the address merge fields used in the template with the field names used in your data source. To match the field names, click the Match Fields button 🖳 on the Mail Merge toolbar, then use the list arrows in the Match fields dialog box to select the field name in your data source that corresponds to each address field component in the main document.

Designing a Data Source

Once you have identified the main document, the next step in the mail merge process is to identify the data source, the file that contains the information that will differ in each version of the merge document. You can use an existing data source that already contains the records you want to include in your merge, or you can create a new data source. When you create a new data source you must determine the fields to include—the categories of information, such as a first name, last name, city, or a zip code—and then add the records. Alice creates a new data source that includes fields for the name, address, and MediaLoft store location of each new member of the Coffee Club.

1. **Make sure the Mail Merge task pane displays Step 3 of 6 at the bottom**
   Step 3 of 6 involves selecting a data source to use for the merge. You can use an existing data source, a list of contacts created in Microsoft Outlook, or a new data source.

2. **Select the Type a new list option button, then click Create**
   The New Address List dialog box opens, as shown in Figure H-4. You use this dialog box both to design your data source and to enter records. The Enter Address information section of the dialog box includes fields that are commonly used in form letters, but you can customize your data source by adding and removing fields from this list. A data source can be merged with more than one main document, so it's important to design a data source to be flexible. The more fields you include in a data source, the more flexible it is. For example, if you include separate fields for a person's title, first name, middle name, and last name, you can use the same data source to create an envelope addressed to "Mr. John Montgomery Smith" and a form letter addressed to "Dear John."

3. **Click Customize**
   The Customize Address List dialog box opens, as shown in Figure H-5. You use this dialog box to add, delete, rename, and reorder the fields in the data source.

4. **Click Company Name in the list of field names, click Delete, then click Yes in the warning dialog box that opens**
   Company Name is removed from the list of field names. The Company Name field will not be part of the data source.

5. **Repeat step 4 to delete the Address Line 2, Home Phone, Work Phone and E-mail Address fields**
   The fields are removed from the data source.

6. **Click Add, type Store in the Add Field dialog box, then click OK**
   A field called "Store," which you will use to indicate the location of the MediaLoft store where the customer joined the Coffee Club, is added to the data source.

7. **Select Store in the list of field names if necessary, then click Move Up eight times**
   The field name "Store" is moved to the top of the list. Although the order of field names does not matter in a data source, it's convenient to arrange the field names logically to make it easier to enter and edit records.

8. **Click OK**
   The New Address List dialog box shows the customized list of fields, with the Store field first in the list. The next step is to enter each record you want to include in the data source. You will add records to the data source in the next lesson.

FIGURE H-4: **New Address List dialog box**

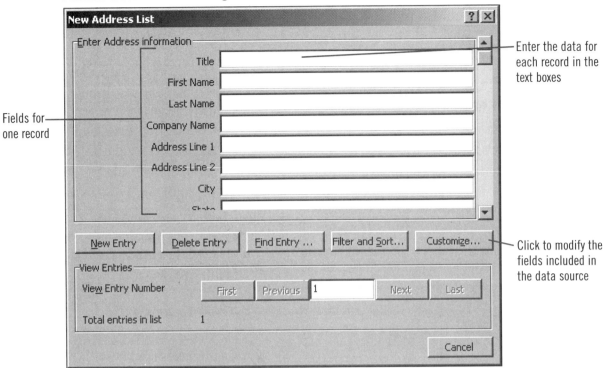

Fields for one record

Enter the data for each record in the text boxes

Click to modify the fields included in the data source

FIGURE H-5: **Customize Address List dialog box**

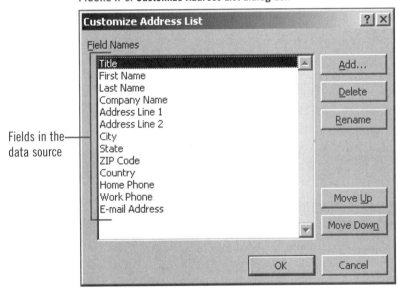

Fields in the data source

Merging with an Outlook data source

If you maintain lists of contacts in Microsoft Outlook, you can use one of your Outlook contact lists as a data source for a merge. To merge with an Outlook data source, click the Select from Outlook contacts option button in the Step 3 of 6 Mail Merge task pane, then click Choose Contacts Folder to open the Select Contact List folder dialog box. In this dia-

log box, select the contact list you want to use as the data source, then click OK. All the contacts included in the selected folder appear in the Mail Merge Recipients dialog box. Here you can refine the list of recipients to include in the merge by sorting and filtering the records. When you are satisfied, click OK in the Mail Merge Recipients dialog box.

Entering and Editing Records

Word 2002

Once you have established the structure of a data source, the next step is to enter the records. Each record includes the complete set of information for each individual or item you include in the data source. Alice creates a record for each new member of the Coffee Club.

QuickTip

Be careful not to add spaces or extra punctuation after an entry in a field, or these will appear when the data is merged.

1. Place the insertion point in the Store text box in the **New Address List** dialog box, type **Seattle**, then press **[Tab]**

   "Seattle" appears in the Store field and the insertion point moves to the next field in the list, the Title field.

2. Type **Ms.**, press **[Tab]**, type **Linda**, press **[Tab]**, type **Barker**, press **[Tab]**, type **62 Cloud St.**, press **[Tab]**, type **Bellevue**, press **[Tab]**, type **WA**, press **[Tab]**, type **83459**, press **[Tab]**, then type **US**

   Compare your New Address List dialog box with Figure H-6.

QuickTip

It's OK to leave a field blank if you do not need it for a record.

3. Click **New Entry**

   The record for Linda Barker is added to the data source and the dialog box displays empty fields for the next record, record 2.

4. Enter the following four records, pressing **[Tab]** to move from field to field, and clicking **New Entry** at the end of each record except the last:

Store	Title	First Name	Last Name	Address Line 1	City	State	ZIP Code	Country
Boston	Mr.	Bob	Cruz	23 Plum St.	Boston	MA	02483	US
Chicago	Ms.	Joan	Yatco	456 Elm St.	Chicago	IL	60603	US
Seattle	Ms.	Anne	Butler	48 East Ave.	Vancouver	BC	V6F 1AH	CANADA
Boston	Mr.	Fred	Silver	56 Pearl St.	Cambridge	MA	02139	US

5. Click **Close**

   The Save Address List dialog box opens. Data sources are saved by default in the My Data Sources folder so that you can easily locate them to use in other merge operations. Data sources you create in Word are saved in Microsoft Office Address Lists (*.mdb) format.

Trouble?

If a check mark appears in the blank record under Fred Silver, click the check mark to eliminate the record from the merge.

6. Type **New Coffee Club Data** in the File name text box, use the Save in list arrow to navigate to the drive and folder where your Project Files are located, then click **Save**

   The data source is saved, and the Mail Merge Recipients dialog box opens, as shown in Figure H-7. The dialog box shows the records in the data source in table format. You can use the dialog box to edit, sort, and filter records, and to select the recipients to include in the mail merge. You will learn more about sorting and filtering in a later lesson. The check marks in the first column indicate the records that will be included in the merge.

7. Click the **Joan Yatco record**, click **Edit**, select **Ms.** in the Title text box in the New Coffee Club Data.mdb dialog box, type **Dr.**, then click **Close**

   The data in the Title field for Joan Yatco changes from "Ms." to "Dr." and the New Coffee Club Data.mdb dialog box closes.

QuickTip

If you want to add new records or modify existing records, click Edit recipient list in the task pane.

8. Click **OK** in the Mail Merge Recipients dialog box

   The dialog box closes. The file type and filename of the data source attached to the main document now appear under Use an existing list in the Mail Merge task pane, as shown in Figure H-8. The Mail Merge toolbar also appears in the program window when you close the data source. You'll learn more about the Mail Merge toolbar in later lessons.

FIGURE H-6: Record in New Address List dialog box

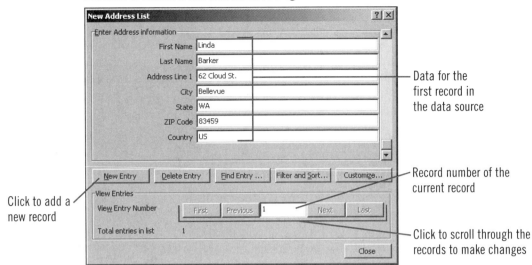

Click to add a new record

Data for the first record in the data source

Record number of the current record

Click to scroll through the records to make changes

FIGURE H-7: Mail Merge Recipients dialog box

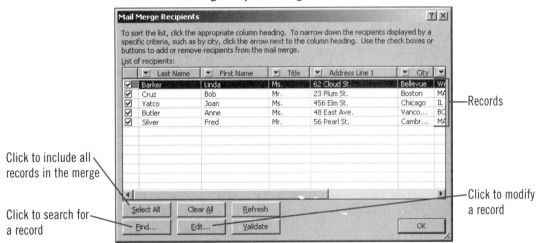

Click to include all records in the merge

Click to search for a record

Records

Click to modify a record

FIGURE H-8: Data source attached to the main document

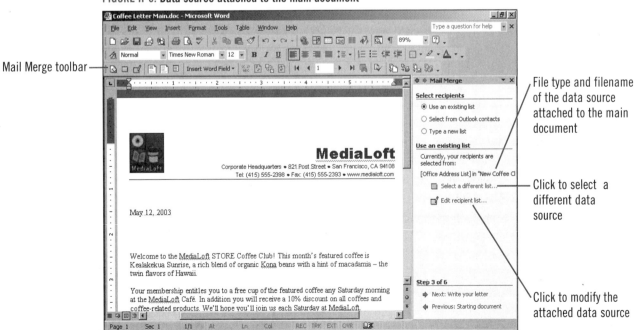

Mail Merge toolbar

File type and filename of the data source attached to the main document

Click to select a different data source

Click to modify the attached data source

Adding Merge Fields

After you have created and identified the data source, the next step is to insert the merge fields in the main document. Merge fields serve as placeholders for text that will be inserted when the main document and the data source are merged. The names of merge fields correspond to the field names in the data source. You can insert merge fields using the Mail Merge task pane or the Insert Merge Field button on the Mail Merge toolbar. You cannot type merge fields into the main document. Alice uses the Mail Merge task pane to insert merge fields for the inside address and greeting of her letter. She also inserts a merge field for the store location in the body of the letter.

1. Click the **Show/Hide ¶ button** ¶ on the Standard toolbar to display formatting marks, then click **Next: Write your letter** in the Mail Merge task pane
   The Mail Merge task pane shows the options for Step 4 of 6: writing the letter and inserting the merge fields in the main document. Since your form letter is already written, you are ready to add the merge fields to it.

QuickTip

You can also click the Insert Address Block button 📄 on the Mail Merge toolbar to insert an address block.

2. Place the insertion point in the blank line above the first body paragraph, then click **Address block** in the Mail Merge task pane
   The Insert Address Block dialog box opens, as shown in Figure H-9. You use this dialog box to specify the fields you want to include in an address block. In this merge, the address block is the inside address of the form letter. An address block automatically includes fields for the street, city, state, and postal code, but you can select the format for the recipient's name and indicate whether to include a company name or country in the address.

3. Scroll the list of formats for a recipient's name to get a feel for the kinds of formats you can use, then click **Mr. Joshua Randall Jr.** if necessary
   The selected format uses the recipient's title, first name, and last name.

4. Click the **Only include the country/region if different than: option button**, then type **US** in the text box
   You only need to include the country in the address block if the country is different from the United States, so you indicate that all entries in the Country field except "US" should be included in the printed address.

QuickTip

You cannot simply type chevrons around a field name. You must insert merge fields using the Mail Merge task pane or the buttons on the Mail Merge toolbar.

5. Click **OK**, then press **[Enter]** twice
   The merge field AddressBlock is added to the main document. Chevrons (<< and >>) surround a merge field to distinguish it from the boilerplate text.

6. Click **Greeting line** in the Mail Merge task pane
   The Greeting Line dialog box opens. You want to use the format "Dear Mr. Randall:" (the recipient's title and last name, followed by a colon) for a greeting. The default format uses a comma, so you have to change the comma to a colon.

7. Click the **, list arrow**, click **:**, click **OK**, then press **[Enter]**
   The merge field GreetingLine is added to the main document.

QuickTip

You can also click the Insert Merge Fields button 🗒 on the Mail Merge toolbar to insert a merge field

8. In the body of the letter select **STORE**, then click **More items** in the Mail Merge task pane
   The Insert Merge Field dialog box opens and displays the list of field names included in the data source.

9. Select **Store** if necessary, click **Insert**, click **Close**, press **[Spacebar]** to add a space between the merge field and Coffee if necessary, save your changes, then click ¶ to turn off the display of formatting marks
   The merge field Store is inserted in the main document, as shown in Figure H-10. You must type spaces and punctuation between merge fields if you want spaces and punctuation to appear between the data in the merged documents. You will preview the merged data and perform the merge in the next lesson.

FIGURE H-9: Address Block dialog box

Formats for the recipient's name

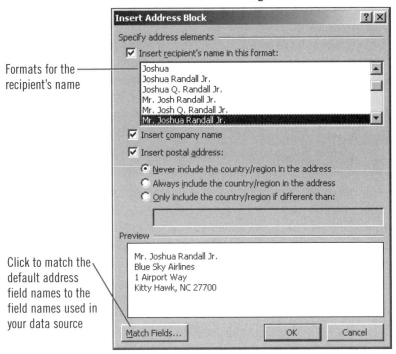

Click to match the default address field names to the field names used in your data source

FIGURE H-10: Merge fields in the main document

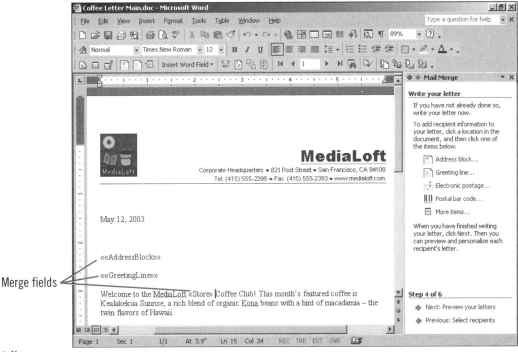

Merge fields

Matching fields

The merge fields you insert in a main document must correspond with the field names in the associated data source. If you are using the Address Block merge field, you must make sure that the default address field names correspond with the field names used in your data source. If the default address field names do not match the field names in your data source, click Match Field in the Insert Address Block dialog box, then use the list arrows in the Match Fields dialog box to select the field name in the data source that corresponds to each default address field name.

Merging Data

Once you have added records to your data source and inserted merge fields in the main document, you are ready to perform the merge. Before merging, it's a good idea to preview the merged data to make sure the printed documents will appear as you want them to. You can preview the merge using the wizard or the View Merged Data button on the Mail Merge toolbar. When you merge the main document with the data source, you must choose between merging to a new file or directly to a printer. ✎ Before merging the form letter with the data source, Alice previews the merge to make sure each customized letter looks as she intended. She then merges the two files to a new document.

Steps

1. Click **Next: Preview your letters** in the Mail Merge task pane

   The data from the first record in the data source appears in place of the merge fields in the main document, as shown in Figure H-11. Always check the preview document to make sure the merge fields, punctuation, page breaks, and spacing all appear as you intend before you perform the merge.

2. Click the **Next Recipient button** ⟩⟩ in the Mail Merge task pane

   The data from the second record in the data source appears in place of the merge fields.

3. Click in the **Go to Record text box** on the Mail Merge toolbar, press **[Backspace]**, type **4**, then press **[Enter]**

   The data for the fourth record appears in the document window. The non-US country name, in this case Canada, is included in the address block, just as you specified. You can also use the First Record ⟨◀, Previous Record ◀, Next Record ▶, and Last Record ▶⟩ buttons on the Mail Merge toolbar to preview the merged data. Table H-1 describes other buttons on the Mail Merge toolbar.

4. Click **Next: Complete the Merge** in the Mail Merge task pane

   The options for Step 6 of 6 appear in the Mail Merge task pane. Merging to a new file allows you to edit the individual letters.

5. Click **Edit individual letters** to merge the data to a new document

   The Merge to New Document dialog box opens. You can use this dialog box to specify the records to include in the merge.

6. Make sure the **All option button** is selected, then click **OK**

   The main document and the data source are merged to a new document called Letters1, which contains a customized form letter for each record in the data source. You can now further personalize the letters without affecting the main document or the data source.

7. Click the **Zoom list arrow** on the Standard toolbar, click **Page Width**, scroll to the fourth letter (addressed to Ms. Anne Butler), place the insertion point before **V6F** in the address block, then press **[Enter]**

   The postal code is now consistent with the proper format for a Canadian address.

8. Click the **Save button** 🖫 on the Standard toolbar to open the Save As dialog box, then save the merge document as **Coffee Letter Merge** to the drive and folder where your Project Files are located

   You may decide not to save a merged file if your data source is large. Once you have created the main document and the data source, you can create the letters by performing the merge again.

9. Click **File** on the menu bar, click **Print**, click the **Current Page option button** in the Page Range section of the Print dialog box, click **OK**, then close all open Word files, saving changes if prompted

   The letter to Anne Butler prints.

FIGURE H-11: Preview of merged data

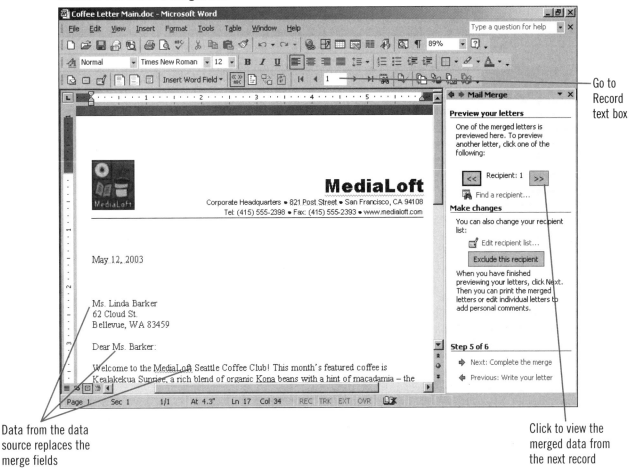

Go to
Record
text box

Data from the data
source replaces the
merge fields

Click to view the
merged data from
the next record

TABLE H-1: Buttons on the Mail Merge toolbar

button	use to
	Change the main document to a different type, or convert it to a normal Word document
	Select an existing data source
	Edit, sort, or filter the associated data source
	Insert an Address Block merge field
	Insert a Greeting Line merge field
	Insert a merge field from the data source
	Switch between viewing the main document with merge fields and with merged data
	Highlight the merge fields in the main document
	Match address fields with the field names used in the data source
	Search for a record in the merged documents
	Check for errors in the merged documents
	Merge the data to a new document and display it on screen
	Print the merged documents without first reviewing them on screen

Creating Labels

You can also use the Mail Merge Wizard to create mailing labels or print envelopes for a mailing. When you create labels or envelopes, you must select a standard label or envelope size to use as the main document, select a data source, and then insert the merge fields in the main document before performing the merge. In addition to mailing labels, you can use mail merge to create labels for diskettes, CDs, videos, and other items, and to create documents that are based on standard or custom label sizes, such as business cards, nametags, and postcards. ⟨⟨⟨⟨ Alice uses the Mail Merge Wizard to create mailing labels for a brochure she needs to send to all members of the Coffee Club. She creates a new label main document and attaches an existing data source.

Steps

1. Click the **New Blank Document button** ▢ on the Standard toolbar, click the **Zoom list arrow** on the Standard toolbar, click **Page Width**, click **Tools** on the menu bar, point to **Letters and Mailings**, then click **Mail Merge Wizard**
   The Mail Merge task pane opens.

Trouble?

If your dialog box does not show Avery standard, click the Label products list arrow, then click Avery standard.

2. Click the **Labels option button** in the Mail Merge task pane, click **Next: Starting document** to move to step 2 of 6, make sure the **Change document layout option button** is selected, then click **Label options**
   The Label Options dialog box opens, as shown in Figure H-12. You use this dialog box to select a label size for your labels and to specify the type of printer you plan to use. The default brand name Avery standard appears in the Label products list box. You can use the Label products list arrow to select other label products or a custom label. The many standard types of Avery labels for mailings, file folders, diskettes, post cards, and other types of labels are listed in the Product number list box. The type, height, width, and paper size for the selected product is displayed in the Label information section.

Trouble?

If your gridlines are not visible, click Table on the menu bar, then click Show Gridlines.

3. Scroll down the Product number list, click **5161 – Address**, then click **OK**
   A table with gridlines appears in the main document, as shown in Figure H-13. Each table cell is the size of a label for the label product you selected.

4. Save the label main document with the filename **Coffee Labels Main** to the drive and folder where your Project Files are located
   Next you need to select a data source for the labels.

5. Click **Next: Select recipients** to move to Step 3 of 6, click the **Use an existing list option button** if necessary, then click **Browse**
   The Select Data Source dialog box opens.

6. Use the Look in list arrow to navigate to the drive and folder where your Project Files are located, then open the file **WD H-2.mdb**
   The Mail Merge Recipients dialog box opens and displays all the records in the data source. In the next lesson you will sort and filter the records before performing the mail merge.

FIGURE H-12: Label Options dialog box

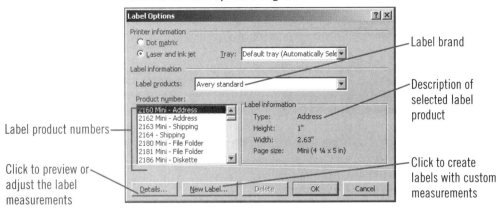

Label brand

Description of selected label product

Label product numbers

Click to preview or adjust the label measurements

Click to create labels with custom measurements

FIGURE H-13: Label main document

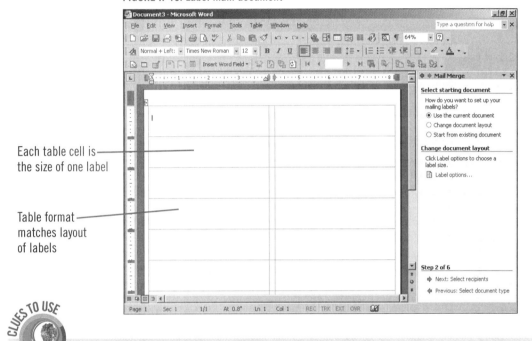

Each table cell is the size of one label

Table format matches layout of labels

Printing individual envelopes and labels

The Mail Merge Wizard allows you to easily print envelopes and labels for mass mailings, but you can also quickly format and print individual envelopes and labels using the Envelopes and Labels dialog box. To open the Envelopes and Labels dialog box, point to Letters and Mailings on the Tools menu, then click Envelopes and Labels. On the Envelopes tab, shown in Figure H-14, type the recipient's address in the Delivery address box and the return address in the Return address box. Click Options to open the Envelope Options dialog box, which you can use to select the envelope size, change the font and font size of the delivery and return addresses, and change the printing options. When you are ready to print the envelope, click Print in the Envelopes and Labels dialog box. The procedure for printing an individual label is similar to printing an individual envelope:

Enter the recipient's address on the Labels tab, click Options to select a label product number, click OK, then click Print.

FIGURE H-14: Envelopes tab in the Envelopes and Labels dialog box

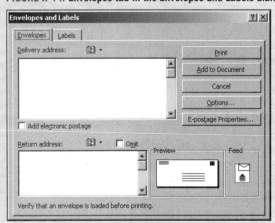

Sorting and Filtering Records

If you are using a large data source, you might want to sort and/or filter the records before performing a merge. **Sorting** the records determines the order in which the records are merged. For example, you might want to sort an address data source so that records are merged alphabetically by last name or in zip code order. **Filtering** the records pulls out the records that meet specific criteria and includes only those records in the merge. For instance, you might want to filter a data source to send a mailing only to people who live in the state of New York. You can use the Mail Merge Recipients dialog box both to sort and to filter a data source. Alice applies a filter to the data source so that only United States addresses are included in the merge. She then sorts those records so that they merge in zip code order.

QuickTip
For more advanced sort and filter options, click Filter and Sort in the New Address List dialog box when you create or edit the data source.

1. In the Mail Merge Recipients dialog box, scroll right to display the Country field, click the **Country column heading list arrow**, then click **US** on the menu that opens
A filter is applied to the data source so that only the records with "US" in the Country field will be merged. You can filter a data source by as many criteria as you like. To remove a filter, click a column heading list arrow, then click "All."

QuickTip
You can click a column heading again to reverse the sort order.

2. Scroll right, click the **ZIP Code column heading**, then scroll right again to see the ZIP Code column
The Mail Merge Recipients dialog box now displays only the records with a US address sorted in zip code order, as shown in Figure H-15.

3. Click **OK**, then click **Next: Arrange your labels** in the Mail Merge task pane
The sort and filter criteria you set are saved for the current merge, and the options for Step 4 of 6 appear in the task pane.

QuickTip
You use the Insert Postal Bar Code dialog box to select the field names for the zip code and street address in your data source. Postal bar codes can be inserted only for U.S. addresses.

4. Click **Postal Bar Code** in the task pane, then click **OK** in the Insert Postal Bar Code dialog box
A merge field for a U.S. postal bar code is inserted in the first label in the main document. When the main document is merged with the data source, a customized postal bar code determined by the recipient's zip code and street address will appear on every label.

5. Press [→], press [Enter], click **Address Block** in the task pane, then click **OK** in the Insert Address Block dialog box
The Address Block merge field is added to the first label.

6. Point to the **down arrow** at the bottom of the task pane to scroll down, then click **Update all labels** in the task pane
The merge fields are copied from the first label to every label in the main document.

QuickTip
To change the font or paragraph formatting of merged data, format the merge fields before performing a merge.

7. Click **Next: Preview your labels** in the task pane
A preview of the merged label data appears in the main document. Only U.S. addresses are included, and the labels are organized in zip code order.

8. Click **Next: Complete the merge** in the task pane, click **Edit individual labels**, then click **OK** in the Merge to New Document dialog box
The merged labels document is shown in Figure H-16.

9. In the first label replace **Ms. Clarissa Landfair** with your name, save the document with the filename **US Coffee Labels Zip Code Merge** to the drive and folder where your Project Files are located, print the labels, save and close all open files, then exit Word

FIGURE H-15: US records sorted in zip code order

Click the column heading to sort the records

Click the list arrow to filter the records

All records with a US address are sorted by zip code in ascending order

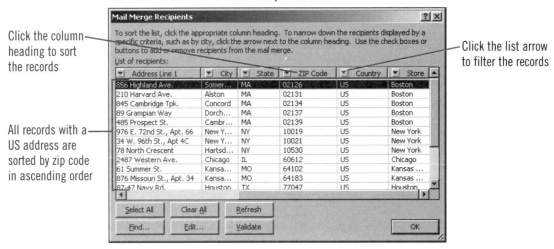

FIGURE H-16: Merged labels

Postal bar code

Labels are sorted by zip code

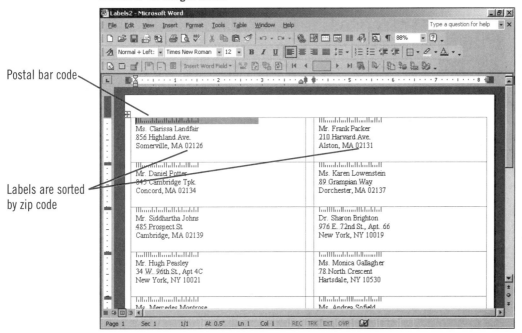

Inserting individual merge fields

You must include proper punctuation, spacing, and blank lines between the merge fields in a main document if you want punctuation, spaces, and blank lines to appear between the data in the merge documents. For example, to create an address line with a city, state, and zip code, you would insert the City merge field, type a comma and a space, insert the State merge field, type a space, and then insert the Zip Code merge field: <<City>>, <<State>> <<Zip Code>>.

You can insert an individual merge field by selecting the field name in the Insert Merge Fields dialog box, clicking Insert, and then clicking Close. You can also insert several merge fields at once by clicking a field name in the Insert Merge Field dialog box, clicking Insert, clicking another field name, clicking Insert, and so on. When you have finished inserting the merge fields, click Close. You can then add spaces, punctuation, and lines between the merge fields you inserted in the main document.

Practice

▶ Concepts Review

Label each toolbar button shown in Figure H-17.

FIGURE H-17

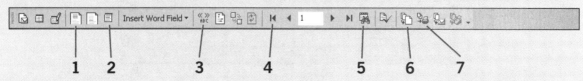

Match each term with the statement that best describes it.

8. **Main document**   a. The standard text that appears in every version of a merged document
9. **Merge field**   b. A complete set of information for one item or individual
10. **Data field**   c. To organize records in a sequence
11. **Boilerplate text** d. A file that contains boilerplate text and merge fields
12. **Data source**   e. A file that contains customized information for each item or individual
13. **Data record**   f. To pull out records that meet certain criteria
14. **Filter**   g. A placeholder for merged data in the main document
15. **Sort**   h. A category of information in a data source

Select the best answer from the list of choices.

16. **In a mail merge, which type of file contains the information that varies for each individual or item?**
    a. Main document   c. Merge document
    b. Data source   d. Label document
17. **Which of the following buttons can be used to insert a merge field for an inside address?**
    a. 🖺   c. 🖺
    b. 🖺   d. 🔠
18. **Which of the following buttons can be used to preview the merged data in the main document?**
    a. 🖹   c. 🖋
    b. ▦   d. 🔠
19. **Which command is used to merge two documents to create a third document that shows the difference between the two?**
    a. AutoSummarize   c. Track Changes
    b. Mail Merge Wizard   d. Compare and Merge Documents
20. **Which of the following is included in a data source?**
    a. Boilerplate text   c. Merge fields
    b. Records   d. Labels

Skills Review

1. Create a main document.

    a. Start Word, then open the Mail Merge task pane.

    b. Use the Mail Merge Wizard to create a letter main document, click Next, then select the current (blank) document.

    c. At the top of the blank document, press [Enter] four times, type today's date, press [Enter] five times, then type **We are delighted to receive your generous contribution of AMOUNT to the New England Humanities Council (NEHC).**

    d. Press [Enter] twice, then type **Whether we are helping adult new readers learn to read or bringing humanities programs into our public schools, senior centers, and prisons, NEHC depends upon private contributions to ensure that free public humanities programs continue to flourish in CITY and throughout the REGION region. I hope we will see you at a humanities event soon.**

    e. Press [Enter] twice, type **Sincerely**, press [Enter] four times, type your name, press [Enter], then type **Executive Director.**

    f. Save the main document as **Donor Thank You Main** to the drive and folder where your Project Files are located.

2. Design a data source.

    a. Click Next; in the Step 3 of 6 Mail Merge task pane, select the Type a new list option button, then click Create.

    b. Click Customize in the New Address List dialog box, then remove the fields from the data source: Company Name, Address Line 2, Country, Home Phone, Work Phone, and E-mail Address.

    c. Add an **Amount** field and a **Region** field to the data source. Be sure these fields follow the Zip Code field.

    d. Rename the Address Line 1 field **Street**, then click OK to close the Customize Address List dialog box.

3. Enter and edit records.

    a. Add the following records to the data source:

Title	First Name	Last Name	Street	City	State	Zip Code	Amount	Region
Mr.	John	Conlin	34 Mill St.	Exeter	NH	03833	$250	Seacoast
Mr.	Bill	Webster	289 Sugar Hill Rd.	Franconia	NH	03632	$1000	Seacoast
Ms.	Susan	Janak	742 Main St.	Derby	VT	04634	$25	North Country
Mr.	Derek	Gray	987 Ocean Rd.	Portsmouth	NH	03828	$50	Seacoast
Ms.	Rita	Murphy	73 Bay Rd.	Durham	NH	03814	$500	Seacoast
Ms.	Amy	Hunt	67 Apple St.	Northfield	MA	01360	$75	Pioneer Valley
Ms.	Eliza	Perkins	287 Mountain Rd.	Dublin	NH	03436	$100	Pioneer Valley

    b. Save the data source as **Donor Data** to the drive and folder where your Project Files are located.

    c. Change the region for record 2 (Bill Webster) from Seacoast to **White Mountain**.

    d. Click OK to close the Mail Merge Recipients dialog box.

4. Add merge fields.

    a. Click Next, then in the blank line above the first body paragraph, insert an Address Block merge field.

    b. In the Insert Address Block dialog box, click Match Fields.

    c. Click the list arrow next to Address 1 in the Match Fields dialog box, click Street, click OK, then click OK in the Insert Address Block dialog box to accept the default address block format.

    d. Press [Enter] twice, insert a Greeting Line merge field using the default greeting line format, then press [Enter].

    e. In the first body paragraph, replace AMOUNT with the Amount merge field.

    f. In the second body paragraph, replace CITY with the City merge field and REGION with the Region merge field. (*Note:* Make sure to insert a space before or after each merge field as needed.)

    g. Save your changes to the main document.

5. Merge data.

   a. Click Next to preview the merged data, then scroll through each letter.

   b. Click the View Merged Data button on the Mail Merge toolbar, then make any necessary adjustments.

   c. Place the insertion point before "I hope" in the second sentence of the second body paragraph, then press [Enter] twice to create a new paragraph.

   d. Combine the first and second body paragraphs into a single paragraph, then save your changes.

   e. Click Next, click Edit individual letters, then merge all the records to a new file.

   f. Save the merged document as **Donor Thank You Merge** to the drive and folder where your Project Files are located, print a copy of the first letter, then save and close all open files.

6. Create labels.

   a. Open a new blank document, then start the Mail Merge Wizard.

   b. Create a label main document, click Next, then select Change the document layout if necessary in the Step 2 of 6 Mail Merge task pane.

   c. Open the Label Options dialog box, select Avery 5162 – Address labels, then click OK, save the label main document as **Donor Labels Main** to the drive and folder where your Project Files are located, then click Next.

   d. Use an existing list, click Browse, then open the Donor Data.mdb file you created.

7. Sort and filter records.

   a. Filter the records so that only the records with NH in the State field are included in the merge.

   b. Sort the records in zip code order, then click OK.

   c. Click Next, insert a Postal Bar Code merge field using the default settings, press [→], then press [Enter].

   d. Insert an Address Block merge field using the default settings, then click the View Merged Data button.

   e. Click the View Merged Data button again, click the Address Block merge field in the upper-left table cell to select it if necessary, then click Address Block in the Mail Merge task pane.

   f. Click Match Fields in the Insert Address Block dialog box, click the list arrow next to Address 1, click Street, click OK, then click OK again.

   g. Click the View Merged Data button to preview the merged data, click Update All Labels in the Mail Merge task pane, then click Next to move to Step 5 of the Mail Merge Wizard.

   h. Preview the merged data, then click Next to move to Step 6 of the Mail Merge Wizard.

   i. Click Edit individual labels, merge all the records, then save the merged file as **NH Donor Labels Merge** to the drive and folder where your Project Files are located.

   j. In the first label, change Ms. Eliza Perkins to your name, save the document, then print it.

   k. Save and close all open Word files, then exit Word.

► Independent Challenge 1

You are the director of the Emerson Arts Center (EAC). The EAC is hosting an exhibit of ceramic art in the city of Cambridge, MA, and you want to send a letter advertising the exhibit to all EAC members with a Cambridge address. You'll use Mail Merge to create the letter. If you are able to print envelopes on your printer, you will also use Word to print an envelope for one letter that you need to separate from the mass mailing.

   a. Start Word, then use the Mail Merge Wizard to create a letter main document using the file WD H-3, found on the drive and folder where your Project Files are located.

   b. Replace Your Name with your name in the signature block, then save the main document as **Member Letter Main** to the drive and folder where your Project Files are located.

   c. Use the file WD H-4, found on the drive and folder where your Project Files are located, as the data source. Alternatively, if you maintain a list of contacts in Outlook, use your Outlook contact list as the data source.

   d. Sort the data source by last name, then filter the data so that only records with Cambridge as the city are included in the merge. (*Note*: If you are using an Outlook data source, select different filter criteria.)

e. Insert an address block and a greeting line merge field in the main document, preview the merged letters, then make any necessary adjustments. (*Note*: If you are using an Outlook data source, you might need to match the fields.)

f. Merge all the records to a new document, then save it as **Member Letter Merge** to the drive and folder where your Project Files are located. (*Note*: If you are using an Outlook data source, merge only the first four records.)

g. Print the first letter. If you can print envelopes on your printer, continue with the next step. If you cannot print envelopes, close all open Word files, saving changes, and then exit Word.

h. If you can print envelopes, select the inside address in the first merge letter, click Tools on the menu bar, point to Letters and Mailings, then click Envelopes and Labels.

i. On the Envelopes tab, type your name in the Return address text box, type **60 Crandall Street, Concord, MA 01742**, click Options, make sure the Envelope size is set to Size 10, then change the font of the Delivery address and the Return address to 12-point Times New Roman.

j. On the Printing Options tab, select the appropriate Feed method for your printer, then click OK.

k. Click Print, then click No to save the return address as the default.

l. Save the merge document, close it, save the main document, close it, then exit Word.

▶ Independent Challenge 2

One of your responsibilities at DSI Enterprises, a growing computer software company, is to create business cards for the staff. You use mail merge to create the cards so that you can easily produce standard business cards for future employees.

a. Start Word, then use the Mail Merge Wizard to create labels using the current blank document as the main document.

b. Select Avery standard 3612 – Business Card labels.

c. Create a new data source that includes the following fields: Title, First Name, Last Name, Phone, Fax, E-mail, and Hire Date. Add the following records to the data source:

Title	First Name	Last Name	Phone	Fax	E-mail	Hire Date
President	Sandra	Bryson	(312) 555-3982	(312) 555-6654	sbryson@dsi.com	1/12/01
Vice President	Philip	Holm	(312) 555-2323	(312) 555-4956	pholm@dsi.com	1/12/01

d. Add six more records to the data source, including one with your name as the Administrative Assistant.

e. Save the data source with the filename **Employee Data** to the drive and folder where your Project Files are located, then sort the data by Title.

f. In the first table cell, create the DSI Enterprises business card. Figure H-18 shows a sample DSI business card, but you should create your own design. Include the company name, a street address, and the Web site address www.dsi.com. Also include a First Name, Last Name, Title, Phone, Fax, and E-mail merge field. (*Hint*: If your design includes a graphic, insert the graphic before inserting the merge fields. Use the Insert Merge Field dialog box to insert each merge field, adjusting the spacing between merge fields as necessary.)

g. Format the business card with fonts, colors, and other formatting features. (*Note*: Use the Other Task Panes list arrow to reopen the Mail Merge task pane if necessary.)

h. Update all the labels, preview the data, make any necessary adjustments, then merge all the records to a new document.

i. Save the merge document with the filename **Business Cards Merge** to the drive and folder where your Project Files are located, print a copy, then close the file.

j. Save the main document with the filename **Business Cards Main** to the drive and folder where your Project Files are located, close the file, then exit Word.

FIGURE H-18

DSI Enterprises

Sandra Bryson
President

234 Walden Street, Dublin, PA 32183
Tel: (312) 555-3982; Fax: (312) 555-6654
E-mail: sbryson@dsi.com
www.dsi.com

Independent Challenge 3

You need to create a team roster for the children's softball team you coach. You use mail merge to create both the team roster and mailing labels.

a. Start Word, then use the Mail Merge Wizard to create a directory using the current blank document.

b. Create a new data source that includes the following fields: First Name, Last Name, Age, Position, Parent First Name, Parent Last Name, Address, City, State, Zip Code, and Home Phone.

c. Enter the following records in the data source:

First Name	Last Name	Age	Position	Parent First Name	Parent Last Name	Address	City	State	Zip Code	Home Phone
Sophie	Wright	8	Shortstop	Kerry	Wright	58 Main St.	Camillus	NY	13031	555-2345
Will	Jacob	7	Catcher	Bob	Jacob	32 North Way	Camillus	NY	13031	555-9827
Brett	Eliot	8	First base	Olivia	Eliot	289 Sylvan Way	Marcellus	NY	13032	555-9724
Abby	Herman	7	Pitcher	Sarah	Thomas	438 Lariat St.	Marcellus	NY	13032	555-8347

d. Add five additional records to the data source using the following last names and positions: O'Keefe, Second base; George, Third base; Goleman, Left field; Siebert, Center field; Choy, Right field. Make up the remaining information for the records.

e. Save the data source as **Softball Team Data** to the drive and folder where your Project Files are located.

f. Sort the records by last name, then click Next in the Mail Merge task pane.

g. Insert a table that includes five columns and one row in the main document.

h. In the first table cell, insert the First Name and Last Name merge fields, separated by a space.

i. In the second cell, insert the Position merge field.

j. In the third cell, insert the Address and City merge fields, separated by a comma and a space.

k. In the fourth cell, insert the Home Phone merge field.

l. In the fifth cell, insert the Parent First Name and Parent Last Name merge fields, separated by a space.

m. Preview the merged data and make any necessary adjustments. (*Hint*: Only the first record will display when you preview the data.)

n. Merge all the records to a new document, then save the document with the filename **Softball Roster Merge** to the drive and folder where your Project Files are located.

o. Press [Ctrl][Home], press [Enter], type **Tigers Team Roster** at the top of the document, press [Enter], type **Coach:**, followed by your name, then press [Enter] twice.

p. Insert a new row at the top of the table, then type the following column headings in the new row: **Name, Position, Address, Phone, Parent Name**.

q. Format the roster to make it attractive and readable, save your changes, print a copy, then close the file.

r. Close the main document without saving changes.

s. Open a new blank document, then use the Mail Merge Wizard to create mailing labels using Avery 5162 – Address labels.

t. Use the Softball Team data source you created, and sort the records in zip code order.

u. In the first table cell, create your own address block using the Parent First Name, Parent Last Name, Address, City, State, and Zip Code merge fields. Be sure to include proper spacing and punctuation.

v. Update all the labels, preview the merged data, merge all the records to a new document, then type your name centered in the document header.

w. Save the document with the filename **Softball Labels Merge** to the drive and folder where your Project Files are located, print a copy, close the file, close the main document without saving changes, then exit Word.

Independent Challenge 4

Your boss has given you the task of purchasing mailing labels for a mass mailing of your company's annual report. Your company plans to use Avery standard 5160 white labels for a laser printer, or their equivalent, for the mailing. The annual report will be sent to 55,000 people. In this independent challenge, you will search for Web sites that sell Avery labels, compare the costs, and then write a memo to your boss detailing your purchasing recommendations.

a. Use your favorite search engine to search for Web sites that sell Avery labels. Use the keywords **Avery labels** to conduct your search. If your search does not result in appropriate links, try looking at the following Web sites: www.staples.com, www.officeworld.com, www.worldlabel.com.

b. Find at least three Web sites that sell Avery 5160 white labels for a laser printer, or their equivalent. Note the URL of the Web sites and the price and quantity of the labels. You need to purchase enough labels for a mailing of 55,000, plus enough extras in case you make mistakes.

c. Start Word, then use the Professional Memo template to create a memo to your boss. Save the memo as **5160 Labels Memo** to the drive and folder where your Project Files are located.

d. In the memo, make up information to replace the placeholder text in the memo header, then type the body of your memo.

e. In the body, include a table that shows the URL of each Web site, the product name, the unit cost, the number of labels in each unit, the number of units you need to purchase, and the total cost of purchasing the labels. Also make a brief recommendation to your boss.

f. Format the memo so it is attractive and readable, save your changes, print a copy, close the file, then exit Word.

▶ Visual Workshop

Using the Mail Merge Wizard, create the post cards shown in Figure H-19. Use Avery standard 3611—Post Card labels for the main document and create a data source that contains at least four records. Save the data source as **Party Data**, save the main document as **Party Card Main**, and save the merge document as **Party Card Merge**, all to the drive and folder where your Project Files are located. (*Hint:* Use a table to lay out the postcard; the clip art graphic uses the keyword "party;" and the font is Comic Sans MS.) Print a copy of the postcards.

FIGURE H-19

You're invited to a
surprise party!

For: Claudette Summer
When: August 3rd, 7:00 p.m.
Where: The Wharf Grill
Given by: Your Name

Grace Pappas
186 Buena Vista Terrace
Apt. 5C
San Francisco, CA 94117

You're invited to a
surprise party!

For: Claudette Summer
When: August 3rd, 7:00 p.m.
Where: The Wharf Grill
Given by: Your Name

Mika Takeda
456 Parker Ave.
San Francisco, CA 94118

Project Files List

Read the following information carefully!

It is very important to organize and keep track of the files you need for this book.

1. **Find out from your instructor the location of the Project Files you need and the location where you will store your files.**

   - To complete many of the units in this book, you need to use Project Files. Your instructor will either provide you with a copy of the Project Files or ask you to make your own copy.

   - If you need to make a copy of the Project Files, you will need to copy a set of files from a file server, stand-alone computer, or the Web to the drive and folder where you will be storing your Project Files.

   - Your instructor will tell you which computer, drive letter, and folders contain the files you need, and where you will store your files.

   - You can also download the files by going to www.course.com. See the inside back cover of the book for instructions on how to download your files.

2. **Copy and organize your Project Files.**

   ### Floppy disk users

   - If you are using floppy disks to store your Project Files, the list on the following pages shows which files you'll need to copy onto your disk(s).

   - Unless noted in the Project Files List, you will need one formatted, high-density disk for each unit. For each unit you are assigned, copy the files listed in the **Project File Supplied column** onto one disk.

   - Make sure you label each disk clearly with the unit name (e.g., Word Unit A).

   - When working through the unit, save all your files to this disk.

   ### Users storing files in other locations

   - If you are using a zip drive, network folder, hard drive, or other storage device, use the Project Files List to organize your files.

   - Create a subfolder for each unit in the location where you are storing your files, and name it according to the unit title (e.g., Word Unit A).

   - For each unit you are assigned, copy the files listed in the **Project File Supplied column** into that unit's folder.

   - Store the files you modify or create for each unit in the unit folder.

3. **Find and keep track of your Project Files and completed files.**

   - Use the **Project File Supplied column** to make sure you have the files you need before starting the unit or exercise indicated in the **Unit and Location column**.

   - Use the **Student Saves File As column** to find out the filename you use when saving your changes to a Project File that was provided.

   - Use the **Student Creates File column** to find out the filename you use when saving a file you create new for the exercise.

Unit and Location	Project File Supplied	Student Saves File As	Student Creates Files
Word Unit A			
Lessons			Marketing Memo.doc
Skills Review			Lacasse Fax.doc
Independent Challenge 1			Zobel Letter.doc
Independent Challenge 2			Smart Tags Memo.doc
Independent Challenge 3			Komata Letter.doc
Independent Challenge 4			Business Letters.doc
Visual Workshop			Publishing Cover Letter.doc
Word Unit B			
Lessons	WD B-1.doc	NY Press Release.doc	
			NYT Fax.doc
Skills Review	WD B-2.doc	CAOS Press Release.doc	
			CAOS Fax.doc
Independent Challenge 1	WD B-3.doc	Lyric Theatre Letter.doc	
Independent Challenge 2			Global Dynamics Letter.doc
Independent Challenge 3	WD B-4.doc	Computer Memo.doc	
Independent Challenge 4	WD B-5.doc	Web References.doc	
Visual Workshop			Visa Letter.doc
Word Unit C			
Lessons	WD C-1.doc	Chicago Marketing Report.doc	
Skills Review	WD C-2.doc	EDA Report.doc	
Independent Challenge 1	WD C-3.doc	Zakia Construction.doc	
Independent Challenge 2	WD C-4.doc	Membership Flyer.doc	
Independent Challenge 3	WD C-5.doc	Solstice Memo.doc	
Independent Challenge 4	WD C-6.doc	Fonts.doc	
Visual Workshop	WD C-7.doc	Rosebud Specials.doc	
Word Unit D			
Lessons	WD D-1.doc	MediaLoft Buzz.doc	
Skills Review	WD D-2.doc	Amherst Fitness.doc	
Independent Challenge 1	WD D-3.doc	Bon Appetit.doc	
Independent Challenge 2	WD D-4.doc	Parking FAQ.doc	
Independent Challenge 3	WD D-5.doc	Stormwater.doc	
Independent Challenge 4	WD D-6.doc	MLA Style.doc	
			MLA Sample Format.doc
Visual Workshop	WD D-7.doc	Gardener's Corner.doc	

Unit and Location	Project File Supplied	Student Saves File As	Student Creates Files
Word Unit E			
Lessons			Boston Ad Budget.doc
Skills Review			Mutual Funds.doc
Independent Challenge 1	WD E-1.doc	40K Relay.doc	
Independent Challenge 2			Business Cards.doc
Independent Challenge 3	WD E-2.doc	Ad Dimensions.doc	
Independent Challenge 4			My Resume.doc
Visual Workshop			March 2003.doc
Word Unit F			
Lessons	WD F-1.doc Mloft.jpg	Ad Tips.doc	
	WD F-2.doc	Age and Gender.doc	Genre Sales.doc
Skills Review	WD F-3.doc Farm.jpg	Farm Flyer.doc	
			Realty Sales.doc
Independent Challenge 1			Letterhead.doc
Independent Challenge 2			GoTropper Ad.doc
	Vacation.jpg		
Independent Challenge 3			Bookmarks.doc
Independent Challenge 4	WD F-4.doc	Copyright Info.doc	
Visual Workshop			Surf Safe.doc
	WD F-5.doc Surfing.jpg		

Word Unit G: If you are saving your solution files to a floppy disk, then the files for the Lessons, Skills Review, each Independent Challenge, and the Visual Workshop must be stored on separate disks. Copy the files you need for the exercise you are completing onto one disk, and label it clearly (e.g. Word Unit G Lessons).

Unit and Location	Project File Supplied	Student Saves File As	Student Creates Files
Lessons			swfhome.htm
	mloft.jpg WD G-1.doc	swfevent.htm	
Skills Review			literacy.htm
	WD G-2.doc reader.gif WD G-3.doc	whattodo.htm	
Independent Challenge 1			longwalk.htm
	WD G-4.doc rwolf.jpg jackson.jpg		
Independent Challenge 2			default.htm Monet's Garden Home.htm
	WD G-5.doc	Products and Prices.htm	
Independent Challenge 3	WD G-6.doc WD G-7.doc WD G-8.doc WD G-9.doc	tri_home.htm tri_view.htm tri_get.htm tri_athl.htm	

Unit and Location	Project File Supplied	Student Saves File As	Student Creates Files
Independent Challenge 4			my_web.htm
Visual Workshop			azulhome.htm azulexhb.htm
	rest.jpg bridge.jpg studlamp.jpg		
Word Unit H			
Lessons	WD H-1.doc	Coffee Letter Main.doc	
			New Coffee Club Data.mdb Coffee Letter Merge.doc Coffee Labels Main.doc US Coffee Labels Zip Code Merge.doc
	WD H-2.mdb		
Skills Review			Donor Labels Main.doc Donor Thank You Main.doc Donor Data.mdb Donor Thank You Merge.doc NH Donor Labels Merge.doc
Independent Challenge 1	WD H-3.doc WD H-4.mdb	Member Letter Main.doc	
			Member Letter Merge.doc
Independent Challenge 2			Employee Data.mdb Business Cards Main.doc Business Cards Merge.doc
Independent Challenge 3			Softball Team Data.mdb Softball Roster Merge.doc Softball Labels Merge.doc
Independent Challenge 4			5160 Labels Memo.doc
Visual Workshop			Party Data.mdb Party Card Main.doc Party Card Merge.doc

Microsoft Word 2002 MOUS Certification Core Objectives

Below is a list of the Microsoft Office User Specialist program objectives for the Core Word 2002 skills, showing where each MOUS objective is covered in the Lessons and Practice. For more information on which Illustrated titles meet MOUS certification, please see the inside cover of this book.

MOUS standardized coding number	Activity	Lesson page where skill is covered	Location in lesson where skill is covered	Practice
W2002-1	**Inserting and Modifying Text**			
W2002-1-1	Insert, modify, and move text and symbols	WORD B-4 WORD B-5 WORD B-6 WORD B-7 WORD B-8 WORD B-9 WORD B-10 WORD B-11 WORD B-14 WORD B-15 WORD D-12	Steps 1–8 Clues to Use Steps 1–7 Clues to Use Steps 1–8 Clues to Use Steps 1–9 Clues to Use Steps 1–9 Clues to Use Steps 2–3	Skills Review Independent Challenges 1–4 Visual Workshop Skills Review Independent Challenges 2, 3
W2002-1-2	Apply and modify text formats	WORD C-2 WORD C-3 WORD C-4 WORD C-5	Steps 2–9 Clues to Use Steps 1–9 Clues to Use	Skills Review Independent Challenges 1–3 Visual Workshop
W2002-1-3	Correct spelling and grammar usage	WORD B-12	Steps 1–9	Skills Review Independent Challenges 1–4 Visual Workshop
W2002-1-4	Apply font and text effects	WORD C-4 WORD C-5 WORD C-16	Steps 1–9 Clues to Use Clues to Use	Skills Review Independent Challenges 1–3 Visual Workshop
W2002-1-5	Enter and format date and time	WORD D-8 WORD D-10 WORD D-11	Clues to Use Steps 2–3, Quick Tip Clues to Use	Skills Review Independent Challenge 3
W2002-1-6	Apply character styles	WORD C-3 WORD C-7	Clues to Use Clues to Use	Independent Challenge 3
W2002-2	**Creating and Modifying Paragraphs**			
W2002-2-1	Modify paragraph formats	WORD C-6 WORD C-7 WORD C-8 WORD C-9 WORD C-10 WORD C-12 WORD C-16	Steps 1–9 Clues to Use Steps 1–9 Clues to Use Steps 1–9 Steps 1–6, Table Steps 1–8	Skills Review Independent Challenges 1–3 Visual Workshop
W2002-2-2	Set and modify tabs	WORD C-10	Steps 1–9	Skills Review Independent Challenges 1–3
W2002-2-3	Apply bullet, outline, and numbering format to paragraphs	WORD C-14 WORD C-15	Steps 1–8 Clues to Use	Skills Review Independent Challenges 1–3
W2002-2-4	Apply paragraph styles	WORD C-7	Clues to Use	Independent Challenge 3

MOUS standardized coding number	Activity	Lesson page where skill is covered	Location in lesson where skill is covered	Practice
W2002-3	**Formatting Documents**			
W2002-3-1	Create and modify a header and footer	WORD D-10 WORD D-11 WORD D-12	Steps 1–7, Quick Tip Table Steps 1–9	Skills Review Independent Challenges 1–4
W2002-3-2	Apply and modify column settings	WORD D-4 WORD D-5 WORD D-6 WORD D-14	Steps 4–5 Clues to Use Clues to Use Steps 1–8, Quick Tip	Skills Review Independent Challenges 1, 2 Visual Workshop
W2002-3-3	Modify document layout and Page Setup options	WORD D-2 WORD D-3 WORD D-4 WORD D-5 WORD D-6 WORD D-7 WORD D-8	Steps 1–6 Clues to Use Steps 1–6, Quick Tip Clues to Use Steps 1–5, Clues to Use Table Steps 1–6, Quick Tip	Skills Review Independent Challenges 1–4 Visual Workshop
W2002-3-4	Create and modify tables	WORD C-11 WORD E-2 WORD E-3 WORD E-4 WORD E-5 WORD E-6 WORD E-10 WORD E-14 WORD E-15 WORD E-16 WORD E-17	Clues to Use Steps 1–8 Clues to Use Steps 1–9 Clues to Use Steps 1–8 Steps 1–9 Steps 1–5 Clues to Use Steps 3–9 Clues to Use	Skills Review Independent Challenges 1–4 Visual Workshop
W2002-3-5	Preview and Print documents, envelopes, and labels	WORD A-12 WORD H-14 WORD H-16 WORD H-17	Steps 1–4, 6–7 Steps 1–6 Steps 1–10 Clues to Use	Skills Review Independent Challenges 1–4 Visual Workshop Skills Review Independent Challenges 1–3 Visual Workshop
W2002-4	**Managing Documents**			
W2002-4-1	Manage files and folders for documents	WORD B-3	Clues to Use	Independent Challenge 2
W2002-4-2	Create documents using templates	WORD B-16	Steps 1–9	Skills Review Independent Challenge 3 Visual Workshop
W2002-4-3	Save documents using different names and file formats	WORD A-10 WORD A-11 WORD B-2 WORD B-3	Steps 1–5 Table Steps 5–6 Clues to Use	Skills Review Independent Challenges 1–4 Visual Workshop Skills Review Independent Challenges 1–4 Visual Workshop

MOUS standardized coding number	Activity	Lesson page where skill is covered	Location in lesson where skill is covered	Practice
W2002-5	**Working with Graphics**			
W2002-5-1	Insert images and graphics	WORD D-16	Steps 1–8	Skills Review Independent Challenges 1, 2 Visual Workshop
		WORD F-2	Steps 1–8	Skills Review
		WORD F-3	Clues to Use	Independent Challenges 1–4
		WORD F-4	Steps 1–6, Table	Visual Workshop
		WORD F-5	Clues to Use	
		WORD F-6	Steps 1–8	
		WORD F-8	Steps 1–10	
		WORD F-10	Steps 1–8	
		WORD F-12	Steps 1–8	
		WORD F-13	Clues to Use	
		WORD F-14	Steps 1–8	
W2002-5-2	Create and modify diagrams and charts	WORD F-16	Steps 1–10	Skills Review
		WORD F-17	Clues to Use	
W2002-6	**Workgroup Collaboration**			
W2002-6-1	Compare and Merge documents	WORD H-2	Details	Skills Review
		WORD H-3	Clues to Use	Independent Challenges 1–3
		WORD H-4	Steps 1–7	Visual Workshop
		WORD H-5	Clues to Use	
		WORD H-6	Steps 1–8	
		WORD H-7	Clues to Use	
		WORD H-8	Steps 1–8	
		WORD H-10	Steps 1–9	
		WORD H-11	Clues to Use	
		WORD H-12	Steps 1–9	
		WORD H-13	Table	
		WORD H-17	Clues to Use	
W2002-6-2	Insert, view, and edit comments	WORD G-14	Clues to Use	Independent Challenge 2
W2002-6-3	Convert documents into web pages	WORD G-2	Steps 7–10	Skills Review
		WORD G-3	Clues to Use	Independent Challenges 1–4
		WORD G-4	Steps 1–10	Visual Workshop
		WORD G-5	Clues to Use	
		WORD G-6	Steps 1–9	
		WORD G-7	Clues to Use	
		WORD G-8	Steps 1–6	
		WORD G-9	Clues to Use	
		WORD G-10	Steps 1–3	
		WORD G-11	Clues to Use	
		WORD G-12	Table	
		WORD G-13	Clues to Use	
		WORD G-14	Steps 1–6, Clues to Use	
		WORD G-16	Steps 1–10	
		WORD G-17	Clues to Use	

Glossary

Word 2002

Adjustment handle Used to change the shape, but not the size, of many Autoshapes.

Alignment The position of text in a document relative to the margins.

Anchored The state of a floating graphic that will move with a paragraph if the paragraph is moved; an anchor symbol appears with the floating graphic when formatting marks are displayed.

Application See *Program*.

Ascending order Lists data alphabetically or sequentially (from A to Z, 0 to 9, or earliest to latest).

Ask a Question box The list box at the right end of the menu bar in which you can type or select questions for the Help system.

AutoComplete A feature that automatically suggests text to insert.

AutoCorrect A feature that automatically detects and corrects typing errors, minor spelling errors, and capitalization, or inserts certain typographical symbols as you type.

Autoshapes Drawing objects, such as rectangles, ovals, triangles, lines, block arrows, stars, banners, lightning bolts, hearts, and suns, that you create using the tools on the Drawing toolbar.

AutoText A feature that stores frequently used text and graphics so they can be easily inserted into a document.

Bitmap graphic A graphic that is composed of a series of small dots called "pixels."

Boilerplate text Text that appears in every version of a merged document.

Bold Formatting applied to text to make it thicker and darker.

Border Lines that can be added above, below, or to the sides of paragraphs, text, and table cells; lines that divide the columns and rows and help you see the grid-like structure of a table.

Browser A software program used to access and display Web pages.

Bullet A small graphic symbol used to identify items in a list.

Cell reference Identifies a cell's position in a table. Each cell reference contains a letter (A, B, C, and so on) to identify its column and a number (1, 2, 3, and so on) to identify its row.

Center Alignment in which an item is centered between the margins.

Character spacing Formatting that changes the width or scale of characters, expands or condenses the amount of space between characters, raises or lowers characters relative to the line of text, and adjusts kerning (the space between standard combinations of letters).

Character style A named set of character format settings that can be applied to text to format it all at once.

Chart A visual representation of numerical data, which is usually used to illustrate trends, patterns, or relationships.

Click and Type pointer A pointer used to move the insertion point and automatically apply the paragraph formatting necessary to insert text at that location in the document.

Clip art A collection of graphic images that can be inserted into documents, presentations, Web pages, spreadsheets, and other Office files.

Clipboard A temporary storage area for items that are cut or copied from any Office file and are available for pasting. *See also* Office Clipboard and System Clipboard.

Column break A break that forces text following the break to begin at the top of the next column.

Copy To place a copy of an item on the Clipboard without removing it from a document.

Cut To remove an item from a document and place it on the Clipboard.

Cut and paste To move text or graphics using the Cut and Paste commands.

Data field A category of information, such as last name, first name, street address, city, or postal code.

Data record A complete set of related information for a person or an item, such as a person's name and address.

Data source In a mail merge, the file with the unique data for individual people or items.

Delete To permanently remove an item from a document.

Descending order Lists data in reverse alphabetical or sequential order (Z to A, 9 to 0, or latest to earliest).

Dialog box A window that opens when a program needs more information to carry out a command.

Document The electronic file you create using Word.

Document window The workspace in the program window that displays the current document.

Drawing canvas A workspace for creating your own graphics.

Field A code that serves as a placeholder for data that changes in a document, such as a page number.

Field name The name of the data field.

File An electronic collection of information that has a unique name, distinguishing it from other files.

Filename The name given to a document when it is saved.

Filtering In mail merge, pulls out records that meet specific criteria and includes only those records in the merge.

First line indent A type of indent in which the first line of a paragraph is indented more than the subsequent lines.

Floating graphic A graphic to which a text wrapping style has been applied which makes the graphic independent of text and able to be moved anywhere on a page.

Font The typeface or design of a set of characters (letters, numbers, symbols, and punctuation marks).

Font effects Font formatting that applies special effects to text, such as shadow, outline, small caps, or superscript.

Font size The size of characters, measured in points (pt).

Footer Text or graphics that appears at the bottom of every page in a document or a section.

Format Painter A feature used to copy the format settings applied to text to other text.

Formatting marks Nonprinting characters that appear on-screen to indicate the ends of paragraphs, tabs, and other formatting elements.

Formatting toolbar A toolbar that contains buttons for frequently used formatting commands.

Frame A section of a Web page window in which a separate Web page can be displayed.

Gutter Extra margin space left for a binding at the top or left side of a document.

Hanging indent A type of indent in which the second and subsequent lines of a paragraph are indented more than the first.

Hard page break A page break inserted to force the text following the break to begin at the top of the next page.

Header Text or graphics that appears at the top of every page in a document or a section.

Highlighting Transparent color that can be applied to text to call attention to it.

Home page The main page of a Web site and the first page Web page viewers see when they open a site.

Horizontal ruler A ruler that appears at the top of the document window in Print Layout, Normal, and Web Layout view.

HTML (Hypertext Markup Language) The programming language used to code how each element of a Web page should appear when viewed with a browser.

Hyperlink Text or a graphic that opens a file, Web page, or other item when clicked. Also known as a link.

I-beam pointer The I pointer, used to move the insertion point and select text.

Indent The space between the edge of a line of text or a paragraph and the margin.

Indent markers Markers on the horizontal ruler that show the indent settings for the active paragraph.

Inline graphic A graphic that is part of a line of text in which it was inserted.

Insertion point The blinking vertical line that shows where text will appear when you type in a document.

Italic Formatting applied to text to make the characters slanted.

Justify Alignment in which an item is flush with both the left and right margins.

Keyboard shortcut A combination of keys or a function key that can be pressed to perform a command.

Landscape orientation Page orientation in which the page is wider than it is tall.

Left-align Alignment in which the item is flush with the left margin.

Left indent A type of indent in which the left edge of a paragraph is moved in from the left margin.

Line spacing The amount of space between lines of text.

Main document In mail merge, the document with the standard text.

Margin The blank area between the edge of the text and the edge of a page.

Menu bar The bar beneath the title bar that contains the names of menus, that when clicked, open menus from which you can choose program commands.

Merge To combine adjacent cells into a singer larger cell.

Merge field A placeholder that you insert in the main document to indicate where the data from each record should be inserted when you perform the merge.

Mirror margins Margins used in documents with facing pages, where the inside and outside margins are mirror images of each other.

Negative indent A type of indent in which the left edge of a paragraph is moved to the left of the left margin.

New Document task pane A task pane that contains shortcuts for opening documents and for creating new documents.

Normal view A view that shows a document without margins, headers and footers, or graphics.

Nudged The action of moving a graphic a small amount in one direction; use the arrow keys to nudge a graphic.

Office Assistant An animated character that appears to offer tips, answer questions, and provide access to the program's Help system.

Office Clipboard A temporary storage area shared by all Office programs that can be used to cut, copy and paste multiple items within and between Office programs. The Office Clipboard can hold up to 24 items collected from any Office program. *See also* Clipboard and System Clipboard.

Open To use one of the methods for opening a document to retrieve it and display it in the document window.

Outline view A view that shows the headings of a document organized as an outline.

Overtype mode A feature that allows you to overwrite existing text as you type.

Paragraph spacing The amount of space between paragraphs.

Paragraph style A named set of paragraph and character format settings that can be applied to a paragraph to format it all at once.

Paste To insert items stored on the Clipboard into a document.

Pixels Small dots that define color and intensity in a graphic.

Point The unit of measurement for text characters and the space between paragraphs and characters; $1/72$ of an inch.

Portrait orientation Page orientation in which the page is taller than it is wide.

Print Layout view A view that shows a document as it will look on a printed page.

Print Preview A view of a file as it will appear when printed.

Program Task-oriented software (such as Excel or Word) that enables you to perform a certain type of task such as data calculation or word processing.

Reset usage data An option that allows adapted toolbars and menus to be returned to their default settings.

Right-align Alignment in which an item is flush with the right margin.

Right indent A type of indent in which the right edge of a paragraph is moved in from the right margin.

Sans serif font A font, such as Arial, whose characters do not include serifs.

Save To store a file permanently on a disk or to overwrite the copy of a file that is stored on a disk with the changes made to the file.

Save As Command used to save a file for the first time or to create a new file with a different filename, leaving the original file intact.

Scale Describes the way a graphic can be resized so the height to width ratio remains the same.

ScreenTip A label that appears on the screen to identify a button or to provide information about a feature.

Scroll To use the scroll bars or the arrow keys to display different parts of a document in the document window.

Scroll arrows The arrows at the ends of the scroll bars that are clicked to scroll a document one line at a time.

Scroll bars The bars on the right and bottom edges of the document window that are used to display different parts of the document in the document window.

Scroll box The box in a scroll bar that can be dragged to scroll a document.

Section A portion of a document that is separated from the rest of the document by section breaks.

Section break A formatting mark inserted to divide a document into sections.

Select To click or highlight an item in order to perform some action on it.

Serif font A font, such as Times New Roman, whose characters include serifs—small strokes—at the ends.

Shading A background color or pattern that can be applied to text, tables, or graphics.

Shortcut key See *Keyboard shortcut*.

Sizing handles The black squares or white circles that appear around a graphic when it is selected; used to change the size or shape of a graphic.

Smart tag A purple dotted line that appears under text that Word identifies as a date, name, address, or place.

Smart Tag Actions button The button that appears when you point to a smart tag.

Soft page break A page break that is inserted automatically at the bottom of a page.

Sorting In mail merge, determines the order in which records are merged.

Standard toolbar A toolbar that contains buttons frequently used for operating and editing commands.

Status bar The bar at the bottom of the Word window that shows the vertical position, section, and page number of the insertion point, the total number of pages in a document, and the on/off status of several Word features.

Style A named collection of character and/or paragraph formats that are stored together and can be applied to text to format it quickly.

Subscript A font effect in which text is formatted in a smaller font size and placed below the line of text.

Superscript A font effect in which text is formatted in a smaller font size and placed above the line of text.

Symbols Special characters that can be inserted into a document using the Symbol command.

System Clipboard A clipboard that stores only the last item cut or copied from a document. *See also* Clipboard and Office Clipboard.

Tab See *Tab stop*.

Tab leaders Lines that appear in front of tabbed text.

Tab stop A location on the horizontal ruler that indicates where to align text.

Table A grid made up of rows and columns of cells that you can fill with text and graphics.

Tags HTML codes placed around the elements of a Web page to describe how each element should appear when viewed with a browser.

Template A formatted document that contains placeholder text you can replace with your own text.

Text box A container that you can fill with text and graphics.

Theme A set of complementary design elements that you can apply to Web pages, e-mail messages, and other documents that are viewed on-screen.

Title bar The bar at the top of the program window that indicates the program name and the name of the current file.

Toggle button A button that turns a feature on and off.

Toolbar A bar that contains buttons that you can click to perform commands.

Undo To reverse a change by using the Undo button or command.

URL (Uniform Resource Locator) A Web address.

Vertical alignment The position of text in a document relative to the top and bottom margins.

Vertical ruler A ruler that appears on the left side of the document window in Print Layout view.

View A way of displaying a document in the document window; each view provides features useful for editing and formatting different types of documents.

View buttons Buttons on the horizontal scroll bar that are used to change views.

Web Layout view A view that shows a document as it will look when viewed with a Web browser.

Web page A document that can be stored on a computer called a Web server and viewed on the World Wide Web or on an intranet using a browser.

Web site A group of associated Web pages that are linked together with hyperlinks.

Wizard An interactive set of dialog boxes that guides you through a task.

WordArt A drawing object that contains text formatted with special shapes, patterns, and orientations.

Word processing program A software program that includes tools for entering, editing, and formatting text and graphics.

Word program window The window that contains the Word program elements, including the document window, toolbars, menu bar, and status bar.

Word wrap A feature that automatically moves the insertion point to the next line as you type.

Word 2002

Index

Index